Debates in Economic History

Edited by Peter Mathias

Capital Formation in
the Industrial Revolution

Capital Formation in the Industrial Revolution

edited with an introduction by
FRANÇOIS CROUZET

METHUEN & CO LTD
11 NEW FETTER LANE LONDON EC4

First published in 1972 by Methuen & Co Ltd
Introduction © 1972 by François Crouzet
Printed in Great Britain by
Richard Clay (The Chaucer Press), Ltd,
Bungay, Suffolk

SBN 416 15770 X hardbound
SBN 416 18150 3 paperback

Distributed in the USA by
HARPER & ROW PUBLISHERS, INC.
BARNES & NOBLE IMPORT DIVISION

Contents

Preface

Professor Crouzet's introduction and this collection of articles contain evidence for what has been virtually a revolution in the interpretation of the role of capital in the British Industrial Revolution, with wide implications for other case histories of industrialization and for capital theory about development economies. As so often, a complex interplay between changing theory and the empirical results of seeking to test theory lies behind the reassessment. With the basic premiss, eloquently asserted by Professor Postan as early as 1935 and now generally accepted and tested, that there was no overall shortage of savings for productive investment in eighteenth-century England, many implications follow.

With the rate of capital accumulation rising only very slowly, if steadily, over a century, it cannot now be claimed that the need to switch a higher proportion of the national income from consumption to investment of necessity pulled down living standards for the masses in the early phases of this sequence of industrialization. War and ostentatious expenditure absorbed many more times resources than productive investment. Interest consequently switched (as it is switching in capital theory) away from the quantitative measurement of capital–inputs (irrespective of their nature and quality) to less linear relationships. We know from more recent analyses how capital–output ratios, and incremental capital–output ratios, vary much in relation to the quality of capital–inputs. We now consider how capital is embodied in technology as instrumental for any assessment of its economic efficiency. Greater interest is focused upon development of the mechanisms – the institutional means and the financial intermediaries – by which extant savings and hoards could be deployed towards those needing capital and credit. Social values are also revealed as instrumental to capital accumulation: the attitudes which led the land-owning, professional and mercantile groups in Britain, in whose hands most of the savings were accruing, to bring productive investment into their pattern of disposing of resources (or at least to allow their savings to be held by a banker), and the imperatives by which individuals and families requiring very high rates of accumulation for investment in enterprise – at least initially – abstained from lavish personal consumption.

The modesty of rates of capital accumulation also enhances the importance of certain aspects of processes of investment, and emphasizes the very profound differences between the context within which industrialization was proceeding in eighteenth-century England and that of many poor countries in our own day. The initial capital requirements for entering even the most capital intensive industries were astonishingly small; technology was simple; many devices were employed for economizing in fixed capital (such as renting buildings, converting existing buildings and plant, hiring power, drawing credit from raw materials suppliers); fixed capitals were very modest in relation to short-term credit needs.

In the economy as a whole, similarly, many special features eased the pressure on capital requirements. Rates of growth were very modest indeed, compared with twentieth-century levels of expectation; the absolute level of national wealth was high in relation to the demands on it for investment; the demands made on the pool of capital by the state (except in wartime) and for social investment were very low by twentieth-century standards, whether in the capital requirements of urbanization or transport or in national systems of health and education. In other ways the earlier position was less favourable – it was a world without international agencies, without massive foreign borrowing (the temporary Dutch stake in British government funds was exceptional), without the state acting as an effective instrument for productive investment in modernization; with very underdeveloped institutional means for mobilizing capital; with the expenditure pattern of social groups receiving most savings being more prejudicial to productive investment.

With such profoundly different institutional assumptions it is clearly dangerous to equate the problems of capital accumulation, or the means whereby they could be resolved, in eighteenth-century England with the more desperate of twentieth-century developing countries. But in this, as in other ways, history provides no repeat performances for the direct guidance of those concerned with similar problems in other contexts. If the analysis is perceptive in relation to the problem in hand, however, it should widen the range of awareness, and this is the beginning of wisdom.

All Souls College, Oxford   PETER MATHIAS
16 February 1972

Acknowledgements

The editor and publishers wish to thank the following for permission to reproduce the articles listed below:

The *Business History Review* and the author for 'Financing the Industrial Revolution', by Professor Herbert Heaton (*Bulletin of the Business Historical Society*, XI, 1937); Frank Cass & Co. Ltd for 'The Attorney and the Early Capital Market in Lancashire', by B. L. Anderson (in J. R. Harris, ed., *Liverpool and Merseyside: Essays in the Economic and Social History of the Port and its Hinterland*, 1969); the Economic History Association and the author for 'Fixed Capital in the Industrial Revolution in Britain', by Professor Sidney Pollard (*Journal of Economic History*, XXIV, 1964); the International Economic History Association for 'Capital Formation in Great Britain during the Industrial Revolution', by Professor François Crouzet (in *Second International Conference of Economic History. Aix-en-Provence, 1962*, II, 1965); Professor Sidney Pollard for 'Capital Accounting in the Industrial Revolution' (*Yorkshire Bulletin of Economic and Social Research*, XV, 1963); Professor M. M. Postan for 'Recent Trends in the Accumulation of Capital' (*Economic History Review*, VI, 1935); the University of Chicago Press and the author for 'Capital Formation in Britain before the Railway Age', by Miss Phyllis Deane (*Economic Development and Cultural Change*, IX, 1961).

Editor's Introduction[1]

AN ESSAY IN HISTORIOGRAPHY
I

Capital played a central part in the classical economists' theory of development; to Adam Smith, Ricardo and their followers, the accumulation of capital was the fundamental determinant of economic growth and progress:

Every increase or diminution of capital . . . naturally tends to increase or diminish the real quantity of industry, the number of productive hands, and consequently the exchangeable value of the annual produce of the land and labour of the country, the real wealth and revenue of all its inhabitants. Capitals are increased by parsimony, and diminished by prodigality and misconduct. . . . Every prodigal appears to be a public enemy, and every frugal man a public benefactor.[2]

[1] As this volume includes a previous article by the present writer, a different point of view has been chosen for this introduction, which attempts to survey the course of discussions on the problem of capital formation during the industrial revolution.

Most of the reading for this essay was done during a two months' stay in Cambridge, in 1969, as a Leverhulme Research Fellow at University College. The author wants to thank the College authorities, and especially its President, Mr John Morrison, for having made this stay possible. He also wants to pay a tribute to the memory of the late Professor David Joslin, with whom he had many fruitful and stimulating discussions. Finally, he owes a great deal to Professor Peter Mathias, who gave valuable suggestions and encouragements, and took the trouble of revising the manuscript stylistically but who, of course, has no responsibility in its content.

For a definition of capital formation, one can adopt that given by J. Hibbert, in J. P. P. Higgins and S. Pollard (eds), *Aspects of Capital Investment in Great Britain, 1750–1850. A Preliminary Survey* (London, 1971), p. 11: 'Additions made during a particular period of time to the stock of goods which are for use in future production.'

[2] Adam Smith, *An Inquiry into the Nature and Causes of the Wealth of Nations* (ed. J. R. M'Culloch, Edinburgh, 1850), pp. 149, 151, and chap. III of book II, 'Of the Accumulation of Capital, or of productive and unproductive Labour', pp. 145–55. Cf. also J. Hicks, *Capital and Labour* (Oxford, 1965), p. 36; G. L. S. Tucker, *Progress and Profits in British Economic Thought, 1650–1850* (Cambridge, 1960), pp. 4, 54–5, 57, 80 ff., 105, 107, 162, 169; R. M. Hartwell, *The Causes of*

However, the early historians of the industrial revolution did not pay much attention to the question of capital formation; they were far more interested in the institutional, technical and social aspects of the industrial revolution than in its economic problems;[1] they concentrated on the rise of the factory system, of industrial capitalism, on the 'hegemony' which capital established over industry.[2] Still they put forward unsystematically a number of basic ideas relative to capital formation. They stressed that the introduction into industry of new machinery or new processes involved a considerable expenditure of capital,[3] and most of these writers argued therefore that the abundance, the 'ready command of capital', the rapid accumulation which England enjoyed during the eighteenth century, had been a decisive factor of the industrial revolution;[4] but some others pointed out that innovators had

---

the Industrial Revolution in England (London, 1967), pp. 65–6; G. M. Meier and R. Baldwin, *Economic Development. Theory, History, Policy* (New York, 1957), pp. 21, 24, 26, 35, 44.

[1] Their approach was descriptive rather than analytical and lacked any theoretical framework. However, though economic history developed in reaction against the sterility of neo-classical economics, and several of its early practitioners had socialist leanings, it is likely that their views on capital formation were influenced by A. Smith and the classical school, where they found both the concept of industrialization as the result of increasing capital accumulation, and the implicit idea that capital was a scarce commodity, i.e. that eighteenth-century England suffered from a capital shortage. Cf. F. A. Hayek (ed.), *Capitalism and the Historians* (London, 1954), pp. 21–3, 54–5; R. M. Hartwell, *The Industrial Revolution in England*, rev. ed. (London, 1968: Historical Association Pamphlets), p. 7.

K. Marx had of course stressed the importance of capital accumulation (see below, pp. 57–9), but he had little influence on British writers at this stage.

[2] Quite often they seem to consider 'capital' and 'capitalism' as identical. Cf. W. J. Ashley, *The Economic Organisation of England. An Outline History* (London, 1914), p. 141; W. Cunningham, *The Growth of English Industry and Commerce in Modern Times*, 4th ed. (London, 1907), vol. III, pp. 614, 618; P. Mantoux, *The Industrial Revolution in the Eighteenth Century* (London, 1928), pp. 93 ff., 374.

[3] Cunningham, op. cit., vol. III, p. 610; Ashley, op. cit., pp. 155–6; C. K. Hobson, *The Export of Capital* (London, 1914), p. 86; L. C. A. Knowles, *The Industrial and Commercial Revolutions in Great Britain during the Nineteenth Century*, 2nd ed. (London, 1922), p. 34.

However, Mantoux (op. cit., pp. 375–7) and W. Bowden (*Industrial Society in England towards the End of the Eighteenth Century*, New York, 1925, p. 139) pointed out that the new machinery was simple and cheap and that some large undertakings had been established with a small initial capital.

[4] For instance, Knowles, op. cit., p. 34; J. A. Hobson, *The Evolution of Modern Capitalism. A Study of Machine Production*, rev. ed. (London, 1906), p. 24.

been hampered by difficulties in raising the capital they needed,[1] which implied some shortage of capital.[2]

The inter-war period saw the publication of a number of monographs, on a regional or sectoral basis, which brought to light many useful data about the various sources from which the pioneers of the industrial revolution had drawn their initial capital, and the process of accumulation within industrial concerns through the regular ploughing back of profits. Of special importance in this respect was T. S. Ashton's book on the iron industry, the conclusions of which were generalized in his later works. He described how the Nonconformist and Quaker ironmasters rose 'by dint of constant industry and unremitting thrift', and he stressed their 'frugality, austerity, constant re-investment'. 'The practice of taking but a small part of the profits for their personal needs and leaving the remainder to accumulate in the business led to a rapid growth of capital.'[3]

However, none of these works dealt systematically with capital formation, and the first writer to attempt an overall, though sketchy, study was J. Lord. In his book on Boulton and Watt,[4] Lord stressed the increase in fixed capital as a vital component of the industrial revolution:[5] from being commercial, a preponderant amount of capital became industrial, and from being floating, circulating capital, the development of machinery, especially steam-power, caused it to become increasingly fixed capital. There was a 'tremendous increase' in the volume of Britain's national capital, which Lord, using Giffen's figures, estimated to have grown ninefold from 1700 to 1800.[6] But Lord's main point was to emphasize the difficulties

[1] Mantoux, op. cit., pp. 375–7; Cunningham, op. cit., vol. II, p. 621.

[2] And while Cunningham (vol. II, pp. 442, 445–6) stated that the development of the banking system gave a great impulse to the formation of capital, made trading on borrowed capital a usual practice, and helped the introduction of new and costly appliances, Ashley (op. cit., pp. 157–9) stressed that the country banks did not supply any resources to entrepreneurs to start their business.

[3] T. S. Ashton, *Iron and Steel in the Industrial Revolution*, (Manchester, 1924), pp. 48, 156–61, 209–11. Ashley (op. cit., pp. 157–9) had already stressed the self-denial, abstinence and parsimony of early industrialists.

[4] J. Lord, *Capital and Steam-Power, 1750–1800* (London, 1923). 2nd ed., 1966, with a bibliographical introduction by W. H. Chaloner.

[5] Earlier writers had only mentioned the increase in capital, without distuinguishing fixed and circulating capital.

[6] Exclusive of land; Lord, op. cit., pp. 60–2, 182–4, 222, 231. However, in another passage, Lord writes that 'the capital of the country had more than doubled itself' from 1740 to 1800.

which the Boulton and Watt partnership experienced in finding capital for financing the development of the steam engine;[1] and his conclusion that in the eighteenth century 'the capitalization of a large industrial firm was difficult' had a deep influence on the thinking of economic historians. As it was strengthened by some other monographs,[2] the prevalent feeling during the inter-war period seems to have been that capital had been a serious problem during the industrial revolution, and that innovators and entrepreneurs had been hampered by its scarcity.[3]

This idea clashed, of course, with the other widespread view of an abundance of capital as one of the main factors of the industrial revolution, but most writers do not appear to have been conscious of this contradiction,[4] and it was left to M. M. Postan to untie elegantly this Gordian knot in an article of 1935, reprinted in this volume,[5] as it was the first serious discussion of the problem of capital formation in a historical perspective and in economic terms.[6] Postan pointed out that in eighteenth-century Britain there was no shortage of capital on a nationwide or aggregate basis: 'There were enough rich people in the country to finance an economic effort far in

[1] Lord, op. cit., pp. 27, 104, 108; still, he also wrote that after 1750 there was plenty of capital and it easily became available through the banking houses (pp. 65, 69). J. E. Cule, 'Finance and Industry in the Eighteenth Century: The Firm of Boulton and Watt', *Economic History*, IV, no. 15 (February 1940), pp. 319–25, was to demonstrate later that Lord had over-estimated Boulton and Watt's difficulties, that Boulton's financial troubles came from his hardware manufactory, and that he was in fact saved from disaster by help from Watt and the steam engine enterprise; see the introduction by Chaloner, to Lord, op. cit., p. vii.

[2] Such as Eric Roll, *An Early Experiment in Industrial Organization, being a History of the Firm of Boulton and Watt, 1775–1805* (London, 1930); G. Unwin, *Samuel Oldknow and the Arkwrights. The Industrial Revolution at Stockport and Marple* (Manchester, 1924). L. H. Jenks, *The Migration of British Capital to 1875* (New York, 1927; 2nd ed., London, 1963), pp. 12–15, had stressed the business as well as social cleavage between industry and finance, the stock market being entirely divorced from any important connexion with industrial life.

[3] See, for instance, C. R. Fay, *Great Britain from Adam Smith to the Present Day. An Economic and Social Survey* (London, 1928), pp. 128, 174. The late David Joslin suggested also an influence from the 1931 'Macmillan Report', which stressed the importance of investment and criticized the inadequacies of the existing facilities for the financing of British industry, and the lack of integration of the financial and industrial worlds.

[4] Contradictory statements are to be found sometimes in the same book.

[5] M. M. Postan, 'Recent Trends in the Accumulation of Capital', *Economic History Review*, VI, no. 1 (October 1935), pp. 1–12; see below pp. 70—83.

[6] Though part of it only is devoted to the period of the industrial revolution.

excess of the modest activities of the leaders of the Industrial Revolution.' But, on the other hand, the imperfections of the capital market were such that 'the new enterprises, in their search for capital, were not much assisted by the fact that England happened to be at the time the richest land in Christendom'. She had no 'general reservoir of national savings', but 'a multiplicity of small disjointed pools', and, though they were 'full enough . . . conduits to connect them with the wheels of industry were few and meagre', so that 'within industry almost every enterprise was restricted to its own private supplies' of capital, the shortage of which 'must have been acute'. 'But on the whole the insufficiency of capital was local rather than general and social rather than material.'[1] Shortly afterwards Herbert Heaton, in a short but stimulating article which is also reprinted in this volume, synthesized a number of data on 'Financing the Industrial Revolution'. He pointed out that the initial capital requirements for eighteenth-century would-be factory masters were very modest, especially as far as fixed capital was concerned, and that a variety of sources were tapped to supply them, with family ties playing a predominant part.[2]

These two seminal articles had put the study of capital formation on the right path, but unfortunately some other writers drew red herrings across the track. In 1929 Earl J. Hamilton had stated that during the price revolution, resulting from the inflow of American treasure, wages had so much lagged behind prices that stupendous windfall profits accrued to traders and manufacturers, and furnished the means to build up capital equipment. So the price revolution contributed directly to the progress of capitalism and prepared the way for the industrial revolution.[3] This hypothesis received support

---

[1] Postan, op. cit., pp. 2–5, and below, pp. 71–5. Postan seems, however, to have believed that industry suffered from an effective capital shortage. He stressed also the personal character of capital in the eighteenth century. It was only after 1850 that it very nearly became the perfect factor of production envisaged by textbooks of economics.

[2] H. Heaton, 'Financing the Industrial Revolution', *Bulletin of the Business Historical Society*, XI, no. 1 (February 1937), pp. 1–10; see below, pp. 84–93.

[3] E. J. Hamilton, 'American Treasure and the Rise of Capitalism (1500–1700)', *Economica*, IX, no. 27 (November 1929), pp. 338–57, especially pp. 338, 348–50, 355–6. No evidence is brought forward in this article to substantiate such extremely general statements.

and a theoretical rationale from J. M. Keynes, who, in *A Treatise on Money*, maintained that 'the wealth of nations is enriched not during Income inflation but during Profit inflation, at times . . . when prices are running away from costs' and especially from wages, so that there is an abnormal growth of capital wealth, partly at the expense of current consumption.[1] This blessing may have encouraged Hamilton to elaborate his suggestion and to lay down in 1942[2] the principle 'that profit inflation through a lag of wages behind prices . . . facilitated the Industrial Revolution during the second half of the eighteenth century'.[3] This lag, due to the fast price rise of this period, brought large profits to industrialists and widened the margin of earnings to be ploughed back for the development of their enterprises, thus alleviating the scarcity of capital,[4] and also stimulating the investment of savings as they took place, so that the invention and utilization of machinery was accelerated.

This explanation of the industrial revolution through forced savings[5] and the exploitation of labour was for a long time popular with many writers,[6] possibly because it could be made to fit with the experience of Soviet Russia, and with the view

[1] J. M. Keynes, *A Treatise on Money* (London, 1930), vol. II, pp. 152–63.

[2] E. J. Hamilton, 'Profit Inflation and the Industrial Revolution, 1751–1800', *Quarterly Journal of Economics*, LVI, no. 2 (February 1942), pp. 256–73, especially pp. 257, 262–5, 272. This thesis was later generalized in his 1952 presidential address to the Economic History Association: 'Prices and Progress', *Journal of Economic History*, XII, no. 4 (Autumn 1952), pp. 325–49, especially pp. 327, 339–41, 347–9.

[3] However, he admitted that a favourable wage–price ratio was neither the sole nor the only important cause of the industrial revolution.

[4] Hamilton adopted the view that there was an absolute scarcity of capital in the eighteenth century, as the development of inventions required heavy investments, and he pointed to several 'classical' examples of inventors being crippled by lack of capital. But, thanks to profit inflation, savings, investment and the capital supply 'rose phenomenally' after 1750, and there was a close relationship between this increased supply of capital and the outburst of mechanical inventions.

[5] Hamilton used the expression in his 1952 article, but not earlier. He stated then that the creation and utilization of new modes of production required such large amounts of capital that a substantial portion had to be drawn directly or indirectly from the working class, whose real wages fell sharply, to the benefit of capitalists as a class.

[6] It appears for instance in W. A. Lewis, *The Theory of Economic Growth* (London, 1955), p. 235, and even in W. W. Rostow, 'The Take-Off into Self-Sustained Growth', *Economic Journal*, LXVI, no. 261 (March 1956), p. 39.

of inflation as a therapeutic for underdeveloped countries.[1] But it was blown to pieces in 1956 by D. Felix,[2] who pointed out that Hamilton had based his theory on a rash comparison between the courses of agricultural prices and of wages of London building artisans, so that the lag between the two series was no proof of an inflation in industrial profits. As a matter of fact, during the second half of the eighteenth century prices of manufactured goods rose less than money wages and much less than agricultural prices; if anything there was pressure on industrial profits, cost inflation rather than profit inflation. It was increased productivity, thanks to innovation, and not rising prices or a wage lag, which accounted for the expanded profits, the ploughing back of which swelled industrial capital accumulation. Forced saving was not a major factor in the growth of industry.[3]

Another alluring but unfounded and misleading hypothesis was put forward in 1944 by Eric Williams,[4] who maintained that a large part of the capital accumulation which financed the industrial revolution came from the profits of the slave trade. 'The capital accumulated by Liverpool from the slave trade poured into the hinterland to fertilize the energies of Manchester' and supplied 'part of the huge outlay for the construction of the vast plants to meet the needs of the new productive

[1] S. Shapiro, *Capital and the Cotton Industry in the Industrial Revolution* (Ithaca, 1967), appendix 1, pp. 214-15, 221-5. Hamilton had made an explicit parallel with Soviet policy of forced industrialization, and his thesis, though quite different from orthodox Marxism, was sometimes used as a justification of Stalinism.

[2] David Felix, 'Profit Inflation and Industrial Growth: The Historic Record and Contemporary Analogies', *The Quarterly Journal of Economics*, LXX, no. 3 (August 1956), pp. 441-63, especially pp. 442-3, 454-9. See also T. S. Ashton, *An Economic History of England: The Eighteenth Century* (London, 1955), pp. 199-200; P. Deane, *The First Industrial Revolution* (Cambridge, 1965), p. 163; Hartwell, *Causes of Industrial Revolution*, p. 68; D. S. Landes, *The Unbound Prometheus. Technological Change and Industrial Development in Western Europe from 1750 to the Present* (Cambridge, 1969), p. 74.

[3] Landes, op. cit., p. 74, points out also that it is not proven that profit margins did increase over the century, that most of the price increases occurred in the 1790s, and that the very industries that were making the most rapid technological advances were the ones where prices were falling. Deane, *First Industrial Revolution*, p. 163, adds that windfall profits did not go to the innovating industrialists, but to farmers and merchants.

[4] E. Williams, *Capitalism and Slavery* (Chapel Hill, North Carolina, 1944), especially pp. vii, 52, 68, 98-107, 210.

process and the new markets'.[1] However, Williams's rather slight essay did not provide any serious and detailed evidence for his general statements, which at best were based on a few random and unrepresentative examples of West India merchants having become bankers or manufacturers.[2]

After such solitary and sometimes fanciful endeavours, the study of capital formation during the industrial revolution was undertaken more systematically after the Second World War, largely under the growing influence of economists on economic history, or through their own interest in it. While pre-war economics had concentrated on short-term fluctuations and the problem of unemployment, post-Keynesian economists turned to long-term economic growth and to the problems of underdeveloped countries; they revived the classical theory and reassigned to capital accumulation a crucial part in the process of growth, as in the Harrod–Domar models, their relations and offsprings, which made the level of investment the determinant of the rate of growth and industrialization. And for years, the 'almost unanimous and sometimes the only prescription', first for the reconstruction of Europe, later for the development of backward countries, was 'massive injection of capital'.[3]

[1] This opinion had been expressed earlier by W. Sombart, L. Knowles (op. cit., p. 34), L. H. Jenks (op. cit., p. 8), A. P. Wadsworth and J. de Lacy Mann, *The Cotton Trade and Industrial Lancashire, 1600–1780* (Manchester, 1931), pp. 212, 224, 229. Though Williams was certainly influenced by Marxism, the idea of a transfer of capital from colonial trade to industry is not to be found in Karl Marx, who stated only that the colonial system was 'a powerful lever' for 'concentration of capital', and for an increased 'primitive accumulation'; K. Marx, *Capital. A Critical Analysis of Capitalist Production*, 5th ed. (London, 1896), pp. 775–9. Trans. from the third German edition by S. Moore and E. Aveling, and ed. by Frederick Engels.

[2] See below, pp. 175–7, and M. W. Flinn, *Origins of the Industrial Revolution* (London, 1966), pp. 45–6, who points out that Williams juxtaposes two sets of facts rather than analyses the process of interaction between slave trade and industrial revolution. Flinn adds that, assuming that the proportion of the slave trade and the trade in slave-produced commodities to total British trade, and the proportion of industrial capital which was drawn from trading profits were both one-fifth, the share of industrial investment generated by slavery and the slave trade would be a mere 4 per cent; 'obviously *some* industrial capital came from this source, but it must remain questionable whether it ever rose to significant levels'.

Williams was on better ground in simply showing that industrial development was stimulated by the demand for exports to the colonies (pp. 65 ff.).

[3] R. Cameron, 'Some Lessons of History for Developing Nations', *American Economic Review*, LVII, no. 2 (May 1967), p. 313; also Meier and Baldwin, op. cit., p. 101; and below, p. 10 n.1.

This re-emergence of capital to the forefront of economic thinking had a deep influence on economic historians, and the problems of capital formation were treated more thoroughly in many of the monographs on the industrial revolution which were published after 1945; while, at a more general level, there was a sort of consensus on a simple capital accumulation model, in which increasing capital formation led to the industrial revolution, many writers coming down in favour of the abundance of capital as the great unique advantage which explained Britain's early start.[1] More specifically, in his small masterpiece of 1948, Ashton emphasized the importance of the substantial fall in the rates of interest during the first decades of the eighteenth century: 'If we seek – it would be wrong to do so – for a single reason why the pace of economic development quickened about the middle of the eighteenth century', he wrote, 'it is to this we must look. The deep mines, solidly built factories, well-constructed canals, and substantial houses of the industrial revolution were the products of relatively cheap capital.'[2] However, though economic historians had by now a better theoretical training than formerly, they did not analyse systematically the problems of capital formation,[3] and they left this task to some economists, who had become interested in a historical approach, and who tried to analyse the relationship between capital formation and economic development in the past, especially during the industrial revolution. This attempt, which was made with some sophisticated tools and sometimes involved an effort of quantification, was to give a completely new twist to the discussions on capital formation, which for some years were to concentrate on the

[1] Hartwell, *Causes of Industrial Revolution*, op. cit., pp. 6, 10, 58; P. Mathias, *The First Industrial Nation. An Economic History of Britain 1700–1914* (London, 1969), p. 8.

At a conference held in 1959 under the auspices of *Past and Present*, D. C. Coleman observed in his summing up that several speakers had defined the problems of capital formation as the key to the understanding of the industrial revolution; 'The Origins of the Industrial Revolution. Conference's Report', *Past and Present*, no. 17 (April 1960), pp. 74, 75, 78.

[2] T. S. Ashton, *The Industrial Revolution. 1760–1830* (London, 1948), pp. 7–11. On the problem of interest rates, see below, pp. 30-2.

[3] D. S. Landes and C. Fohlen, 'Capital Formation in the Early Stages of Industrialization. Introduction', *Second International Conference of Economic History. Aix-en-Provence, 1962* (Paris–The Hague, 1965), vol. II, p. 564.

question of the proportion which investment bore to national income.

In 1953 Simon Kuznets stated that 'at some phase in the growth of a developed country within the last two centuries there must have been a substantial rise in the capital formation proportions'. Failing such a rise, any acceleration in population growth would have brought about a decline in *per capita* product; and he inferred from a 'comparison with the current situation in underdeveloped countries that the period of rising capital formation proportions marked the shift from the pre-industrial to the modern era in all the old countries'.[1] Then a jump towards quantification was taken by W. A. Lewis, who wrote in 1954:

> The central problem in the theory of economic develop-ment is to understand the process by which a community which was previously saving and investing 4 or 5 per cent of its national income or less, converts itself into an economy where voluntary saving is running at about 12 to 15 per cent of national income or more. This is the central problem because the central fact of economic development is rapid capital accumulation. . . . We cannot explain any 'industrial revolution' (as the economic historians pretend to do) until we can explain why saving increased relatively to national income.[2]

The following year he stated still more sharply: 'All the countries which are now relatively developed have at some time in

[1] S. Kuznets, 'International Differences in Capital Formation and Financing', *Capital Formation and Economic Growth. A Conference of the Universities – National Bureau Committee for Economic Research* (Princeton, 1955), pp. 26–8, 30–2; also his 'Population, Income and Capital', in L. H. Dupriez, with the assistance of D. C. Hague, *Economic Progress. Papers and Proceedings of a Round Table held by the International Economic Association* [at Sta. Margherita Ligure, 1953] (Louvain, 1955), pp. 36–7. The proceedings of this conference show clearly that in the 1950s capital occupied a dominant position in the theory of economic growth, and that for most economists, growth hinged on capital accumulation. See also in this respect: Meier and Baldwin, op. cit., p. 172; Conference on Research in Income and Wealth, *Problems of Capital Formation. Concepts, Measurement and Controlling Factors* (Princeton, 1957), Studies in Income and Wealth, vol. XIX, A Report of the National Bureau of Economic Research, p. 3: 'It is the process of capital formation . . . which has largely made possible the spectacular growth in income and productivity' (during the last two centuries).

[2] W. A. Lewis, 'Economic Development with Unlimited Supplies of Labour', *The Manchester School*, XXII, no. 2 (May 1954), p. 155.

the past gone through a period of rapid acceleration, in the course of which their rate of annual net investment has moved from 5 per cent or less to 12 per cent or more. This is what we mean by an Industrial Revolution',[1] which Lewis defined as a 'sudden acceleration of the rate of capital formation'.[2]

It is clear that this hypothesis was derived from the empirical study of twentieth-century underdeveloped countries, and especially from the case of India, which at the time invested 4 to 5 per cent of its national income per year and obtained an increase of its income of 1·25 per cent, which was the same as its rate of population growth; to increase the income *per capita* by 1 per cent per year, the investment rate ought to be doubled. 'Communities in which the national income per head is not increasing invest 4 or 5 per cent of their national income per annum, whilst progressive economies invest 12 per cent per annum or more.'[3]

This idea that the capital formation proportion doubled during the industrial revolution, first put forward by Lewis, was elaborated and made widely known by W. W. Rostow in his 1956 article on 'the take-off' and in his famous *Stages of Economic Growth* (1960).[4] To Rostow a decisive shift in capital formation was central to the mechanism of change in the industrial revolution (which to him is identical with the take-off), and he located it in the case of Britain during the period 1783–1802.[5]

---

[1] Lewis, *Theory of Economic Growth*, p. 208; also pp. 225–6. Lewis admitted that 'figures do not exist which would enable us to say for any particular case . . . how long the transition took' (Rostow was to go further).

[2] Ibid., p. 235.

[3] Ibid., pp. 201–2, 207–8, 225. Kuznets ('International Differences', pp. 26–7) had pointed out that contemporary proportions of net domestic capital formation to net national product range from 5 to 15 per cent, and calculated that, with a population increasing 1 per cent per year, a constant supply of final output *per capita*, and a capital-output ratio between 2·5 to 1 and 5 to 1, the net domestic capital formation required would be 2·5 to 5 per cent of national product.

See also C. Clark, *The Conditions of Economic Progress*, 2nd ed. (London, 1951), p. 504: the rate of capital accumulation rises with income, and in developing economies, it rises in such a way as to keep net savings about 10 per cent of income.

[4] Rostow, 'The Take-Off', pp. 25–48 (Lewis's article of 1954 is mentioned pp. 33 n. 1 and 39); also, *The Stages of Economic Growth. A Non-Communist Manifesto* (Cambridge, 1960), pp. 8, 20, 27, 41–5.

[5] However, Rostow admitted that the rate of investment may already rise, up to 5 per cent of national income, during the pre-conditions period, and that this actually happened in Britain between 1750 and 1783, when basic capital

The Take-off is defined as the interval during which the rate of investment increases in such a way that real output *per capita* rises. . . . A necessary but not sufficient condition for the Take-off [is] that the proportion of net investment to national income (or net national product) rises from (say) 5 per cent to over 10 per cent, definitely outstripping the likely population pressure (since under the assumed Take-off circumstances the capital–output ratio is low),[1] and yielding a distinct rise in real output *per capita*.[2]

Rostow admitted that quantitative data on the scale and productivity of investment in the early stages of industrialization were 'not now available historically' and that a great deal of research would be necessary before his hypothesis could be regarded as proved or disproved, but he insisted he had a 'logical prima facie case'; in an economy at the beginning of its development, with an aggregate marginal capital–output ratio of 3·5 to 1 and a rise of population of 1 to 1·5 per cent per year, a 3·5 to 5·25 per cent share of net national product must be regularly invested if the net national product is to be sustained, and a rise of 2 per cent per year of the net national product *per capita* requires an investment rate of 10·5 to 12·5 per cent of the net national product. Rostow also put forward a scattering of supporting empirical evidence, especially the cases of Sweden and Canada in the nineteenth century and of various developing countries in the twentieth, but no quantitative data about Britain in the eighteenth century.[3]

Rostow's take-off hypothesis made such a sensation that the International Economic Association held a conference in Konstanz, in September 1960, to discuss it thoroughly; a paper on 'The Take-Off in Britain' was delivered jointly by

---

especially the transport network, was expanded; but it did not do much more than keep ahead of population increase ('The Take-Off', pp. 28, 32–3). A. K. Cairncross, *Factors in Economic Development* (London, 1962), p. 140, has pointed out that it is unclear whether saving habits are assumed to alter before or during the 'take-off'; but Rostow writes that the pre-conditions include an initial ability to mobilize domestic savings productively.

[1] Rostow devotes a long footnote to substantiating this assumption.

[2] Rostow, 'The Take-Off', pp. 25, 30. Rostow does not mention any possibility of a scarcity of capital.

[3] Ibid., pp. 33–8; also his *Stages of Economic Growth*, pp. 41–5.

Phyllis Deane (who had been working for some years on a project on the economic growth of the United Kingdom from the seventeenth to the twentieth century, inspired by Kuznets), and by H. J. Habakkuk.[1] They accepted Rostow's (and Lewis's) basic idea that the investment proportion had roughly doubled during the industrial revolution, as it fits with empirical evidence, i.e. Gregory King's figures, which suggest that *circa* 1688 this proportion was in the region of 5 per cent of net national income, and the modern estimates,[2] which show that in the 'mature' post-1850 economy it averaged 10 per cent or more. As it is unlikely that the substantial investments which occurred during the first three-quarters of the eighteenth century involved an addition to the annual rate of national savings of more than 1 per cent of national income, the shift in the investment proportion took place between the early 1780s and the late 1840s. But Deane and Habakkuk rejected Rostow's thesis that a change of this magnitude should have been largely compressed within the space of the last two decades of the eighteenth century; they presented some quantitative data on the rise of investment in canals and in the industries which are thought to have 'ignited' the industrial revolution, such as cotton and iron, which showed that this rise could not have had much effect on the national rate of capital formation by the beginning of the nineteenth century. Only the 'railway age' fitted into Rostow's hypothesis, as at the peak of the railway boom in 1847 capital formation reached 12 per cent of national income, but during most of the industrial revolution the increase in the rate of investment appears to have been very gradual, and capital was not 'a strategic factor' in take-off.[3]

Deane elaborated these views, with much more supporting

[1] P. Deane and H. J. Habakkuk, 'The Take-Off in Britain', in W. W. Rostow (ed.), *The Economics of Take-Off into Sustained Growth* (London and New York, 1963), pp. 63–82. At the Sta. Margherita Ligure conference (1953), Habakkuk had already expressed his misgivings about the decisive part which capital accumulation was supposed to have played in the industrial revolution: 'Finance was not a major influence on the rate of growth . . . the english priority can not be attributed to greater availability of capital'; Dupriez, op. cit., pp. 155, 161, 163–4.

The criticism of Rostow at Konstanz by Cairncross and Kuznets will be mentioned below, p. 16.

[2] Such as C. H. Feinstein, 'Income and Investment in the United Kingdom, 1856–1914', *The Economic Journal*, LXXI (June 1961).

[3] Deane and Habakkuk, op. cit., pp. 73–7, 80, 440.

evidence, in an article of 1961, which is the first quantitative study of capital formation during the British industrial revolution, and which is reprinted in this volume.[1] She did not attempt to make estimates of aggregate capital formation, but carefully pieced together, sector by sector, the available fragments of evidence, both qualitative and quantitative, about the additions which were made to the nation's capital during the eighteenth and the early nineteenth centuries, and compared them with the growth of population and national income. She stressed that most of her data, drawn from published material, were inadequate, and her conclusions necessarily tentative. They are nevertheless impressive, having been upheld, with minor qualifications, in her two subsequent books,[2] and are widely accepted. They may be summarized as follows:

1. Towards the end of the seventeenth century the annual rate of capital formation may have reached about 6 per cent of national income in a very prosperous year, like 1688, but it was vulnerable to war and other temporary disasters, and the long-term average did not exceed 3 per cent.[3]

2. The investment proportion did not rise during the first half of the eighteenth century, as there was little change in the level of capital accumulation in any major sector.[4]

3. The nation's capital stock rose appreciably after mid-century, but so too did population and income, and it is impossible to say whether capital accumulation grew faster than national income;[5] at best it might have advanced to reach a long-term average of 5 or 6 per cent before the American War.

[1] Phyllis Deane, 'Capital Formation in Britain before the Railway Age', *Economic Development and Cultural Change*, IX, no. 3 (April 1961), pp. 352–68; see below, pp. 94–118.

[2] P. Deane and W. A. Cole, *British Economic Growth, 1688–1959. Trends and Structure*, 2nd ed. (Cambridge, 1967), pp. 260–4, 304–5, 308–9; Deane, *First Industrial Revolution*, pp. 153, 154, 156–8. However, in these two books Miss Deane has rather revised downwards her initial figures.

[3] In *First Industrial Revolution* (p. 153), Deane puts more bluntly the investment proportion at the end of the seventeenth century at 5 per cent.

[4] C. Wilson, *England's Apprenticeship, 1603–1763* (London, 1965), pp. xiii–xiv, points out that the English economy was 'marking time' during most of this period.

[5] But various passages by Deane suggest alternatively an 'acceleration' in capital formation, either in the 1750s, or in the 60s, or in the 70s. See also Hartwell, *Causes of Industrial Revolution*, pp. 26–7.

4. There was undoubtedly an increase in the relative level of capital formation in the last two decades of the eighteenth century, but it is unlikely that it amounted to more than 1 or 1·5 per cent of the national income; the investment proportion may have reached about 6 or 7 per cent around the turn of the century.[1]

5. It is unlikely that this level was maintained during the latter part of the Napoleonic Wars and their aftermath, or that it was appreciably increased in the 1820s.[2]

6. From the mid 1830s onwards, there was at last a radical change in the level and structure of investment, attributable to the railways and the generalization of machinery; the investment rate increased suddenly, perhaps by as much as 2 per cent of national income in the 1830s and 1840s, to reach a permanent 10 per cent or more in the mid 1850s.[3]

On the whole the change had been definitely gradual and the industrial revolution had got well into its stride with an average net investment of under 10 per cent per annum.

This conclusion has been strengthened by Deane's recent estimates of British gross national product for the period 1830–1914, which are calculated on a yearly basis from the expenditure side. They show a surprisingly low percentage of

[1] Deane gave the higher figures in *British Economic Growth* (p. 263), and the lower ones, which are more likely, in *First Industrial Revolution* (p. 154).

[2] In her 1961 article (pp. 366, 368), Deane had stated that capital grew faster than income after 1815, but she gave up this idea in *First Industrial Revolution* (p. 154). See also B. R. Mitchell, 'The Coming of the Railway and United Kingdom Economic Growth', *Journal of Economic History*, XXIV, no. 3 (September 1964), p. 331: 'Reckoning roughly on the basis of her [Deane's] suggested figures for various sectors, it would seem that around the early 1830s' the investment proportion 'was, in fact, a good deal less than 10 per cent – perhaps indeed, only 6 or 7 per cent'. See also A. G. Kenwood, 'Railway Investment in Britain, 1825–1875', *Economica*, N.S., XXXII, no. 127 (August 1965), pp. 313–22.

[3] See Mitchell, op. cit., pp. 321–2, 331–3. Kuznets has elaborated Deane's figures and presented them in tabular form:

Net national capital formation/Net national product.

England and Wales	1700–40	5·0 per cent
	1740–70	5·5 per cent
	1770–1800	6·5 per cent
United Kingdom	1801–11 to 1821–31	7·5 per cent
	1821–31 to 1831–61	9·0 per cent

(for this last period, the net *domestic* capital formation proportion is put at 7·4 per cent.) Cf. Kuznets, 'Long-term Trends' (full reference in n. 3, p. 16), pp. 10 table 3, and 58 table U.K. 1.

national expenditure devoted to gross fixed domestic capital formation (on a decade average, 4·1 per cent for 1830–9, 6 per cent for 1840–9); making allowance for additions to stocks and work in progress would probably increase those percentages by 1 to 2 per cent, and Deane considers it unlikely that 'United Kingdom gross domestic investment exceeded 10 per cent of gross national product for any decade preceding the First World War'.[1]

At the Konstanz conference, Deane and Habakkuk had been joined and supported in their criticism of the Rostow thesis on capital formation during the 'take-off' by two leading economists, A. K. Cairncross and Kuznets, who stressed that Rostow and Lewis had been 'too dramatic' in presenting the 'change in savings habits' during the industrial revolution 'in semi-miraculous terms', while in fact there had been a 'slow and relatively steady rather than a sudden and rapid acceleration' in investment ratios.[2]

As a matter of fact, Deane's findings were in harmony with the results of other empirical studies on the development of advanced countries during the last century – especially those by Kuznets or inspired by him;[3] these indicated that, as in

[1] Deane, 'New Estimates of Gross National Product for the United Kingdom 1830–1914', *The Review of Income and Wealth*, series 14, no. 2 (June 1968), pp. 99–100. The percentage of net foreign investment to GNP is 0·9 per cent for 1830–9 and 0·7 per cent for 1840–9.

Feinstein has built up a yearly series of gross fixed capital formation, 1856–1913, which gives sensibly higher figures than Deane's series, except for 1856–60 and 1867–70, mostly owing to higher estimates of industrial and commercial capital; cf. Higgins and Pollard, op. cit., pp. 44–9.

[2] A. K. Cairncross, 'Capital Formation in the Take-off', in Rostow (ed.), *Economics of Take-Off*, pp. 240–60, especially pp. 248–51 (see also his *Factors in Economic Development*, p. 141); S. Kuznets, 'Notes on the Take-off', ibid., pp. 22–43, especially pp. 31–5 (reprinted in his *Economic Growth and Structure: Selected Essays*, London, 1966, pp. 213–35). See also his 'Capital Formation in Modern Economic Growth (and Some Implications for the Past)', *Third International Conference of Economic History. Munich, 1965* (Paris–The Hague, 1968), vol. I, pp. 19–20, 22–3, where he points out that the richest countries of today have net capital formation proportions at only moderate levels (under 15 per cent), which 'many earlier societies might have found not impossible, and perhaps even not too difficult to obtain . . .' and that even a shift from a 5 to a 15 per cent national savings rate 'can hardly be regarded as a revolutionary and crucial attainment', as it would have 'meant a minor change in the consumption ratio easily offset by the rise in aggregate product *per capita*'. Lewis, *Theory of Economic Growth*, p. 236, makes the same point.

[3] S. Kuznets, 'Quantitative Aspects of the Economic Growth of Nations: V. Capital Formation Proportions: International Comparisons for Recent Years',

Britain during the eighteenth and early nineteenth centuries, net capital formation never approached a level of twice its initial rate in the two or three decades dated as the 'take-off', but climbed at a sustained rate (even though only a few percentage points) for a much longer period, and is presently at a relatively modest level in the most developed economies.[1] Moreover, the relationship between *levels* of capital formation and *rates* of growth in output or incomes appeared neither simple, nor direct, nor uniform. Capital is a factor that yields highly variable and uncertain results in terms of rates of growth. Though a high investment ratio often accompanies a fast growth in productivity and income, this is no proof of any causal relationship between the two variables. Wide variations of experience, both between nations and in the same economy over time, demonstrate that growth does not invariably depend on a high level of capital formation, and differences in the level of capital formation do not necessarily explain differences in the growth rates between various economies. In addition the measurement, by econometric analysis, of the contribution by various factors to the growth of advanced economies, appeared to show that in recent years the increase in physical capital-inputs has accounted for only a limited fraction of the growth of output.[2] In many underdeveloped countries, on the other hand, the recommendations of the

---

Economic Development and Cultural Change, VIII, no. 4, part II (July 1960), pp. 1–96; 'VI. Long-term Trends in Capital Formation Proportions', ibid., IX, no. 4, part II (July 1961), pp. 3–124; also his *Modern Economic Growth. Rate, Structure and Spread* (New Haven and London, 1966).

[1] See Kuznets, *Modern Economic Growth*, pp. 221–2, 231, 426–7. Since the Second World War, *gross* domestic capital formation in developed countries has accounted for between a fifth and a quarter of gross national product; and *net* domestic capital formation for about 15 or 16 per cent of net domestic product. In underdeveloped countries, these proportions are 15 and 10 per cent respectively.

See also ibid., pp. 236, 248: the domestic capital formation proportions for the United Kingdom, 1860–79, are 7·7 net and 9·4 per cent gross.

[2] Such as R. M. Solow, 'Technical Change and Aggregate Production Function', *Review of Economics and Statistics* (August 1957); 'Technical Progress, Capital Formation and Economic Growth', *American Economic Review* (May 1962); also his *Economic Growth. An American Problem* (Englewood Cliffs, N.J., 1964); E. F. Denison, *The Sources of Economic Growth in the United States* (New York, 1962); Denison, assisted by J. P. Poullier, *Why Growth Rates Differ. Post-war Experience in Nine Western Countries* (Washington, 1967); also Kuznets, *Modern Economic Growth*, pp. 82–3, 491.

'capital intensive' economists had failed – massive injections of 'foreign aid' had not triggered off fast and sustained growth.

During the 1960s, therefore, many economists were led to question the views generally accepted during the post-war period about the central role of capital formation in economic growth and industrialization, and which now appeared to them inconsistent with the facts and theoretically inadequate. They did not presume any more that output was limited by capital, that capital accumulation *per se* would necessarily produce economic growth, or more capital formation a corresponding acceleration in production, or that the stock of capital and its rate of increase were the crucial determinants of a country's rate of progress. Though *some* increase in the savings ratio must form part of the process of growth, investment is at best a necessary condition for growth, but neither a *primum movens* nor a sufficient condition. It is one of its many sources, along with technological progress, advances of 'useful knowledge' and investment in human capital (i.e. education), the importance of this 'residual' having been emphasized in recent growth models. The gains in aggregate and *per capita* product derive primarily from improvements in the *quality*, not the quantity of inputs, from greater efficiency per single unit of input. Capital formation does not matter as much as capital utilization. Moreover, a number of economists have turned the causal relationship between savings and growth the other way round and maintained that, as a rise in the savings ratio follows rather than precedes the 'take-off', the growth in income draws capital formation along behind it. Rather than increased savings and investment causing growth, both are more likely to be the result of growth (in the case of eighteenth-century Britain, a main source of capital for industry was reinvested profits; other sources were banks and merchants, who grew with industry). The ability to save is not autonomous: investment is dependent on the rate of growth, and is likely to be strong in a booming, fast-growing economy, and weak in a slow-growing one.[1]

[1] For instance, Cairncross, 'Capital Formation', pp. 243–5, 248; *Factors in Economic Development*, pp. 96–7; Kuznets, 'Notes on Take-off', p. 35; 'Long-term Trends', pp. 12, 56; *Modern Economic Growth*, p. 491; Deane, 'Capital Formation before Railway Age', p. 352; Denison and Poullier, op. cit., pp. 121, 141–2; Cameron, op. cit., pp. 313–14; Hartwell, *Causes of Industrial Revolution*, pp.

With the help of these developments in economic thinking, Deane's conclusions – and especially that there was at no time in the eighteenth century a marked rise in the rate of investment out of national income and that a 10 per cent proportion was not reached before the 1840s – have been widely accepted in recent years by economic historians.[1] Correspondingly, the Rostowian hypothesis of a sharp and dramatic acceleration in capital formation during the 'take-off' has been abandoned, though, as J. R. T. Hughes has pointed out, Rostow was wrong only in his timing – in postulating that the investment proportion was doubled within a short period of about twenty years. Rostow was right in assuming that an increase of this order of magnitude had occurred during the industrial revolution – if it is understood in the usual sense, i.e. the period from the mid eighteenth to the mid nineteenth century; and after all, there was definitely *some* increase in the proportion during the last quarter of the eighteenth century.[2] However, most recent writers have agreed that at present there is little theoretical or historical justification for assuming that the industrial revolution was the result of a notable acceleration in capital accumulation, and that a high investment proportion was required for the starting of 'modern growth'.[3]

However, the debate cannot be considered as completely

66–7; E. D. Domar, 'On the Measurement of Technological Change', *Economic Journal*, LXXI, no. 284 (December 1961), p. 709; D. C. North, 'Capital Formation in the United States during the Early Period of Industrialization: A Re-examination of the Issues', *Second International Conference of Economic History*, vol. II, pp. 644–5, 656; Landes, op. cit., pp. 79–80; Flinn, *Origins of Industrial Revolution*, pp. 39–40.

[1] For instance, Mathias, op. cit., pp. 13–14, 20; Hartwell, *Causes of Industrial Revolution*, p. 17. A dissenting opinion is expressed by Flinn, ibid., pp. 10, 43–4, who criticizes Deane for not taking into account the increase in circulating capital, and maintains that the aggregate demand for capital 'expanded significantly in the late eighteenth century to a degree that placed capital accumulation on an entirely new plane'.

[2] J. R. T. Hughes, 'Measuring British Economic Growth', *Journal of Economic History*, XXIV, no. 1 (March 1964), p. 71. Hughes points out that a rate of net capital formation of 6 per cent (around 1800), and a capital–output ratio of 3:1 (as found by Deane and Cole) would provide net growth *per capita* for a rate of population increase higher than which prevailed in Britain at the end of the eighteenth century; so 'Rostow seems to have his Take-off with room to spare, although not with a 10 per cent rate of net capital formation'.

[3] Hartwell, *Causes of Industrial Revolution*, p. 67; Kuznets, 'Capital Formation in Modern Economic Growth', p. 22.

closed. On the economists' front, the supporters of the 'classical' factors of production – capital and labour – as the main
engine of productivity increases and economic growth have not
given up counter-attacking,[1] and on the side of empirical
historical research, Deane's conclusions might have to be
eventually revised.

Owing to the method she has followed, a good deal of her
argument hinges on her starting point, i.e. a 5 per cent investment proportion for prosperous years in the late seventeenth
(and also early eighteenth) century, a figure which is based only
on the interpretation of Gregory King's data. Deane admits that
this figure is 'highly conjectural', but accepts it as 'an intelligent
contemporary guess'.[2] Though most writers give King high
marks for reliability,[3] one can wonder if such a foundation is
solid enough. Moreover, Kuznets has questioned this magic
5 per cent figure from a logical and theoretical point of view,
as it would mean that the incremental and average capital-
output ratios were very high, while existing evidence suggests
that average capital–output ratios are rather low in present
underdeveloped countries, and were low in the others before
the beginning of industrialization.[4] Assuming, from Deane
and Cole's figures, that in seventeenth- and early eighteenth-
century Britain the rate of growth per annum of aggregate
product was 4 per cent, and that the incremental capital-
output ratio was the same as in modern economic growth
(3 net, 5 gross), Kuznets derives a capital formation proportion

[1] See the survey of recent work in F. Hetman, 'Le progrès technique, une
illusion comptable?', *Analyse et prévision*, IX, no. 3 (March 1970), pp. 168–71;
also OECD, *La croissance de la production. 1960–1980. Expérience, perspectives et
problèmes de politique économique* (Paris, 1970), pp. 52–4: a study of the six major
OECD countries for the period 1955–68 shows that 85 per cent of the variability
in output growth rates can be explained by the differences between investment
rates, and the marginal capital coefficient is much higher than in the previous
studies on the USA.

[2] Deane, 'Capital Formation before Railway Age', p. 354; Deane and Cole,
op. cit., p. 260.

[3] A more critical point of view is adopted by J. P. Cooper, 'The Social
Distribution of Land and Men in England, 1436–1700', *Economic History Review*,
2nd series, XX, no. 3 (December 1967), pp. 427–9, 433.

[4] Kuznets, 'Long-term Trends', pp. 21–2, 24, 60; 'Capital Formation in
Modern Economic Growth', pp. 30–1, 33–5 (this is a conjectural but tightly
reasoned and suggestive article, one of the few attempts by economists to apply
their tools of analysis to pre-industrial economies); also Cairncross, 'Capital
Formation', p. 250.

of 1·2 per cent net, and 2 per cent gross. As for the net average capital–output ratio of 7, which can be extracted from King's data as elaborated by Deane, and which is the most extreme case (as it includes the total value of land),[1] it would yield an implicit net capital formation proportion of 2·8 per cent, and this at the upper end of a range that could vary down to 1 per cent; while a very high and unlikely[2] ratio of 12:5 (for re-producible capital) would be needed to obtain a 5 per cent net capital formation proportion. Kuznets concludes therefore that the average net reproducible capital–output ratios were not high in pre-industrial Britain, and consequently 'it may well be that the net national capital formation proportions . . . were well below 5 per cent'.[3] On the other hand he has sug-gested that the gross capital formation proportion (*including current maintenance*)[4] – and the incremental gross capital–output ratio – were much higher before the industrial revolution (11·7 per cent for the gross investment proportion, if the net one was 1·2 per cent), and not very different from those which prevail in modern economies. This resulted from a high cur-rent consumption of fixed depreciable capital, owing to the short physical life of capital goods and from the very low rate of growth of product.[5] This view appears conjectural[6] but,

[1] For reproducible capital only, Deane has calculated an average ratio of 2:3 for 1688: 'Capital Formation before Railway Age', p. 353.

[2] With greater relative supplies of labour and natural resources, the marginal yield on capital was certainly higher than it is today.

[3] He admits, however, that owing to the wide inequality in the distribution of income, potential savings were quite large, and the possibility of a high long-term incremental capital–output ratio (7:10) cannot be excluded; 'Capital Formation in Modern Economic Growth', pp. 32–3, 36–7, 52.

[4] This is the *gross gross* proportion mentioned in Higgins and Pollard, op. cit., p. 7. The usual definition of gross capital formation does not include running repairs and maintenance.

[5] Kuznets, 'Capital Formation in Modern Economic Growth', pp. 33–9, 43–4, 46–8, 50. The rate of growth of aggregate product has strikingly different effects on the net and gross capital formations, and hence on the net and gross incremental capital–output ratios. The acceleration in the rate of growth of product during the industrial revolution reduced the relative burden of capital consumption and replacement and thus made a higher *net* capital accumulation possible, with the same (or only slightly increased) gross proportion. This would subordinate investment to growth, as maintained by many economists; see above, p. 18.

[6] Kuznets's hypothesis that the physical life for capital goods (except what he calls 'monuments') before the industrial revolution was relatively short, and that they required current maintenance (or replacement) amounting to a high

even for the period of the industrial revolution, it is possible that the margin between the *net* and *gross* (or rather gross gross) capital formation proportions was relatively wider than in modern economies. In the comparatively primitive technology of the eighteenth and early nineteenth centuries, repairs and maintenance of capital equipment may have loomed much larger than genuine net investment. It has been recently stressed, for instance, that the vast expenditure on shoeing horses (which has been estimated at well over £1 million per year, while the 'gross horse formation' may have been something like £1·5 million) would completely dwarf the figures of new investment in, say, cotton machinery. On the other hand, though overall technical change was slow compared to the present, the length of life of new machinery and equipment in the most progressive industries may have been abnormally foreshortened by premature obsolescence, and the expenditure on replacement relatively high. Because replacement of fixed capital generally involved a marked rise in productivity, gross capital formations might be more directly relevant than net to economic growth.[1]

In any event, Kuznets's analysis creates some misgivings:[2]

---

proportion of the original full value, is not absolutely convincing. He may be right about producers' equipment, but, from his own reckoning, it made only 20 per cent of gross capital formation, so that its maintenance was not as heavy a burden as he suggests; as for buildings, which accounted for 70 per cent of gross capital formation, he has probably underestimated their durability. On the other hand, if land is included, the practice of fallow meant enormous maintenance costs.

[1] Higgins and Pollard, op. cit., pp. 6–7, 27, 150, 186–7; also Kuznets, *Modern Economic Growth*, p. 243. Pollard makes a strong plea in favour of the gross gross proportion, as the best indicator of the burden which the economy had to carry during the process of industrialization, and of the necessary shift of resources.

It would certainly be useful to calculate capital consumption coefficients in various sectors and for various types of equipment.

[2] And would show that the definitions of capital formation, which have been devised for contemporary advanced countries, ought to be modified for the study of pre-industrial economies. For instance, they might be widened to include consumer durable goods, and durable military goods, such as warships and fortifications.

On the other hand, the 'broad' definition of capital formation as all uses of current product that contribute to rises in long-term national product *per capita*, and including therefore outlays on education, recreation, health, which contribute to greater productivity (as suggested by Kuznets, 'Population, Income and Capital', p. 21), would not mean much change for the period of the industrial revolution, owing to the low level of such 'investment in human capital'.

if the net capital formation proportion was not above 3 per cent before the mid eighteenth century, it would mean a bigger increase during the second half of the century than Deane has assumed – even if the low figure of 5 per cent around 1800 was adopted.

Deane's work has also been subjected to detailed scrutiny by Sidney Pollard,[1] who pointed out that much of the statistical material on which it was based was highly suspect. Many figures for the late eighteenth and early nineteenth centuries had been borrowed from various writers who had, in fact, copied each other. Therefore, they were not independent estimates but variations on the same theme, and it was not surprising that no trend could be read in them, or only a 'deceptively smooth rise'. The best documented figures were those of Patrick Colquhoun but, none the less, they were often based on pure guesswork and 'heroic assumptions'. Moreover, these writers had used a very different concept of 'capital' from that current today, and Deane did not succeed in reconciling their estimates with modern notions of investment.[2]

Pollard followed those criticisms by computing his own estimates of *gross* capital formation, sector by sector, for various bench-years between 1770 and the 1830s. As can be seen from Table 1, which embodies the gist of his findings, he concluded that the proportions of *gross* British national income which were invested were higher than Deane and Cole had suggested and 'much closer to those postulated in the theoretical schemes of Lewis and Rostow though still not as high before 1815'. The investment rate – at 6·5 per cent – was higher than 5 per cent around 1770, at the 'threshold' of the industrial revolution; it rose quickly during the 'take-off', to reach 9 per cent in the exceptional boom years from 1790 to 1793, was held up by the massive diversion of resources during the French wars (8 per cent in the peak war year of 1813), but 'reached something approaching the postulated 10 to 12 per cent' by the early

---

[1] S. Pollard, 'The Growth and Distribution of Capital in Great Britain, *c.* 1770–1870', *Third International Conference of Economic History*, vol. I, pp. 335–65.
 This paper could not be reprinted in this volume for lack of space and because two articles by the same writer are included. It is none the less very important.
[2] Ibid., pp. 336–41.

B

1830s, just before the first railway mania.[1] Pollard also pointed out that 'it was, in any case, scarcely credible that the British economy towards the end of the eighteenth century should not be more "developed", in terms of investment rates, than

TABLE 1 *Possible order of magnitude of gross capital formation and proportion of gross national income, Great Britain (in £ million)**

		c. 1770	c. 1790–3	c. 1815	c. 1830–5
1 Agriculture:	Enclosures	0·2	0·4	0·6	0·1
	Reclamation	—	—	0·2	—
	General	2·5	3·2	4·5	4·5
2 Transport:	Turnpike roads	0·2	0·3	0·7	1·0
	Other roads	0·3	0·3	1·2	1·2
	Canals, navigation	0·2	0·8	0·4	0·4
	Docks, etc.	—	0·1	0·5	0·6
	Railways	—	—	0·1	2·0
3 Building:	Residential	2·0	4·5	7·5	10·0
	Public, streets, etc.	0·3	0·6	1·0	1·5
4 Manufacture and trade:	Ships	0·6	0·9	1·0	1·5
	Machinery, millwork, etc.	0·8	2·0	4·0	8·0
	Stocks	1·5	2·0	2·5	2·5
	Foreign investment	0·6	0·6	0·6	6·5
	Bullion	0·1	0·1	0·1	—
5 Miscellaneous:		0·1	0·2	0·2	0·2
	Totals	9·4	16·0	25·1	40·0
	Gross National Income†:	140	175	310	360
	GCF⎫ GNI⎭	6·5%	9%	8%	11%

* From Pollard, 'Growth and Distribution', table IV, p. 362.

† Based on various estimates in Deane and Cole, op. cit., and interpolations, bearing in mind price changes.

some of the most backward parts of the world today which certainly could not "take off" into industrialism unaided, as Britain did then'. So historians would 'have been misled into underestimating the investment effort of the British economy during the Industrial Revolution'.

[1] See also S. Pollard and D. W. Crossley, *The Wealth of Britain, 1085–1966* (London, 1968), pp. 196–7: the relatively stable long-term rate of gross domestic fixed capital formation around 7 to 8 per cent of national expenditure, which is fairly well established from 1856 onwards, would have been maintained since about 1830 and probably since 1820.

Pollard's calculations are more comprehensive and systematic than Deane's rather impressionistic estimates, but he admits very fairly that his table 'exhibits . . . nearly all the features to be avoided in the construction of statistics, especially in its lack of accuracy and of comparability', and that some items, 'including several of the crucial larger ones, are very uncertain'. But he maintains that 'the likelihood that all doubtful ones are too large by a margin which would bring them back to the levels postulated in Deane and Cole, is surely very small'.[1] But even a cursory glance at his sectoral estimates seems to reveal some bias towards selecting the highest figures whenever an alternative is available, and pushing upwards many estimates.[2] For instance, he accepts and uses Colquhoun's guess of £60 million for the capital value of 'steam engines and other expensive machinery' in 1811, which seems far too high.[3] On the other hand the figures for investment in enclosures and land reclamation seem fairly reasonable (and those of Deane far too low), as they fit rather well with B. A. Holderness's more recent and thorough estimates;[4] but those for

---

[1] Pollard, 'Growth and Distribution', pp. 362-3.

[2] Pollard has recently admitted that his Munich paper was 'a warning against cursory reworkings . . . it appears already that several of the sums used there will need some major emendations'; Higgins and Pollard, op. cit., p. 2.

[3] Pollard, 'Growth and Distribution', p. 355. Around 1800, Britain had roughly 1,000 steam engines, representing a total capital of less than £500,000 (Deane and Cole, op. cit., p. 262); even if that number had risen to 2,000 ten years later, and if their average value was £500, their total value would be only £1 million. According to S. D. Chapman, 'Fixed Capital Formation in the British Cotton Manufacturing Industry, 1770–1815', *Economic History Review*, 2nd series, XXIII, no. 2 (August 1970), pp. 251–2 (this article is reprinted in Higgins and Pollard, op. cit., pp. 57–107, with some additional paragraphs, pp. 76–81), in 1811, the cotton spinning industry had steam engines totalling 10,000 hp; reckoning £50 per unit horse-power, the net worth would be £500,000 to which an equivalent sum ought to be added for engine houses and transmission systems. The same writer (p. 252), using insurance valuations (see below, p. 29 n. 1), estimates the fixed capital of the cotton industry in 1811 at £6 million while Pollard puts it for 1812 at £10 million ('Growth and Distribution', p. 355 n. 1).

[4] See B. A. Holderness, 'Capital Formation in Agriculture', in Higgins and Pollard, op. cit., pp. 162–6. He has calculated average costs of enclosure per acre (including the 'after-effects'), which are much higher than those of earlier writers, such as W. G. Tate, 'The Cost of Parliamentary Enclosure in England (with special reference to the County of Oxford)', *Economic History Review*, 2nd series, V, no. 2 (December 1952), pp. 258–65; G. E. Mingay, *English Landed Society in the Eighteenth Century* (London, 1963), p. 182; J. D. Chambers and

'general' investment in agriculture are certainly much too high.[1]

In any case, it must be stressed that Pollard has concentrated on *gross* capital formation, and its proportion to *gross* national income;[2] so his investment proportions cannot be considered as a rehabilitation of the assumptions by Lewis and Rostow, who had written about a doubling of the proportions of *net* capital formation to *net* national income; moreover, he emphasizes that in sectors as important as agriculture and road-building, a great deal of expenditure could not be properly termed investment and was just repair and maintenance, and also that in an industry like cotton the rate of obsolescence was rapid, so that *gross* investment would be much higher than the average *net* investment.[3] Pollard has not really closed the gap between empirical findings and the Lewis–Rostow hypothesis,

---

G. E. Mingay, *The Agricultural Revolution. 1750–1880* (London, 1966), p. 85; and Pollard, 'Growth and Distribution', pp. 342–7.

None the less, Holderness's 'Approximate estimates of necessary capital investment following parliamentary enclosure' (tables 2B and 2C, p. 166) are not very high, when calculated on a yearly basis:

	High estimate (£)	Low estimate (£)
1770–89	250,000	180,000
1790–1815	584,000	450,000

As for the 'Putative capital–input' in enclosing waste by parliamentary sanction (p. 169), it would be:

1761–92: £30,000 per year
1792–1815: £210,000 per year

The sharp increase in agricultural investment during the French wars, and especially during their latter part, might have had some consequence on the aggregate investment ratio, as largely offsetting the decline in industrial capital formation.

[1] Holderness (op. cit., pp. 171–6) seems to suggest that the increase in landlord's capital (the two chief components of which were farm buildings and drainage) was quite gradual.

Pollard's figures for investment in inventories ('Growth and Distribution', p. 358), which he justifies on the doubtful basis that industrial output grew faster than the value of overseas trade, and that the holding of industrial stocks increased, owing to more roundabout production methods, seem also far too high. On the other hand, his estimate for road investment in the early nineteenth century (pp. 350–1) is lower than that given by Deane ('Capital Formation before Railway Age', p. 363).

[2] And using for GNI the estimates by Deane and Cole, to which he might have applied the same sort of criticism and upwards revision as for their capital formation figures.

[3] Pollard, 'Growth and Distribution', pp. 346, 348–50, 355.

though one may admit that he has presented a case for judging Deane's capital formation proportions as somewhat too low.[1]

However, we may wonder if this controversy about the proportion of *aggregate* capital formation to *national* income has not been given too much importance.[2] In a criticism of the Rostowian take-off, A. Fishlow pointed out that 'national income is not the proper focus on which to hinge a concept of far-reaching, but temporarily concentrated, change. It is a very insensitive measure of transformation. As a consequence, the predicted acceleration in income *per capita* and the sharp increase in the savings proportion frequently fail of realization', even during rapid industrialization.[3] As a matter of fact, for several decades most of the technological and structural changes which are associated with the industrial revolution were concentrated in a few branches of British industry (such as cotton and iron) which, despite their fast growth, made only a minor contribution to national income, and they cannot be expected to have made a significant impact upon the aggregate savings rate.

Moreover, economists have recently stressed the importance of the rate of increase in the stock of capital, which is not measured by investment ratios, and for which they are poor substitutes.[4] The yearly increment to physical capital appears

[1] But the 1968 calculations by Deane of gross capital formation proportions from 1830 onwards are much lower than those by Pollard (see above, pp. 15–16).

[2] While the practical difficulties of measuring capital formation and capital–output ratios, even in contemporary advanced economies, have been overlooked; on these difficulties, see F. A. Lutz and D. C. Hague, *The Theory of Capital. Proceedings of a Conference held by the International Economic Association* [Corfu, 1958] (London, 1961), for instance, pp. x, 16, 75–94.

Kuznets, 'Notes on Take-off', pp. 221–2, observes that, strictly speaking, it is the proportion between net *domestic* capital formation and net *domestic* product (and not income), which ought to have been considered; but he admits that it would not make much difference. See also his 'Capital Formation Proportions', p. 2, on the inadequacy of such proportions as a tool of analysis, either of the production or of the use of income.

[3] A. Fishlow, 'Empty Economic Stages?', *Economic Journal*, LXXV, no. 297 (March 1965), p. 119; also p. 113. Fishlow points out that the conception of growth (based on the simple Harrod–Domar capital accumulation model), in which the rate of growth of income is the product of an average propensity to save and the inverse of a reasonably stable capital–output ratio, is inappropriate for a society in transformation; the national capital–output ratio lacks behavioural content; its stability is consistent with wide-ranging shifts in industrial composition and investments.

[4] See Denison, op. cit., pp. 121, 138. But the measurement of the capital stock raises very serious difficulties and is still in its infancy; cf. OECD, op. cit., p. 51.

more important for growth than the capital formation proportions. Because technical progress cannot take place without a simultaneous investment in fixed capital, and innovations have to be embodied in new equipment, the decisive factor for effective technical progress is the proportion between new investment and the existing capital stock.[1] A sectoral analysis of such problems might be most fruitful, as the rapid increase in investment in those areas of the economy which were expanding rapidly from the mid eighteenth century onwards must undoubtedly not be overlooked.[2] However, this has not yet been seriously attempted. From some figures collected by Deane and Cole, it would appear that fixed capital increased in the cotton industry at a mean rate of 12 per cent per year from 1783 to 1802, and in the iron industry at a rate of 6 per cent per year from 1791 to 1806.[3] According to S. D. Chapman's more recent and lower estimates, the total fixed capital of the cotton industry would have grown at a rate of 5·6 per cent per year between 1795 and 1811 (5·9 per cent for the spinning sector alone).[4]

---

[1] Hetman, op. cit., pp. 157–8.

[2] Mathias, op. cit., pp. 13–14. The rate of capital formation varied enormously from industry to industry (and from firm to firm).

[3] Deane and Cole, op. cit., p. 262; also Deane and Habakkuk, op. cit., p. 75; Deane, 'Capital Formation before Railway Age', p. 366. These calculations are of course highly tentative, inasmuch as it is not quite clear if the figures refer to the sums which were actually invested between the relevant dates, or to the value of the capital stock at these dates.

These rates of growth can be compared to those of:

– retained imports of raw cotton (Deane and Cole, op. cit., p. 185):

> 1781–3 to 1801–3 : 9·6 per cent per year
> 1795–7 to 1811–13 : 5·8 per cent per year

– output of pig-iron (R. M. Mitchell and P. Deane, *Abstract of British Historical Statistics*, Cambridge, 1962, p. 131):

> 1788–1806: 7·3 per cent per year.

See below, pp. 197–201, for the rates of growth of total capital of a number of 'progressive' and successful firms, which, as can be expected, are frequently 15 per cent per year.

[4] Chapman, 'Fixed Capital Formation', pp. 247, 252. One could also use as a yardstick the horse-power of steam engines used in the cotton industry, which rose from possibly 3,000 hp in 1801, to 10,000 in 1811 and to 41,000 in 1838; the rates of growth would thus be: 11·5 per cent for 1801–11, 5·4 per cent for 1811–38; cf. ibid., and M. Lévy-Leboyer, *Les banques européennes et l'industrialisation internationale dans la première moitié du XIXe siècle* (Paris, 1964), pp. 31–2, and also 37, 343–4: in 1825, the building of cotton-spinning machinery was estimated

Deane's main point none the less seems reasonably secure: the first steps in industrialization did not put any great strain on the supply of capital. Considered in relation to national income, the annual overall cost of the new investment was not heavy. As Cairncross points out, the cotton industry became a large-scale exporter by 1800 (and soon, one may add, the first British industry) on the strength of a total investment of less than £10 million, roughly equivalent to the national income created in a fortnight.[1]

As a matter of fact, the contrast between the acceleration in the rate of economic growth in the late eighteenth century and the modest increase in the level of capital formation has somewhat puzzled Deane and Cole themselves. They have tried to explain it by the lag between initial capital expenditure in agriculture and transport and the time when they were brought into full productive effect under the impact of population increase and war; and by the much more intensive use of existing capital and the elimination of excess capacity, which resulted from the progress of the factory to the detriment of the domestic system.[2] Moreover, a large proportion of the new developments were taking place in industries with a relatively low ratio of capital to income. Most of industrial investment was concentrated in high productivity sectors, in industries with high rates of return, so that the allocation of investment

---

by a witness before a Parliamentary committee at £400,000 per year; and at the end of 1835, the machine-makers of Manchester and its area had orders on their books for 7,000 hp of steam engines, 2,800,000 spinning spindles, 8,500 to 9,000 power-looms, i.e. about one-tenth of the existing equipment.

[1] Cairncross, 'Capital Formation', pp. 248–50, also 245; as a matter of fact, according to Chapman, 'Fixed Capital Formation', pp. 247, 252, the actual figure was much smaller as he estimates the total fixed capital of the cotton industry at £2·5 million in 1795, and a little over £6 million in 1811 – with £2 million and £5 million respectively for the spinning branch.

Deane, 'Capital Formation before Railway Age', pp. 368 and 366: at the end of the eighteenth century the annual flow of new capital in the leading commercial and industrial sectors was not more than about £2 million or perhaps 1 per cent of national income.

And Pollard ('Growth and Distribution', p. 355) estimates that industrial investment was well under £1 million per year *c.* 1770, well over £3 million *c.* 1811 and about £8 million in 1830–5. These figures are certainly too high, but the rate of growth of gross fixed capital formation in industry that can be calculated from the table reproduced on p. 24 is about 3·7 per cent per year for 1770–1835, which is rather moderate.

[2] Deane and Cole, op. cit., pp. 276–7, 308; also Cameron, op. cit., p. 314.

was quite favourable.[1] Habakkuk has also mentioned that there was no population barrier to the supply of savings: the relatively slow growth of Britain's population up to the early nineteenth century allowed a rise in *per capita* income, which in its turn made possible higher savings which increased gradually, without any sharp discontinuity.[2]

A last qualification has to be made. The debate which has just been summarized was concerned with the secular trend in the capital formation proportion, but there is no doubt that investment also underwent considerable short-term fluctuations – in absolute terms, and probably also relatively. Despite the increase of national product in boom years, the investment ratio may have risen substantially at the peaks of 'major' business cycles, such as 1792, 1802, 1825, only to fall sharply in subsequent lean years.[3] This problem of the chronology of investment, and the related questions of the influence upon capital formation of interest rate movements, wars and government borrowing, have been treated at some length in one of the articles reprinted in this volume,[4] while more recently Mathias has wound up the debate in a number of

[1] Denison, op. cit., pp. 155 ff. The problem of the incremental capital–output ratios, during the industrial revolution, remains obscure. However, Kuznets and Cairncross have rejected the Rostowian hypothesis that such ratios were constant, and Kuznets has argued that they fell during the second half of the eighteenth century, so that limited inputs of new capital gave a sustained growth of product. Cf. Kuznets, 'Notes on Take-off', p. 226; 'Long-term Trends, pp. 21, 24; Cairncross, 'Capital Formation', pp. 252–5. See also M. Blaug, 'The Productivity of Capital in the Lancashire Cotton Industry during the Nineteenth Century', *Economic History Review*, 2nd series, XIII, no. 3 (April 1961), pp. 358–60, 366, 367–70; Blaug deals with the post-1830 period, but finds a stable capital–output ratio (at constant prices), owing to the fall in the prices of machinery and the progress of the engineering industry; he warns against the idea that capital-using innovations dominated during the industrial revolution. The rough comparisons, p. 28 n. 3, between the growth rates of fixed capital and physical output (or import of raw materials) would seem to support this view.

[2] H. J. Habakkuk, 'Historical Experience of Economic Development', in E. A. G. Robinson (ed.), *Problems in Economic Development. Proceedings of a Conference held by the International Economic Association* (London, 1965), pp. 112–14, 128.

[3] Pollard, in *Aspects of Capital Investment*, pp. 9–10, stresses the importance of this problem, and mentions the possibility of intra-sectoral shifts, within a relatively constant total investment.

[4] F. Crouzet, 'La formation du capital en Grande-Bretagne pendant la Révolution industrielle', *Second International Conference of Economic History*, vol. II, pp. 626–37, and below, pp. 203–16.

excellent pages, which need only a brief summary.[1] He stresses that investment *decisions* were dependent upon the demand for capital goods by the consumer goods industries, and, as far as transport, public utilities and building were concerned, upon the cost and availability of credit. So they clustered at the peaks of trade cycles, when conditions of confidence, cheap credit, good profits and high demand were realized. However, the investment cycle was longer in its rhythm than the trade cycle (every trade boom did not trigger off an investment boom), and also more intense in its effects on the capital goods industries. As the weight of these basic industries in the economy increased, so the fluctuations inherent in their process of growth became more powerful. Agricultural investment had a different cycle, the long swings of which originated in the trend movement of farm prices: the high grain prices during the French wars engineered a tremendous switch of resources to agricultural investment, while their fall after 1815 was associated with a low level of capital formation in that sector up to the 1830s.[2]

As for investment in transport and public utilities, the minimum scale of initial expenditure was high, the gestation period was long, and interest charges on borrowed capital were an important element in the annual costs of enterprises. Building was also heavily dependent upon credit for mortgages, and mortgage rates moved in harmony with the going rate of interest on government stock. So the timing of projects in those sectors was undoubtedly affected by the shifts in the rate of interest, by the state of the money market and of the Stock Exchange.[3] Investment, roughly speaking, fluctuated inversely to the yield on government stocks; it was badly hit by wars, during which heavy government borrowing (in conjunction with the Usury Laws) abruptly diverted the flow

---

[1] Mathias, op. cit., pp. 42, 44–7, 115–16, 146–7, 228, 231, 234–7.

[2] A. H. John, 'Insurance Investment and the London Money Market of the 18th Century', *Economica*, N.S., XX, no. 78 (May 1953), pp. 156–7, suggests some correlation between enclosure activity and interest rates.

[3] The concentration of transport projects at times of plentiful credit and low rates of interest had appeared before the canal age, as early as the Restoration.

On building, see A. K. Cairncross and B. Weber, 'Fluctuations in Building in Great Britain, 1789–1849', *Economic History Review*, 2nd series, IX, no. 2 (December 1956), pp. 283–97.

of loanable funds and drove up rates of interest.[1] On the other hand, investment in manufacturing industry was little affected by interest rate movements. Differences of a few points in the cost of credit were unlikely to be a decisive consideration for manufacturers, when the advantages of innovation were such as they were during the industrial revolution.[2]

As for Ashton's thesis that the long-term fall in interest rates was a decisive factor of the industrial revolution, it has fallen out of favour. P. G. M. Dickson has argued that the decline in the yields on government stocks during the first half of the eighteenth century was due to special causes – an increase in the savings seeking gilt-edged investment just at the time when the bonds available for purchase were diminishing in amount – and had little significance for the capital market as a whole. Apart from long-term government loans, there is little difference in interest rates between the beginning and the end of the eighteenth century. The cheapest monetary conditions of the century prevailed between 1736 and 1756. After 1759, the yield on government stocks never fell below 4 per cent, except from 1789 to 1793, and 'the period of most rapid economic growth [the last quarter of the century] was not, in fact, one in which capital was generally available at rates particularly favourable.'[3]

The idea that Britain carried out most of her industrial revolution without the massive investment which had been postulated has been supported by some parallel research or reflection on related problems.

To begin with, any attempt at breaking up the aggregate capital formation estimates, or proportions, proves undoubtedly that the largest part of investment went into sectors of

[1] But the construction industries received a boost when the government moved out of the loan market after a war, and the rate of interest fell.

[2] Mathias, op. cit., p. 147; Landes, op. cit., p. 64; John, op. cit., p. 158; L. S. Pressnell, 'The Rate of Interest in the Eighteenth Century', in Pressnell (ed.), *Studies in the Industrial Revolution. Essays presented to T. S. Ashton* (London, 1960), p. 195.

[3] P. G. M. Dickson, *The Financial Revolution in England. A Study in the Development of Public Credit. 1688–1756* (London, 1967), pp. 470, 482–3; John, op. cit., pp. 147, 158; Flinn, *Origins of Industrial Revolution*, pp. 49–51. One can also argue that the fall in interest rates could hardly have acted to attract hoardings and encourage saving. On the other hand, the prevalence of relatively low rates is proof of the relative abundance of capital, and of the fact that it was channelled into productive investment.

the economy outside the direct context of industry – a fact which fits well with the estimated composition of the nation's capital. At the beginning of the nineteenth century over half of it was tied up in land; and if reproducible capital alone is considered, one-third consisted of buildings and public property, one-fifth of farmers' capital and just under half of industrial, commercial, financial and other private capital (including canals, railways and foreign assets).[1]

From Pollard's estimates of gross capital formation at various dates, one can tentatively calculate the following figures and percentages:[2]

TABLE 2 *Possible order of magnitude of gross capital formation in the main sectors of the British economy (in £ million)*

	c. 1770	c. 1790–3	c. 1815	c. 1830–5
Agriculture	2·7	3·6	5·3	4·6
Transport	1·3	2·4	3·9	6·7
Building	2·3	5·1	8·5	11·5
Manufacture and trade:				
Machinery	0·8	2·0	4·0	8·0
Stocks	1·5	2·0	2·5	2·5
Sub total	2·3	4·0	6·5	10·5
Miscellaneous	0·8	0·9	0·9	6·7
Total	9·4	16·0	25·1	40·0

TABLE 3 *Gross capital formation in each sector as percentage of aggregate gross capital formation*

Agriculture	28·6	22·5	21·1	11·5
Transport	14·0	15·0	15·5	16·8
Building	24·5	31·9	33·8	28·8
Manufacture and trade:				
Machinery	8·5	12·5	15·8	20·0
Stocks	16·0	12·5	10·1	6·3
Sub total	24·5	25·0	25·9	26·3
Miscellaneous	8·5	5·6	3·6	16·8

[1] Deane and Cole, op. cit., pp. 271, 308; Deane, *First Industrial Revolution*, p. 155; Kuznets, 'Long-term Trends', p. 62.

[2] Pollard, 'Growth and Distribution', table IV, p. 362 (and above, p. 24). 'Ships' have been regrouped with 'Transport', foreign investment and bullion with 'Miscellaneous'.

Pollard's figures have been criticized above, but, as many of them seem to have an upward bias, their relative proportions could be fairly reasonable, though industrial fixed capital might be overestimated.

The share of aggregate gross investment going into manufacture and trade would have remained almost constant – roughly a quarter – with, however, a sharp rise in the percentage of fixed industrial investment between the 1770s and the 1830s. But much larger sums were invested in agriculture (under the pressure of population increase), in transport,[1] in house building and in other social overheads. As a matter of fact, agriculture and transport may have been the target for many of the first spurts of enlarged investment but, of course, their improvement was vital to the progress of industrialization.[2]

As for Deane's series of gross domestic *fixed* capital formation in Britain, it shows the following distribution for the decade 1830–9 (as percentages of total gross domestic fixed capital formation):

	%
Industrial capital	20
Transport and communications	37
Social capital (including dwellings)	41
Administration and defence	3

'Well over three-quarters of gross fixed domestic capital formation . . . went into constructing the basic infrastructure of a highly industrialized and urbanized economy. . . . Less than a quarter . . . went into more directly productive forms of industrial plant and equipment.'[3]

Another problem which has recently attracted attention is the composition of capital during the industrial revolution, and especially the ratio between fixed and circulating capital. 'One may ask,' writes Simon Kuznets, 'whether there was *any* fixed capital formation, except for the "monuments" in

---

[1] Including shipping, which, from the mid seventeenth century onwards, was one of the most important areas of investment; Mathias, op. cit., p. 94; E. Hobsbawn, *Industry and Empire. An Economic History of Britain since 1750* (London, 1968), p. 11.

[2] Mathias, op. cit., pp. 13, 115, 196; Pollard, 'Growth and Distribution', pp. 342, 363–4; Pollard and Crossley, op. cit., p. 177; Flinn, *Origins of Industrial Revolution*, p. 41.

[3] Deane, 'New Estimates of GNP', pp. 101 table 4, 102.

Even in modern developed economies, the proportion of investment in machinery is relatively small.

pre-modern times . . . the whole concept of *fixed* capital may be a unique product of the modern economic epoch and of modern technology.'[1] Under the domestic system, industrial capital was almost entirely circulating capital – raw materials, goods in process of manufacture, goods which had been sold but not yet paid for. Fixed assets were a very small fraction only, and even in the few large-scale enterprises the ratio of fixed to circulating capital was low. Hence an expansion of output involved few investment problems in the modern sense.[2] Earlier writers had rightly seen that a change in the composition of capital and the emergence, for the first time, of large concentrations of fixed capital were a crucial aspect of the industrial revolution.[3] But the speed of the growth of fixed capital and the difference between the old and the new industrialisms had been overestimated, as was demonstrated by Sidney Pollard in two pioneer articles, which are reprinted in this volume.

The first pointed out that, during the industrial revolution, there was no general 'rationalization' of accounting, as postulated by the 'classical' scheme of Wernert Sombart and Max Weber, in order to fit fixed capital into it. The analysis of textbooks of accountancy and of actual accounts of firms reveals little change from the methods which had crystallized in the sixteenth century. There were an enormous variety of practices in the counting houses, but no clear-cut attempt to adapt them to the notion of capital as generalized, depersonalized property, seeking the highest returns. In fact the concept of capital was little understood; it was treated as an auxiliary to entrepreneurship, instead of the central motive force behind the firm, and it was confused with revenue. The notion of capital as a permanent, autonomous factor was virtually unknown. There was a general tendency to ignore the fixed equipment altogether, and industrial accountants were unable to integrate it in their scheme of things. Additions to fixed assets, as well as repairs or replacement, were normally

---

[1] Kuznets, 'Capital Formation in Modern Economic Growth', p. 48; he notes, however, that the modern trend towards an increase of equipment within capital formation might have appeared some time before the industrial revolution.

[2] Mathias, op. cit., pp. 121, 147.

[3] See above, p. 3; also Ashton, *An Economic History*, pp. 112, 118.

entered in the current accounts, while depreciation was seldom made on a regular basis.[1]

These heresies in accountancy were partly the consequence of the relatively small ratio of fixed capital to firms' total assets, a fact which Pollard emphasized in his second article, the conclusions of which have been widely accepted.[2] Though the coming of the factory system increased the amount of fixed capital, in the small number of industries which were thus transformed this ratio remained low until the 1830s (in the early textile factories and in the breweries, buildings and plant were about one-seventh or one-eighth of total assets); and there was an increase in the proportion of firms with higher fixed capital ratios within each industry, rather than any marked change in this ratio within advanced firms themselves. Contrary to generally accepted opinion, the ironworks and other large metallurgical enterprises had less than half their total assets sunk into fixed equipment.[3] According to Pollard, the cotton-spinning mills were the only concerns where fixed capital became the major component – just a little more than half the capital invested.[4]

[1] S. Pollard, 'Capital Accounting in the Industrial Revolution', *Yorkshire Bulletin of Economic and Social Research*, XV, no. 2 (November 1963), pp. 75–91, and below, pp. 119–44; also his *The Genesis of Modern Management* (London, 1965), pp. 271–90 and 247–8: the accounting system of landed estates – the 'master and steward system' – did not separate capital expenditure from other outlays, and for historical reasons it was widely used in the industrial enterprises which developed out of the estates, such as mines (especially coal mines), ironworks, distilleries, canals, which tended to have no capital accounts and entered any investment in the year's current outlay.

[2] S. Pollard, 'Fixed Capital in the Industrial Revolution in Britain', *Journal of Economic History*, XXIV, no. 3 (September 1964), pp. 299–314, and below, pp. 145–61.

[3] Landes, op. cit., p. 75; from Pollard's data, the proportion of fixed capital to total inventory valuation of assets for several firms in the metal trades vary from 8·8 to 33·2 per cent. M. Lévy-Leboyer, 'Quatre générations de maîtres de forges gallois: les Crawshay', *Revue du Nord*, XLVI, no. 180 (January–March 1964), p. 37 n. 4, gives abstracts from the balance sheets of Cyfarthfa from 1810 to 1835; fixed assets are lower than the total value of stocks, cash and credit in 1810–14, but higher for most of the later years; Cyfarthfa was, of course, an exceptionally big concern, and the period late.

[4] Pollard, 'Fixed Capital', pp. 299–303; also Mathias, op. cit., pp. 147–8; R. Cameron *et al.*, *Banking in the Early Stages of Industrialization. A Study in Comparative Economic History* (London, 1967), pp. 36–7.

However, these conclusions are based on the inventory values in balance-sheets; M. W. Flinn, *Men of Iron. The Crowleys in the Early Industrial Revolution* (Edinburgh, 1962), p. 174, points out that such valuations are not to be always

This view has been corroborated by some recent and detailed research on the cotton industry by S. D. Chapman and M. M. Edwards, though the latter writer suggests that Pollard's estimate is too generous, at least for the period before 1815, and he produces some evidence that even the largest cotton-spinning or calico-printing firms employed a much greater proportion of working than of fixed capital.[1]

These (and other) writers have also stressed some factors which explain that fixed capital was the lesser part only of industry's total capital. First, given the nature of technology at the beginning of the industrial revolution, fixed equipment was relatively simple and cheap: the cost of a jenny *circa* 1795 was £6, of a mule £30 (and over £50 for a large, steam-driven one); around 1811, a hand loom was £5, a stocking-frame £15; a small steam engine could be had for £150 to £200, a large one for £500 to £800. A small spinning mill, using horse-power, was never valued at more than £1,000, an Arkwright type water-mill of the 1780s between £3,000 and £5,000; the large multi-storied steam mills, which appeared in the 1790s, alone were worth £10,000 to £15,000.[2] For the iron industry, A. Birch mentions that, with the exception of a few giants,

---

equated with the extent of the original investment; they were often arbitrary and they allowed for depreciation, whatever the vagaries in calculating it.

Landes, op. cit., p. 75 n. 3, observes also that the low ratio of fixed to circulating capital does not hold for the start of an enterprise, when accounts receivable had not yet accumulated.

[1] S. D. Chapman, *The Early Factory Masters. The Transition to the Factory System in the Midlands Textile Industry* (Newton Abbot, 1967), pp. 125, 127–31, 133–6; M. M. Edwards, *The Growth of the British Cotton Trade. 1780–1815* (Manchester, 1967), pp. 213–14, 257–9, appendix E, tables 1–7; the ratios of fixed capital to total assets in the balance sheets of five firms are: 0·7 per cent (1794), 12 per cent (1802), 14 per cent (1802), 21 per cent (1805), 40 per cent (1814).

[2] Chapman, *Early Factory Masters*, pp. 127–34; also his 'Fixed Capital Formation', pp. 239–40, 247 n. 3, 252–3; Higgins and Pollard, op. cit., pp. 77–81; Landes, op. cit., p. 65. Chapman points out that the application of steam-power to spinning did not make much difference to the cost of entering the manufacture, as the transfer of investment to mule spinning after 1795 in fact reduced plant costs per spindle. And for the following thirty years, the scale of fixed capital investment in individual productive units grew very little; in 1834 a small mill of 6,900 spindles, 20 hp, could be built and equipped for £6,000.

See also Lévy-Leboyer, *Les banques européennes*, p. 89 n. 109, for estimates by a French manufacturer in 1834 of the cost of establishing in England a water-spinning mill of 29,000 spindles (£29,000), a weaving mill with 300 power-looms (£8,800), a large cotton-printing works (£10,800); also p. 446 n. 7.

concerns were not large, and the amounts of capital involved
'very modest' – £12,000 to £30,000 *circa* 1800.[1]

Moreover, Chapman and Edwards have stressed that many
capital economizing devices were used to escape large outlays
of fixed capital. The really costly items were buildings and
power, but, up to the late 1790s, relatively few buildings were
built, specifically for the cotton trade. A cotton factory was
almost any old building which had been set up for some other
purpose – corn mill, farm or dwelling-house, barn, warehouse,
etc. – and converted into a jenny workshop or an Arkwright-
type water-mill. The ease with which existing premises could
be thus converted helped many cotton spinners to start business
with a very modest initial capital. In addition, many of them
just rented the building in which they operated – or even part
of it, the room- or floor-letting system being very common.
Machinery, and even steam engines (which, anyway, did not
exist in large numbers) could also be rented, or bought second-
hand. During the initial stages of the industrial revolution, the
requirements of fixed investment were thus very modest and
the threshold of entry into factory production quite low,
especially in the textile industries, of which, for quite a while,
cotton was the only one to be largely mechanized. As much of
this investment was undertaken by established merchant
houses, they found little difficulty in making the marginal
shifts from working to fixed capital which were necessary for
building and tooling the early factories. Except in a few cases,
there were no 'lumpy' blocks of investment. Most firms grew
by gradually increasing the scale of their activities and the size
of their works as their capital increased, or by the multiplica-
tion of small manufacturing units. Lastly, the 'critical innovations were concentrated at first in a small sector of the economy,
and their appetite for capital was correspondingly limited.'[2]

[1] A. Birch, *The Economic History of the British Iron and Steel Industry, 1784–1879*
(London, 1967), pp. 197–8; also R. H. Campbell, 'Investment in the Scottish
Pig-Iron Trade, 1830–1843', *Scottish Journal of Political Economy*, I, no. 3 (October
1954), p. 247: as late as the 1830s, the total cost of a blast furnace in Scotland
(including all the peripheral equipment) was put near to £10,000.

[2] Chapman, 'Fixed Capital Formation', pp. 236–7, 247, 252–3 (his estimate of
the cotton industry's fixed capital is quoted above, p. 29 n.l); 'The Peels in the
Early English Cotton Industry', *Business History*, XI, no. 2 (July 1969), pp. 75,
81; Edwards, op. cit., pp. 182, 186–8, 193–4, 202–3, 211–14; Lévy-Leboyer, *Les
banques européennes*, p. 446, who writes of a 'democratization' of cotton spinning

Capital goods were, of course, the 'carriers of technological change, the major permissive source of modern economic growth', but recent research strongly suggests that, during the industrial revolution, 'the proportion of total inputs needed to provide the material envelope of modern technical progress was a minor fraction'.[1]

One may add that the total capital of most firms, even in the 'progressive' industries, remained relatively modest,[2] but the existence of a number of 'giants', with total assets and even fixed capital running into tens of thousands (in a few cases hundreds of thousands) of pounds, must not be overlooked.[3] Moreover, this analysis of the ratio between fixed and circulating capital applies to 'private' manufacturing industry; outside it, especially in agriculture, transport and public utilities, most of the investment was in the form of fixed capital.[4] And even within industry the importance of circulating capital[5] must not hide the fact that an essential – and possibly *the* essential – characteristic of the industrial revolution, as Professor Hicks emphasized recently, was the increase in the range and variety of fixed capital, and the relative decline of circulating capital.[6]

II

These various findings on the capital requirements of the British economy were bound to have some influence on the discussions relative to the supply of capital, the financing of the

---

in the 1790s, thanks to such practices; Pollard, *Genesis of Modern Management*, pp. 51–63, on sub-contracting as a capital-economizing device, especially in mining; Mathias, op. cit., pp. 146, 148; Flinn, *Origins of Industrial Revolution*, pp. 37–8; Landes, op. cit., pp. 65, 78.

[1] Kuznets, 'Capital Formation in Modern Economic Growth', p. 20.

[2] Lévy-Leboyer, *Les banques européennes*, p. 447, gives the results of an inquiry made in 1809 among 64 Manchester spinning firms: 52 of them (i.e. 81 per cent of the number, 50 per cent of total capitalization) had a capital under £5,000; 9 a capital between £5,000 and £10,000; only 3 exceeded £10,000.

[3] Pollard, *Genesis of Modern Management*, chap. 3, pp. 78–126, mentions a number of such firms, in industries like coalmining, iron, copper-smelting, gas, brewing, glass.

On the giant enterprises of Thomas Williams, in the copper industry, see J. R. Harris, *The Copper King. A Biography of Thomas Williams of Llanidan* (Liverpool, 1964), especially pp. xv, 141–3.

[4] Pollard, 'Fixed Capital', p. 300.

[5] And consequently, of short-term credit, see below, pp. 44–6.

[6] J. Hicks, *A Theory of Economic History* (London, 1969), pp. 142–3; also Flinn, *Origins of Industrial Revolution*, p. 38.

industrial revolution, and the much debated problem of a 'capital shortage', inasmuch as, at the same time, the old idea that England was already a rich country before industrialization started has been brought to life again.

In the eighteenth century, and even in the late seventeenth century, England was by no means an 'underdeveloped' country. Its average income *per capita* was higher than in many countries of the contemporary Third World, and probably of the same order of magnitude as that of Brazil or Mexico today. As early as the Restoration, its economy tended to generate a surplus which was available for investment, and there were men of all ranks increasingly willing and able to save. The ease with which London was rebuilt after the fire of 1666 and joint-stock companies were floated at the end of the seventeenth century (or even earlier, like the Royal African Company in 1671) is strong evidence that there was no serious capital scarcity; and, in fact, the last forty years of the seventeenth century were marked by a good deal of investment activity – in overseas trade, in shipping, in building, in agricultural improvements – despite the stringencies resulting from the wars. Phyllis Deane suggests, not unreasonably, that there was a shortage of investment opportunities, and a pressure upon available investment outlets, much more than of investible funds – a situation which may have persisted during the first half of the eighteenth century.[1]

Evidence of Britain's wealth in the eighteenth century is overwhelming, the main reason for this being the enormous and easy borrowing by the government during the wars, which were much more demanding than the economy in their claims for loanable funds. From 1688 to 1815, 33 per cent of English war expenditure was raised by loans, to the tune of £671 million (£770 million with the separately accounted Irish debt), £440 million of which was floated between 1793 and 1815;

---

[1] Hartwell, *Causes of Industrial Revolution*, pp. 18, 23–5; Landes, op. cit., p. 13; Kuznets, 'Population, Income and Capital', p. 33; Mathias, op. cit., p. 16; Deane, 'Capital Formation before Railway Age', pp. 354–6, 367; Habakkuk, 'Historical Experience of Economic Development', p. 138; Dickson, op. cit., pp. 244, 401, 486–7; K. G. Davies, 'Joint-Stock Investment in the Later Seventeenth Century', *Economic History Review*, 2nd series, IV, no. 3 (1952), pp. 285–9, 292, 298, 301; Wilson, op. cit., p. 171; Pollard and Crossley, op. cit., pp. 147, 150, who, however, suggest that trade was still hindered by some shortage of capital.

and this borrowing, at least for some periods, could be achieved without competing too much with the requirements of the private sector and without any significant effect on prices. These huge figures must be compared with the estimate of the amount of investment in the whole canal system from 1700 to 1815, which did not exceed £20 million – the easy financing of canals and turnpike roads also being evidence that capital was plentiful and the social context favourable to investment.[1] Later on, after 1815, the plethora of English wealth, in excess of internal profitable investment opportunities, was proved by the massive export of capital in the 1820s.[2]

Several writers have also observed that the distribution of income in eighteenth-century Britain was favourable to saving, as it was highly unequal (and possibly growing more so), with a large share of the national income going to the upper-income groups, the 'automatic savers', and few constraints, like taxation, operating to keep down this share. Such inequality is generally considered as creating high absolute and marginal propensities to save.[3] But this is a theoretical and unhistorical assumption, which overlooks the social realities of eighteenth-century England. An enormous flow of income went to the upper class, which had a higher propensity to consume than those of modern societies, and for which the eighteenth century was in a way the age of extravagance: a great flow of wealth poured into pleasure, luxury goods and travel; a large part of the *personal* savings of the upper-income recipients

[1] Dickson, op. cit., pp. 9–10, 12, 245, 472; Hartwell, *Causes of Industrial Revolution*, p. 67; Mathias, op. cit., pp. 14, 117, 144–5; John, op. cit., pp. 153–4; Flinn, *Origins of Industrial Revolution*, p. 42, who points out that government borrowing was 'largely unproductive', and, as far as economic growth was concerned, this was capital lost.

[2] Deane, 'Capital Formation before Railway Age', p. 365; C. K. Hobson, op. cit., pp. 96–8, 103–6; Hobsbawn, op. cit., pp. 91–2; Jenks, op. cit., p. 64; S. G. Checkland, *The Rise of Industrial Society in England. 1815–1885* (London, 1964), pp. 10, 15–16, 21, 24; Pollard, 'Growth and Distribution', pp. 358–9.

There had been some English investment abroad in the mid eighteenth century, and after 1780 a reimbursement of part of the Dutch-held National Debt; John, op. cit., pp. 151–4; Ashton, *An Economic History*, p. 127.

[3] Dickson, op. cit., p. 301; Hobsbawn, op. cit., p. 24; Cairncross, 'Capital Formation', p. 252; Kuznets, 'Capital Formation in Modern Economic Growth', pp. 32–3; Clark, op. cit., pp. 534, 538; Mathias, op. cit., pp. 40–1, on the highly – and doubly – regressive character of the eighteenth-century taxation system, which did not prejudice capital accumulation and transferred income from the lower to the upper classes.

went into such 'consumer durables' as works of art, into ostentatious building, and into loans to the government. It did not
result in capital formation and did not constitute national
savings as defined in modern social accounting.[1] On the other
hand, the eighteenth-century upper class did invest part of its
income productively, especially in agriculture and transportation, and the rate of saving was high in the traditionally thrifty
mercantile and professional classes (though they were also
prone to conspicuous consumption, especially to acquisitions of
landed estates with a stately home). The utility of capital
accumulation was perceived and there was a willingness to
accord it priority over other, non-productive, uses of
resources.[2]

The view that England was a rich country and that consequently aggregate savings were more than sufficient to finance
the industrial revolution appears, therefore, as purely theoretical and partly unhistorical, because such sufficiency does not
necessarily mean that the redistribution of funds from those
who had resources to spare to those who had productive ideas
for their use took place easily and smoothly. The problem of
capital is not solved by the observation that aggregate savings
were adequate, as social, political or institutional constraints
or gaps could have blocked or slowed down their diversion to
productive uses, as has happened in various countries during
the nineteenth or twentieth centuries.[3]

Under these conditions, there has recently been a consensus
among economic historians that, before and during the industrial revolution, England suffered from neither an absolute
nor a relative shortage of capital. 'Few people would now
think that England was short of aggregate savings for [the]
necessary increase in investment' in the expanding sectors of
the economy, writes Mathias, who adds: 'In aggregate it

[1] Mathias, op. cit., p. 145; Kuznets, 'Capital Formation in Modern Economic
Growth', pp. 35–6; Hobsbawn, op. cit., pp. 57, 62; Flinn, *Origins of Industrial
Revolution*, p. 46; Lewis, *Theory of Economic Growth*, p. 236, on the squandering of
resources by upper-income minorities in underdeveloped societies.

[2] Dickson, op. cit., p. 301; Cairncross, 'Capital Formation', pp. 251–2.

[3] Deane, *First Industrial Revolution*, p. 164; Mathias, op. cit., pp. 14, 145, 158 ff.,
who rightly notes that the habit of productive investment did not need to be
developed in the whole society, but only in some 'enclaves', whence the well-
known importance of the Quaker and Dissenter communities; *Capital Formation
and Economic Growth*, p. 8.

seems clear that no absolute shortage of savings relative to the demand for productive investment threatened to constrain economic growth in eighteenth century Britain.' R. M. Hartwell sees 'no convincing evidence that the lack of savings held back growth', and Habakkuk 'little evidence of a capital bottleneck'.[1] So we have come back to the 'plentifulness' of capital, which had impressed the early economic historians, though, unlike them, recent writers do not see this abundance as the decisive cause of the industrial revolution, but only as a permissive factor, and point out, for instance, that capital was, relatively, even more abundant in eighteenth-century Holland, and rates of interest lower.[2]

On the other hand, economic historians have recently devoted a great deal of attention to the problem which appears most important; that of capital supply and capital mobility – of the conduits or channels, the financial intermediaries, procedures and mechanisms through which the institutional, geographical and sociological gaps between savers and investors were closed.[3]

On the question of the 'sources of capital', i.e. the financing of industrial enterprises, both at their foundation and during their expansion, a large number of data had been collected by various monographs, and an attempt was made by the present writer at synthesizing them in a paper of 1962, which is reprinted in this volume. It recognized the variety of the sources of capital which had been used, the resort by innovators to the resources of their relatives and friends, on a personal basis,

[1] Mathias, op. cit., pp. 14, 40, 144; Hartwell, *Causes of Industrial Revolution*, p. 18; Habakkuk, Historical Experience of Economic Development', p. 138; also Cairncross, 'Capital Formation', pp. 242–3, 250; Hobsbawn, op. cit., p. 24; Flinn, *Origins of Industrial Revolution*, p. 51. Kuznets, 'Capital Formation in Modern Economic Growth', pp. 28–9, and Deane, 'Capital Formation before Railway Age', p. 367, are less positive on this point.

[2] Mathias, op. cit., p. 8; Habakkuk, 'The Historical Experience on the Basic Conditions of Economic Progress', in Dupriez, op. cit., pp. 155, 161–4; Landes, op. cit., p. 66.

[3] Mathias, op. cit., pp. 14, 145; Flinn, *Origins of Industrial Revolution*, pp. 51–2, observes however that much capital 'found its way naturally, and almost automatically into productive uses', for instance landlords' rents into enclosure or transport projects, merchants' capital into industries, the raw materials or finished products of which they handled; but he supposes that such flows tended to account for the 'normal' rate of economic growth and that new channels and new institutions were needed for the sudden augmentation of capital necessary for the industrial revolution.

and the movement of capital between various branches of industry. But most of all it stressed the predominance of 'internal' financing of industry. Most firms were started with a small initial capital, which had been accumulated through pre-factory system manufacturing or merchant-manufacturing activities, or in the trading of industrial raw materials or finished articles; and they were expanded thanks to the steady ploughing back[1] of the large profits which were often possible. Altogether retained profits were seen as the greatest single source of long-term capital, and the role played by 'external' capital, supplied by landowners, overseas traders, banks, etc., was rather played down. The industrial revolution would have involved the creation of new savings and new outlets to absorb them, rather than the tapping of traditional types of savings.[2]

Broadly speaking, these conclusions seem to remain valid,[3] but recent research would qualify them on some points, mainly because of the importance which has now been attributed to circulating capital, in relation to fixed capital, and of which this writer had not been fully aware. This new view of the capital structure of eighteenth-century business leads us to reconsider the problem of financing industry, this time emphasizing the importance of *trade credit* (or book debt) and re-examining the relations between industry and the banking system.

Long-term investment in buildings and machinery being relatively small, short-term credit to finance increases in inventories was quantitatively by far the largest need of

[1] An inaccurate expression, as Mathias, op. cit., p. 149, points out, as profits were never taken out of the business in the first place.

[2] Crouzet, op. cit., pp. 590 ff. and below, pp. 163ff.

[3] See, for instance, Deane, *First Industrial Revolution*, pp. 164 ff.; Mathias, op. cit., p. 149; Pollard, 'Growth and Distribution', pp. 355–6. However, Edwards, op. cit., p. 214, argues that the reinvestment of funds was not as crucial a factor in the development of firms as supposed, and was only one of many avenues open to those who wanted to expand; Cameron *et al.*, *Banking*, p. 39: reinvestment was by no means direct or automatic; Flinn, *Origins of Industrial Revolution*, pp. 44–5, 51–2: most of the new industrial investment in the late eighteenth century took place in *new* industries (such as cotton), and could not be financed out of ploughed-back profits. But in fact a lot of the capital came from neighbouring branches in the domestic system.

The most important new work on the sources of capital is Chapman, *Early Factory Masters*; its conclusions have been summarized in additional footnotes to my article, see below, pp. 165 n. 2, 170 n. 4, 182 n. 4.

industry. The main problem for the early industrialists, as for the employers of the domestic system, was of finding circulating capital, and they could take advantage of the elaborate machinery of credit which was already in existence. Firms beginning in a small way could devote most of their own initial capital resources to fixed investment, and, by inserting themselves in the circular flow of credit, acquire working capital by a process of running creditors' balances of much larger amounts than debtors'.[1] They could buy their raw materials (and sometimes their machinery) on credit from their supplier merchants,[2] and though they had themselves to give credit to the buyers of their manufactured goods, they could either have their drafts on their customers discounted, or get advances from the commission agents to whom those goods were consigned. Quite often they also received accommodation and short-term loans from a 'patron' – generally an established merchant. Many small firms could thus start production with only a fraction of the capital they ultimately used, and in this way accumulate enough to enlarge the base of their operations. Pollard writes that 'this web of credit should be placed near the centre of the exposition of the accumulation of capital'. Merchant firms, which supplied industry with a large part of its circulating capital, thus played a dominant and decisive part in the industrial revolution, and the financing of stocks by mercantile capital was much more important than industry's self-finance, at least up to 1815.[3]

Of course, at some stage the ultimate suppliers had to be paid out of real resources saved, but it was along those extended lines of credit that the savings of non-industrialists could be

---

[1] In firms' balance sheets such accounts are very large in relation to fixed assets and even to the total inventory valuation.

[2] Interest, dividends, royalties and even wages could also be paid on credit.

[3] Pollard, 'Fixed Capital', pp. 305–14; 'Growth and Distribution', pp. 356, 358–61, 365; Chapman, *Early Factory Masters*, p. 117; 'The Peels', p. 82; Edwards, op. cit., pp. 224–6, 228, 230–3; Flinn, *Men of Iron*, p. 8; Heaton, op. cit., pp. 2–5, 10, and below, pp. 85–8, 93; Mathias, op. cit., pp. 147–8, 150; B. L. Anderson, 'Money and the Structure of Credit in the Eighteenth Century', *Business History*, XII, no. 2 (July 1970), pp. 90–100; Lévy-Leboyer, 'Quatre générations', pp. 29, 34, 36–7, 39, 50: in the late eighteenth century, the London and Bristol iron merchants were supplying the short-term (and even long-term) credit needs of the South Wales ironworks, but around 1800 the latter became independent and Cyfarthfa had generally a credit balance with George Yard, which it eventually absorbed.

mobilized. However, some writers leave the impression that a firm could grow and prosper with practically no capital resources of its own, though this was a straight way to the bankruptcy court, inasmuch as trade credit was highly unstable. Others seem to believe in an inflationary creation of 'capital', of which there is little evidence, except during some speculative manias or at times during the restriction period. The importance of trade credit is unquestionable, but must not be overrated.[1]

As for the relationship between banks and industry in the eighteenth century, the traditional or textbook view was that they lived in two separate worlds and that the contribution of the banking system to the industrial revolution was therefore quite insignificant. However, various case histories of industrial firms, and the important book on country banking by L. S. Pressnell,[2] revealed that this was far from the truth, and in his 1962 paper the present writer argued that the banks had been much more instrumental than had been generally thought in the financing of industry.[3] These suggestions were, however, criticized as too cautious by R. Cameron in his *Banking in the Early Stages of Industrialization*, which is the main recent contribution to the debate.[4] Though he may have gone too far, especially as regards Scottish banking,[5] there has recently been a tendency to stress the part played by eighteenth-century banks in capital formation.

However, a clear distinction must be made between the provision by banks of short-term and of long-term capital. The traditional view that English banks, cautious and liquidity-conscious, lent on a short- rather than a long-term basis, and did not, as a general rule, finance long-term investments like buildings, machinery and land improvements, remains roughly

[1] Flinn, *Origins of Industrial Revolution*, p. 38, points out that circulating capital is still capital, and that the main difference between fixed and working capital lies simply in the ease with which the respective needs can be met.

[2] L. S. Pressnell, *Country Banking in the Industrial Revolution* (Oxford, 1956).

[3] Crouzet, op. cit., pp. 605–6, 615–17, and below, pp. 180–2, 192–5.

[4] Cameron *et al.*, *Banking*, pp. 18, 41 n. 45.

[5] Ibid., pp. 73, 75, 92, 97–8. Cameron stresses the superiority of the Scottish banking system over the English, and its many innovations in bank policy and practice. But his thesis that this system played a major role in Scotland's more rapid industrialization is not quite convincing – it overlooks the very low level from which Scottish industry started – and does not really demonstrate the banks' contribution to capital formation.

valid, but with some serious qualifications. 'As more case histories reveal the number of instances in which this generalization about the banks not financing industrial investment was broken, the generalization may itself come under suspicion' (Mathias).[1] Many of the industrial firms which have been investigated show some instances of direct loans from bankers,[2] but these are fairly isolated, and few firms seem to have depended on banks for a high proportion of their invested capital, or have taken very long loans. However, borrowing from the banks, though not a regular feature of capital formation, was crucial at certain times of great need, either for survival or for expansion. Moreover, the device of the short-term loan often became an instrument of long-term investment, as it was renewed by agreement, or unwillingly from the bank's point of view when the borrower was unable to repay. There are also instances either of rich bankers investing part of their private fortunes into industrial ventures,[3] or of industrialists turning bankers – a rather dangerous practice, which was none the less frequent in some trades, like the iron industry, as it solved the payments problem and enabled banker-industrialists to raise capital from the public at a zero rate of interest. The old idea of a separation between banking and industry must give way to that of a partial intermingling of the two sectors.[4]

[1] For this paragraph, see Mathias, op. cit., pp. 151, 168, 175–7; Cameron *et al.*, *Banking*, pp. 52, 54–8. Bank lending may also have been important in the finance of enclosures, turnpike trusts, river and canal companies, etc.; Flinn, *Origins of Industrial Revolution*, p. 52.

[2] These loans were secured by mortgages, other securities or a mere promissory note. To the examples quoted by Mathias, op. cit., pp. 151, 168, 175–7; and Crouzet, op. cit., pp. 605–6, 615–17, one must add the involvement of Smith's Bank, of Nottingham, in the development of the local cotton-spinning industry, which has been described by Chapman, *Early Factory Masters*, pp. 138–41. In the peak building year of 1792, Smith's granted overdrafts for a total of £29,921 to cotton and worsted spinners and their partners; this sum represented 30 per cent of the total advances by the Nottingham office to its customers.

[3] Chapman, *Early Factory Masters*, pp. 142–3, concludes to a 'close association' between the banks and the Midlands spinning industry, with numerous partnerships and family connexions overlapping the two sectors. The banks 'almost certainly' played a crucial role in the supply of funds for the development of the large steam-powered factories.

[4] Cameron *et al.*, *Banking*, pp. 52, 54, sees the country banker not as 'a broker' between depositor and borrower but as 'an engine of credit', pumping out a stream of new money.

It remains true, none the less, that English bankers dealt primarily in short-term credit, but the recent emphasis upon circulating capital and trade credit gives added importance to short-term financing, which was undoubtedly the main contribution by the banks to capital formation. As Pollard puts it: 'The banks provided little long-term capital because little long-term capital was demanded. What was needed was a sufficient injection of short-term credit into the system to allow the mutual extension of credit to be developed.' The banks did not only release the manufacturer's own capital for fixed investment by discounting bills, granting overdrafts or short-term loans and thus making possible a faster rate of expansion; by the credit they gave to merchants, both suppliers and customers of industry, they underpinned the whole trade credit system. It was the willingness of banks to discount bills of exchange which gave them currency and helped them to play a vital part in the eighteenth century economy, especially in Lancashire.[1] It has been maintained, therefore, that the banks financed not only the *movement* of goods and the holding of stocks, not merely commodity sales, but also commodity *production*.[2]

Moreover, the progressive integration of the nation's financial system, which was not merely geographical, but social and industrial as well, created mounting inter-regional flows of short-term credit, by which the savings of the landed classes and their subsidiary groups (widows, lawyers, clergymen) were activated and injected through the banking system into the capital provision of the economy at large and especially of the manufacturing districts. The banking system helped to mobilize savings which, in its absence, would not have been utilized; it channelled them towards capital formation as it used them to finance trade, and through this provided some of industry's working capital.[3]

One must remark, however, that this integration (and

[1] Pollard, 'Fixed Capital', pp. 307–8; Mathias, op. cit., pp. 148–9, 175; Cameron *et al.*, *Banking*, pp. 41, 49–52; Edwards, op. cit., pp. 217–22.

[2] Pollard, 'Fixed Capital', p. 309, and Checkland, op. cit., pp. 202, 204, diverge on this point.

[3] Mathias, op. cit., pp. 17, 148–9, 174–5; Pollard, 'Growth and Distribution', pp. 364–5; Cameron *et al.*, *Banking*, pp. 23 n. 13, 30–1, 58; Deane, *First Industrial Revolution*, p. 164.

especially the emergence of the bill-brokers and the London discount market) was achieved relatively late, that the rise of country banking itself is a phenomenon of the late eighteenth century (though many businessmen had earlier exercised banking functions without being properly bankers), and that for a long time country banks were not deposit banks. 'The English banking system was largely a response to industrialization rather than a causal factor, the banks were capital-servicing rather than capital-forming institutions' (B. L. Anderson).[1]

Whatever the importance of circulating capital and short-term credit, long-term finance could still be a problem for industrialists. The imperfect but active eighteenth-century capital market therefore deserves serious attention, more particularly in order to elaborate its 'imperfectibility'.

A capital market had emerged in London in the late seventeenth century, but it was an 'unorganized' market, 'in which the left hand seldom knew what the right was doing, so that it is only with reservations that we should speak of a rate of interest in the seventeenth century'.[2] During the first decades of the eighteenth century, the market in securities developed a great deal and became much more efficient – this is a basic aspect of Dickson's 'financial revolution' – but it remained imperfect, with a separation between its 'public' and 'private' sectors. On one hand, the gaps between government loan rates and private rates of interest in London, and between long- and short-term rates, which had been very wide in the early eighteenth century, had narrowed down by 1750, while both kinds of rates had followed the same declining tendency. On the other hand, there was no close link between private interest rates and the yield on government stocks,[3] while contemporaries denied that rates on the London market were necessarily

[1] Mathias, op. cit., pp. 17, 171; Cameron *et al.*, *Banking*, pp. 23–4; Flinn, *Origins of Industrial Revolution*, p. 53; Landes, op. cit., p. 349; Edwards, op. cit., pp. 216–17; John, op. cit., pp. 139, 143; B. L. Anderson, 'The Attorney and the Early Capital Market in Lancashire', in J. R. Harris (ed.), *Liverpool and Merseyside* (Liverpool, 1969), pp. 71–4, and below, pp. 250–4.

[2] Davies, op. cit., p. 287.

[3] The fall of which resulted from special causes, which were probably political – the increasing stability of the Hanoverian regime, the long peace, the diminishing amount of bonds available for purchase. Even in the second half of the century, complexity in interest rates made the yield on Consols an uncertain barometer of the needs and prices of the capital market as a whole.

indicative of those elsewhere. They complained that the bulk of the nation's liquid resources were concentrated in London, so that private interest rates there had fallen,[1] but that, except in the Home Counties, they were notably higher in the provinces. However, though the public and private markets were financed from separate flows of savings, seeking different forms of investment, 'the two markets were not entirely separate, nor did they coincide'. Savings flowing into government securities were partly derived from, or administered by, sources like London banks or insurance companies which were also concerned in mortgages, the finance of trade, etc., so that there were possibilities of arbitrage between public and private capital requirements. On the other hand, there were some clearly specialized sectors of finance which did not compete for the kind of savings which were put into government securities. In the second half of the eighteenth century this trend towards the unification of a series of relatively separate and imperfect money markets accelerated, and led eventually to the creation of a single market.[2]

The question is, however, what influence this improvement in the London market may have had on the economy, and especially on capital formation. Public borrowing created a whole range of securities in which mercantile and financial houses could safely invest, and from which they could easily disinvest; these varied and flexible facilities for investment were the foundation on which the London money market was built.[3] Government and allied stocks became the first line of financial reserve of the business community, the basis for a pyramid of loans between merchants. Without them, according to Dickson, the City's complex structure of services, and with it the whole system of mercantile credit (the importance of which has been previously emphasized), could not have been established.[4] On the other hand, in the early eighteenth

---

[1] On this inequality between London and the provinces, cf. Pollard and Crossley, op. cit., pp. 149–51; R. Grassby, 'The Personal Wealth of the Business Community in Seventeenth Century England', *Economic History Review*, 2nd series, XXIII, no. 2 (August 1970), pp. 229, 233.

[2] Dickson, op. cit., pp. 452, 472–3, 477, 483–5; John, op. cit., pp. 143, 147, 158.

[3] Of which the best organized and largest component served the issue and jobbing of Government stock; Mathias, op. cit., p. 146.

[4] Dickson, op. cit., pp. 11–12, 245, 247; John, op. cit., pp. 138–40.

century contemporaries were complaining that the diversion of savings into government stock was harmful to the landed interest; but more because it affected the price of land and the landlords' social position, than because it deprived them of risk capital for improvements. Moreover, the domestic capital invested in government loans came mostly from London and its neighbourhood, and within the metropolis from the mercantile oligarchy in the City. Though provincial fund-holding was growing, it did not become important before the Napoleonic Wars, and the landed classes as a whole were not significant contributors of new capital for public loans. So the diversion of savings from the land and from the provinces seems to have been limited, while it is not clear that the savers who were investing in government securities would willingly have switched their money into risky industrial ventures.[1]

Still, the London capital market did not make – partly because of the Bubble Act[2] – any significant *direct* contribution to capital formation. But an important, though little investigated, phenomenon was the existence and development of a partly autonomous provincial capital market (or rather markets), centring on family resources and the activities of local business consortia with expert knowledge of local conditions, and underpinned by the rise of provincial banking houses deeply involved in local trade.[3]

Most of the capital for the turnpike trusts, joint stock canals, docks and bridges companies, was raised locally through the floatation of shares, loans and annuities.[4] And the predominance of local capital in transport projects – associated with an imperfection of the capital market – was to remain true in the early Railway Age, at least in the 1830s.[5] But one of the most important and efficiently organized sides of the capital market

[1] Dickson, op. cit., pp. 25, 29–30, 300–2, 337, 452–3; John, op. cit., pp. 142–3.
[2] See Crouzet, op. cit., p. 610, and below, pp. 185–6.
[3] Dickson, op. cit., p. 484, who dates this phenomenon from the mid eighteenth century and relates it to larger provincial incomes resulting from the expansion of Atlantic trade and Midlands industry. But there is strong evidence of its existence for an earlier period.
[4] Ashton, *An Economic History*, p. 175; Mathias, op. cit., pp. 116–17.
[5] Checkland, op. cit., p. 203; Deane, *First Industrial Revolution*, pp. 166–7; S. A. Broadbridge, 'The Early Capital Market: The Lancashire and Yorkshire Railway', *Economic History Review*, 2nd series, VIII, no. 2 (December 1955), pp. 200–12.

was the mortgage market, and though London was 'the main cross-roads' for the large transactions of this kind, there was also a great deal of local lending on mortgage. This problem has recently been studied for Lancashire by B. L. Anderson, in an unpublished thesis, on which have been based three articles, one of them being reprinted in this volume.[1] It deals with the key role which local attorneys often played as financial intermediaries, in managing the market for long-term loans with which they accommodated all sorts of people, and in forging the mortgage market into something approaching a capital market. The practice of mortgaging was very widespread in Lancashire (being made easier by the large number of small landowners), and the habit of borrowing and lending had penetrated all classes of society quite early on, involving a complex pattern of capital movements between individuals and trades. Of course the specific uses to which funds raised by mortgages were put are not generally known, and it is quite possible that they were mainly used for consumption, and also for house-building. None the less, the existence and activity of this rudimentary but flexible capital market, the mobilization of dormant funds (especially rural savings) and the large facilities for borrowing which resulted from it, cannot have been unimportant for agricultural and industrial capital formation, and for the economic growth of Lancashire. Anderson writes, therefore, that the English provinces went through a financial revolution during the first decades of the eighteenth century, which was at least as significant as the contemporaneous one in the public sector in London.[2] Much more work remains to be done on these local capital markets and on the financial intermediaries other than banks, but they were undoubtedly most important.[3]

[1] B. L. Anderson, *Aspects of Capital and Credit in Lancashire during the Eighteenth Century* (Liverpool M.A. thesis, 1966); 'Provincial Aspects of the Financial Revolution in the Eighteenth Century', *Business History*, XI, no. 1 (January 1969), pp. 11–12; 'The Attorney', and below, pp. 223–55; 'Money and the Structure of Credit', pp. 85–101.

[2] Anderson, 'Provincial Aspects', pp. 11–12, 15–16, 18–19; 'The Attorney', pp. 50, 54, 69, 74; Mathias, op. cit., p. 150. The mortgaging of real estate holdings was a springboard for many young men going into trade or manufacturing, and the source of many fortunes.

[3] Cairncross, 'Capital Formation', pp. 257–8; Edwards, op. cit., pp. 214–15, argues however that, as manufacturers did not need any large initial fixed capital,

In the personal, non-institutionalized world of eighteenth-century business, where kinship was the organizing principle and the private provision of credit depended on personal contact, capital markets remained imperfect, and capital supplies did not move freely between them. Local markets were greatly, though not entirely, influenced by local factors and local variations in credit conditions. There was not *one*, but several interest rates, with no close connexion between them, and it is not certain that they – and especially the yield on government stocks – had much influence, except in wartime, on the direction and flow of investment. Saving was specific, capital heterogeneous, investment localized. Phyllis Deane has even maintained that the capital market became more imperfect once the industrial revolution had started than in the mobile, unspecialized economy of the early eighteenth century, when men and their funds moved freely from one industry to another. Later on, savings tended to be generated by the industries or even the enterprises which invested them.[1] But after all, if provincial enterprises did not have much access to the resources of London,[2] they had more or less a monopoly of local funds, and the imperfection of the capital market limited the competition for capital, which could have been disadvantageous for infant industries or firms.

The emphasis which most recent writing has put upon trade credit, a closer relationship between banks and industry, and the early capital market, has tended to show that in eighteenth- and early nineteenth-century Britain, with its sophisticated and innovating financial system, capital supply was not a serious

---

they probably seldom resorted to 'professional investors', like merchants or attorneys, and raised small loans from their relatives, local friends and business contacts; his appendix E, pp. 255-6, analyses the borrowing of a Blackburn cotton firm: from the 1780s until 1812 it totalled £36,008, raised locally in ninety-seven separate instalments (fifty-one of them from £1 to £100), most of them secured by a mere promise to pay, and with no time limit stipulated (usually the principal remained with the firm for a considerable time). Many of those investors were clergymen, widows, spinsters, trustees and executors, who are often regarded as investors in government securities only.

[1] Mathias, op. cit., pp. 162-3; John, op. cit., pp. 139-40, 143; Deane, *First Industrial Revolution*, p. 165; Shapiro, op. cit., pp. 58-9, 153.

[2] Though there was some movement of long-term capital from London towards the provinces; Ashton, *An Economic History*, p. 26; John, op. cit., pp. 138, 144-5, 148, 157.

problem – though of course there were certainly hard-luck stories and many individual firms may have found it difficult to raise the capital they wanted. But, from a more general point of view, it has also tended to bridge the gap which had been formerly assumed to exist between industry and the other sectors of the economy at the time of the industrial revolution. It is part of the broader development of thinking among economic historians which sees the industrial revolution as a phenomenon of 'balanced growth', as a gradual advance on a broad front, rather than as a sudden breakthrough in a limited sector. Specifically, it relates industrial capital formation to previous capital accumulation in the economy as a whole.[1] The various small disjointed pools, which Postan had visualized in 1935, were neither so few, so meagre, nor so isolated as he had supposed, and they were united by a network of conduits: 'Many direct conduits existed whereby landowning and farming wealth flowed to investment for improving land and transport, while commercial wealth flowed to industry.'[2] However, the problem of the intersectoral flows of capital, especially in and out of land,[3] and of the relationship between industrial society and the landed classes, is still much debated.

Mathias writes that it is impossible to say if the net flow of capital was towards or away from the land.[4] On one hand, there were constantly new recruits to the landed classes, from commerce, industry and the professions, who invested in land the fortunes they had made in business.[5] On the other hand, an important direct flow of savings from the land, created from farmers' profits and from landlords' rents,[6] contributed capital not only for agricultural improvements but also for investment

[1] Pollard, 'Growth and Distribution', p. 357.

[2] Mathias, op. cit., p. 144.

[3] Which were crucial, agriculture being by far the largest sector of the economy and providing the biggest single contribution to the nation's savings; ibid., p. 65.

[4] This balance may also have changed in direction and volume over time, as pointed out by Landes, op. cit., p. 77; from 1793 to 1814 the net flow of resources was probably towards the land.

[5] The dowries of merchants' daughters who married into the gentry must also be considered.

[6] Flinn, *Origins of Industrial Revolution*, p. 47, stresses that of all the sectoral incomes, it was these of the landed classes which rose most rapidly in the second half of the eighteenth century.

in mining, turnpike roads and canals. Moreover, direct investment by groups in the landed sector was supplemented by a
much more widespread connexion once the country banking
system began to tap the savings of agricultural districts more
widely, and when landowners and farmers began to bank their
balances rather than keep them hoarded at home.[1]

Habakkuk observes that the flow of capital into landownership from other sectors must not be overestimated, as far as the
second part of the eighteenth century is concerned, owing to
the 'closure' of the land market. However, he stresses that 'the
best opinion, that of Malthus for example, assumed that landowners were pre-eminently consumers. And this still remains
the most reasonable generalization. . . . Only when the family
built or enlarged the great house did capital expenditure
absorb a large part of their resources.[2] Expenditure on improvements . . . appears in most cases to have been relatively small.'
Landowners were also 'characteristically the borrowing class',
and most of the money they raised by mortgage was not used
for productive enterprises. Agricultural improvements other
than enclosures were generally financed out of income, but
very possibly absorbed less than 10 per cent of landlords' gross
income.[3] Enclosures, on the other hand, which presented a
more serious financial problem, were commonly financed out
of capital, in many cases with borrowed money; but such
borrowing was 'usually a small part of total indebtedness'. As
for the working of mineral resources, direct working by landlords was most prominent in the early stages of the development of a region, when they provided a large part of the initial
capital, but this gave way to leasing as the area developed.
The development of urban sites was done generally through

[1] Mathias, op. cit., pp. 53, 57, 65.

[2] Flinn, *Origins of Industrial Revolution*, p. 48, has made an interesting attempt
to estimate roughly the chronology of investment in country house building,
from a two counties sample: the two main periods were from the 1690s to the
1730s and from 1780 to 1830 – so that in the key half-century 1740–90, the
reduction in this unproductive investment might have freed capital for other
employment.

[3] Mingay, op. cit., pp. 163–88, shows that the majority of landlords were
not taking an active part in improvements other than enclosures; Holderness,
in Higgins and Pollard, op. cit., p. 178, doubts whether 'the generality of
rentier estates is found to have laid out more than 5 per cent of gross rents
at most before 1790', with new capital expenditure almost always forming the
smaller part of the total outlay.

C

building leases to speculators who built at their own expense. And though landowners played an important part in promoting turnpike trusts and canal construction, Habakkuk wonders how often they provided the real initiative: genuine aristocratic canal or port entrepreneurs, like the Duke of Bridgewater or the Lowther family, were not at all common. Dr J. R. Ward has recently calculated that landowners provided just under one-third of the shareholding of eighteenth-century English canals.[1] Many of the landlords' economic activities were the by-product of the pursuit of predominantly non-economic purposes or a response to pressure from tenants. 'The main point about landowners . . . is that they did not acquire land in order to develop it, but in order to enjoy it.' However, Habakkuk admits that there were many exceptions, and he does not accept the view that the ability of an 'extravagant' class to borrow 'for spendthrift purposes' (owing to its possession of the type of assets which were the best security for loans) decreased the percentage of national income which was productively invested and diverted capital from industry. He also stresses that the relatively small sums which landowners invested for productive purposes may have been of critical importance, especially in the construction of a transport system which was a prerequisite of industrial advance. Landlords put their power of borrowing on the security of their estates at the disposal of transport improvements.[2] But, as far as industry is concerned, one is tempted to keep to Postan's view that 'surprisingly little' of the wealth of rural England 'found its way into the new industrial enterprises'.[3]

[1] J. R. Ward (Oxford D.Phil. thesis, 1971).

[2] H. J. Habakkuk, 'Economic Functions of English Landowners in the Seventeenth and Eighteenth Centuries', in H. G. J. Aitken (ed.), *Explorations in Enterprise* (Cambridge, Mass., 1965), pp. 330–40; 'The English Land Market in the Eighteenth Century', in J. S. Bromley and E. H. Kossmann (eds), *Britain and the Netherlands* (London, 1960), pp. 154–73; 'England', in A. Goodwin (ed.), *The European Nobility in the Eighteenth Century*, 2nd ed. (London, 1967), pp. 8–9, 16; 'La disparition du paysan anglais', *Annales ESC*, XX, no. 4 (July–August 1965), pp. 661–3.

[3] Postan, op. cit., p. 2; also Landes, op. cit., pp. 76–7. Mingay, op. cit., pp. 189–201, and Chambers and Mingay, op. cit., pp. 202–3, are not convincing when stating 'the aristocratic origin of much of the industrial enterprise north of the Trent'. In fact, though land was relatively unremunerative purely as an investment, capital was not attracted thereby towards industry, but rather towards the national debt and the long-term mortage.

In connexion with the problem of the flow of capital between agriculture and the rest of the economy, one may mention the Marxist views on 'primitive accumulation', as they assign to agricultural change a leading part in the rise of industrial capitalism in eighteenth-century Britain, i.e. in the industrial revolution.[1] However, this 'so-called primitive accumulation', which is postulated by Marx and his followers as the necessary 'pre-condition' for industrial development, is quite different from capital accumulation or formation in the usual sense. It was defined by Marx as the historical process by which was achieved the basic condition of the capitalist system, which is the polarization of the market between owners of the means of production and 'free' labourers, freed both from 'feudal' bondages and from all property in the means of production by which they realize their labour.[2] In this respect, 'the expropriation of the agricultural producer, of the peasant, from the soil, is the basis of the whole process'; and this was achieved by the sixteenth- and eighteenth-century enclosures which, either by 'forcible means' or by a 'Parliamentary form of robbery', conquered the field for capitalist agriculture and created for the town industries the necessary supply of a 'free and outlawed proletariat'.[3]

However, Marx also stressed a different aspect of primitive accumulation, which is closer to the literal meaning of the expression: the looting and exploitation of colonies in America and the East Indies, the slave trade, 'commercial wars' between European powers, the protectionist system, the creation of the National Debt and of the 'modern mode of taxation' – all factors which focused into 'a systematic combination' in late seventeenth-century England. They increased and concentrated capital, especially merchant capital; and as they relied upon 'brute force' and robbery, or at least 'the power of the State', capital came into the world 'dripping from head to foot, from every pore, with blood and dirt'. But Marx comes

[1] See Marx, op. cit., book I, part VIII, chaps. XXVI–XXXII.

[2] Ibid., pp. 737–8. It is called 'primitive', because it precedes capitalist accumulation and is not the result of the capitalist mode of production but its starting point, the 'pre-historic stage of capital' (p. 736).

[3] Ibid., pp. 739–40, 757–86. Marx adds (chap. XXX, pp. 769–74) that another result of this agricultural revolution was the creation of the home market for industrial capital owing to the destruction of rural domestic industries.

back to his first meaning of capitalist accumulation when he points out that these factors tended to hasten the expropriation of independent peasants and artisans, and the capitalizing (i.e. the transformation into capital) of the natural means of production.[1] On the other hand, he stressed that the existence and development of merchant capital, though being an historical premiss for the development of capitalist production, are incapable by themselves of promoting and explaining the transition from the feudal to the capitalist mode of production and the rise of industrial capitalism. Its predominance is symptomatic of a backward situation and tends to preserve it.[2]

A recent writer has bravely stated that this 'complete model of the pre-conditions for industrial development' has been 'broadly confirmed in its fundamental correctness by later research'.[3] The uniqueness of British history, which explains why the industrial revolution took place in Britain and not elsewhere, lies in the early transformation of the social structure, which virtually eliminated the independent peasantry and replaced it by a landless proletariat working for wages; and which, on the other hand, achieved a 'concentration of property into relatively few hands and *its conversion into capital for industrial development*'[4] (my italics). This sentence is a neat sleight of hand: neither Marx nor his followers have ever put forward any proof that such a 'conversion' took place and, as a matter of fact, little of the wealth which was concentrated into landlords' hands was converted into industrial capital. As for the 'central fact' of the formation of a growing proletariat in the countryside, its relationship with the industrial

[1] Marx, op. cit., pp. 774–82, 785–6. To Marx, the means of production are not capital while they remain the property of the 'immediate producers'; they become capital only when they serve as means of exploitation of the labourers (p. 792).

[2] Marx, vol. III (Moscow, 1959), book III, part IV, chap XX, pp. 318–31. M. Dobb, *Papers on Capitalism, Development, Planning* (London, 1967), pp. 5, 7–8, 15–16, points out also that merchant capital does not generally have a 'progressive role' and that 'manufactures' or the putting-out system are not forms of transition towards industrial capitalism.

[3] J. Saville, 'Primitive Accumulation and Early Industrialization in Britain', *The Socialist Register* (London, 1969), pp. 265–7. He admits, however, that Marx has overestimated the social consequences of sixteenth-century enclosures, and that a rural proletariat could emerge by ways other than forcible expropriation, under the pressures of the market economy; pp. 254–5, 258, 263.

[4] Ibid., pp. 250–1, 266.

revolution is far from clear, though one can readily agree that there was a 'dialectical relationship between the growth of a capitalistic agriculture . . . and the development of the rest of the economy.'[1]

A more sophisticated Marxist analysis, which attempts to find the 'missing link' (which Marx had not provided) between 'primitive accumulation' and capital formation during the industrial revolution, has been given by Maurice Dobb, but he admits honestly that his question marks remain unanswered. For instance, Dobb stresses that 'primitive accumulation', i.e. the mere piling up of wealth (mostly in precious metals and durable consumer goods) and the enrichment of the bourgeoisie through expropriation of small producers and colonial plunder, did not help the growth of capitalist production and could even hinder it. A mere transfer of the property of existing wealth cannot be considered as a creation of real capital and as productive investment. Bourgeois wealth so acquired was not necessarily used to promote the growth of production. It was *dis*-accumulation, in order to provide for investment in means of production, which could stimulate growth. For the previous enrichment to be instrumental in preparing the industrial revolution, there ought to have been 'a final stage of realization'. But Dobb admits that there is no evidence of any such stage in which former bourgeois wealth, previously accumulated, was sold or realized in order to find the means for investing in industry and financing the new instruments of production of the period of technical innovation. Therefore the whole notion of enrichment *per se* as a precursor of the industrial revolution ought to be dismissed as a myth, inasmuch as the new techniques were pioneered mainly by small men, with comparatively little capital of their own.[2]

Another debate which does not lack ideological undertones

[1] Ibid., p. 267.

[2] Dobb, op. cit., pp. 26–30. However, Dobb defends Marx's view that 'primitive accumulation', i.e. the concentration of ownership through the expropriation of small-owners and the creation of a proletariat, was a condition *sine qua non* for the capital investing process, as it provided a superabundant supply of the commodity labour-power, which was the *fons et origo* of capitalist profits and therefore of capital investment by the plough-back method (ibid., pp. 31–2, 59). But it has been maintained that the proletariat was an additional population which was enabled to grow up by the new opportunities for employment which capitalism provided; Hayek, op. cit., p. 16.

is concerned with the relationship between capital formation and consumption, i.e. standards of living, during the industrial revolution.[1] Many of its early historians, from Arnold Toynbee to the Hammonds, who were critical of *laissez-faire* capitalism and had socialist leanings, had commented with severity upon the policies of the early industrialists, who had extracted, by hard and ruthless means, from a people who were already hard-pressed to make ends meet, the savings required for increased capital investment. More conservatively-minded writers had accepted this concept of 'forced savings' at the expense of the working class' current living standards, but had pointed out that a programme of national industrialization could not be carried out without great hardship for the masses, as heavy investment was a necessary pre-condition of a rise in incomes.[2] These views persisted during the pre- and post-Second World War period, as economists and economic historians postulated that the industrial revolution had involved very large investments, and, following Lewis and Rostow, a sharp increase in the percentage of the national income devoted to capital formation within a comparatively short period. As a relative shortage of capital was supposed to have prevailed at the same time, this investment effort could not have been achieved without a heavy pressure upon consumption, especially for the working class.[3]

The most articulate statement of these views is to be found in an article of 1958 by Pollard.[4] He stressed the 'exceptional' burden which the British economy had to bear during the crucial stages of industrialization, in order to accumulate, in real terms, the large resources required for substantial and

[1] As it is out of the question to reopen here the 'standard of living controversy', these few pages will deal only with some works which have approached it in relation to capital formation.

[2] W. H. B. Court, *A Concise Economic History of Britain from 1750 to Recent Times* (Cambridge, 1954), pp. 88–9; see above, pp. 5–7 on Hamilton's profit inflation theory.

[3] It has been pointed out above (p. 7 n. 1) that these views were partly a reverberation of the forced industrialization of the USSR, with its deliberate squeezing of consumption standards. According to the politics of their proponents, they could be used as a justification, either of laissez-faire capitalism or of Stalinism – either system having not behaved in a worse manner towards the workers than its opposite number!

[4] S. Pollard, 'Investment, Consumption and the Industrial Revolution', *Economic History Review*, 2nd series, XI, no. 2 (December 1958), pp. 215–26.

simultaneous investment in several important sectors,[1] at a
time when its output was very little above subsistence level for
a large part of the population. Investment plans tended to
out-run available savings, there was a 'formidable' stress on
resources, aggravated by the burden of a growing population
which absorbed much of the increased investment without
raising equipment *per capita*.[2] It is not surprising therefore that
'even the most optimistic assumptions' cannot make the rise
in real wages during the British industrial revolution 'anything
but disappointing'. But Pollard asserts that 'a victorious economic development . . . needed, for a critical period, the greatest
amount of output and the lowest level of personal consumption,
which could be imposed on the population'; an expansion of
consumption 'would have run counter to the crying needs of
an industrializing economy'. In a recent book Pollard has maintained the same views: in the early stages of industrialization,

> The growing productivity depends on growing industrial
> investment . . . and this investment (together with the needs
> of a rising population) may well . . . swallow up all the
> modest increase. . . . Thus the first generation of industrial-
> izers may be sacrificed to the second, and even the second,
> if its investment is significantly larger than of its predeces-
> sors, may not enjoy the increase in consumption, but use
> it all up for even better future performances.[3]

Some other writers, like Lewis and Rostow, have put
forward a slightly different line of argument, by reviving and
elaborating the classical economists' model of capital accumulation – that 'the central fact of economic development is that
the distribution of income is altered in favour of the saving
class'. They have asserted that the increase in savings, which
they postulated as necessary to finance the industrial revolution,

[1] The idea that the industrial revolution was a 'balanced growth', with an
'advance on a broad front', and capital often required in large 'lumps', is basic
to Pollard's argument (ibid., pp. 216–17).

[2] Pollard criticizes writers who play down their difficulties, and especially
Lewis for arguing that 'no nation is so poor' that it could not raise its savings
ratio from 5 to 12 per cent of national income, 'if it wanted to do so'.

[3] Pollard and Crossley, op. cit., pp. 181, also 182, 187, 197: costly investments,
like canals and railways, had a long gestation period; rising productivity was
limited at first to a small sector of industry, while its benefits were lost by
diffusion among the whole economy.

came largely from shifts in income flows, which considerably enlarged the share of capitalist profits (which are the main source of savings in any economy) in national income. Given an unlimited supply of labour at a subsistence wage at the beginning of the industrial revolution, practically all the 'benefits of rising productivity . . . go not to the classes who would increase their consumption – peasants, wage-earners – but into private profits . . . [which] are used for further capital formation'.[1]

Eric Hobsbawn has also stated that industrialization means a relative diversion of income from consumption to investment, i.e. largely from the non-investing classes to the potentially investing ones, from the poor to the rich; and he observes that early nineteenth-century economic theory and economic practice stressed the crucial importance of capital accumulation by capitalists (i.e. of the maximum rate of profit) and the maximum diversion of income from the workers to their employers.[2] Such views rested on two assumptions: that industrial progress required heavy investment, and that insufficient savings were available for it without holding down the incomes of the masses. Hobsbawn admits that these assumptions were wrong, as there never was the slightest general shortage of capital; but he salvages the 'pessimist' thesis on the standards of living, the idea of 'immiserizing growth', by pointing out that the richest classes and the largest potential investors (landlords, merchants, financiers) invested their money outside direct industrial development or else wasted it. Thus the rest of the (smaller) entrepreneurs, such as the cotton manufacturers, who 'had little access to the big money', were forced to press more harshly upon labour, for instance by massive use of children and women as cheap labour, thus enforcing a successful diversion of incomes from labour to capital.[3]

---

[1] Lewis, 'Economic Development', pp. 156–7; *Theory of Economic Growth*, pp. 226, 231–6; Rostow, 'The Take-Off', pp. 38–40; *Stages of Economic Growth*, pp. 46–50. Lewis writes: 'The essential feature of the conversion from 5 to 12 per cent saving is an *enormous* increase in the share of profits in the national income' [my italics].

[2] See also Pollard, 'Investment, Consumption', pp. 223–4, on the classical economists' 'unconscious reflection' of this problem.

[3] Hobsbawn, op. cit., pp. 51, 56–7, 72.

This substitution of a sectoral for a global approach, which moreover takes into account the imperfections of the capital market, is worth considering. None the less any discussion on the investment–consumption problem has now to start from the basic fact, which, following Phyllis Deane's work, is generally accepted, that the rise in the net investment proportion from around 5 per cent to around 10 per cent of national income was gradual and extended over three-quarters of a century. Little remains of the argument that a steep increase in the investment rate at the beginning of industrialization gives a strong *a priori* reason for anticipating a decline or a stagnation in average consumption levels.[1] Moreover, there is no evidence of a substantial redistribution of income which would have reduced absolutely the real incomes of the working classes, and, as Hartwell has suggested,

> Investment in capital goods was made in the expectation of increasing productivity, at least in the next period; over the fifty to one hundred years of the industrial revolution – a very long period – if capital accumulation did not increase productivity, with a large increase in output and incomes, it must have been largely unproductive, which it patently was not. There is no evidence . . . that investment was anything but highly productive with consequential effects on employment and incomes.[2]

One may add also that, even in the most prosperous concerns within the progressive industries, the returns on capital employed, though certainly high, were not exorbitant enough in the long run to leave much room for a substantial increase in wages at the expense of the ploughing-back of profits.[3]

The decisive factor in the undoubtedly low standards of living and widespread poverty of the working classes in the

---

[1] Mathias, op. cit., p. 214; Hartwell, *Causes of Industrial Revolution*, p. 67.

[2] R. M. Hartwell (ed.), *The Industrial Revolution* (Oxford, 1970: Nuffield College Studies in Economic History, no. 1), pp. 176–7; also Flinn, *Origins of Industrial Revolution*, pp. 64–5.

[3] There was a secular fall in profit per unit of output from the early nineteenth century; Crouzet, op. cit., p. 619.

eighteenth and early nineteenth centuries, was the pressure of a rising population, Lewis's 'unlimited supplies of labour' at a subsistence wage, not the pressure of investment.[1]

III

This survey of some problems concerning capital formation during the industrial revolution has shown that many of them remain unsolved, largely because of the lack of detailed research at the grass roots level and of reliable quantitative data. On 'the basic issue of the quantities of capital involved',[2] writers have used doubtful guess-estimates by earlier authors and a few elementary series, like statistics of the number of enclosure or turnpike acts, of the amount of authorized capital for canal and railway companies, or Shannon's brick index. However, as Pollard pointed out at the Munich conference in 1965, 'there is likely to be sufficient information in surviving records to make estimates possible, but the shameful fact is that so far the required spadework has not yet been undertaken', and he made 'a plea to use the wealth of surviving material' to calculate some estimates of capital formation.[3] Thanks to the support of the Social Science Research Council, Pollard has subsequently been able to launch a large-scale research project on capital formation in Britain from 1750 to 1850, with a quantitative approach and the ultimate target of calculating the rates of capital formation on a much more solid basis than in the estimates which have been discussed earlier in this paper.[4] In January 1969 a conference was held in Sheffield which brought the local research team and a number of experts together to hear progress reports and to pool ideas. The proceedings were published in 1971.[5] At this early stage in the

---

[1] Hartwell, *The Industrial Revolution*, p. 177, suggests that capital formation was in fact too low, especially in social infrastructure, which 'explains some of the distress of the period'.

[2] Higgins and Pollard, op. cit., p. 1.

[3] Pollard, 'Growth and Distribution', p. 362.

[4] Higgins and Pollard, op. cit., pp. 6–7: in many sectors the best figures likely to be obtained will be for *gross gross* investment; but Pollard intends to calculate also the gross and net capital formations and their proportions to national income.

[5] Higgins and Pollard, op. cit.

research work, the conference was 'a departure rather than the arrival', and its proceedings are mostly methodological, dealing with the analysis and discussion of sources and with methods of exploiting them.[1] The general impression they leave is that formidable difficulties are to be encountered (as Pollard admits very frankly), even for sectors like canals or shipbuilding, which one would have thought of as relatively plain sailing.[2] The sectoral series will have to be built from below, instead of being derived from above, as in research on post-1850 capital formation. There are few comprehensive official statistics which can provide a solid basis for time-series,[3] especially for the earlier part of the period; and at the grass roots level, original documents (records of canal companies, turnpike trusts, parishes, enclosure commissions, estates or farms) have partly disappeared or are so massive and scattered that complete analysis is impossible. So work will have to be concentrated on samples and the results grossed up or extrapolated. Moreover, such documents are not too easy to use, because of antiquated methods of book-keeping, for instance, and it is frequently impossible to separate new work from maintenance. Pollard considers that the best series – which it will be possible to calculate on a year-to-year basis – will be for canals, turnpikes, docks, some urban road networks and shipping. On the other hand, for such sectors as investment in agricultural stocks and increases in work in progress, any data are very scarce and yearly figures will be impossible to obtain. In between, there will be 'some reliable information' for house-building, most manufacturing industries, mining and parish road-building, 'but this will usually refer to either a tiny proportion of the expenditure, which will have to be grossed up

[1] Two exceptions are the papers by Chapman ('Fixed Capital Formation', which was the product of independent research), and by Holderness on agriculture, which present factual data. One of the merits of the various papers is to pay a great deal of attention to technical change and its consequences for capital formation.

[2] They also shed a most critical light upon previous estimates. For instance, J. E. Ginarlis (pp. 121–2) criticizes the use of the maximum amounts of capital authorized by private Acts of Parliament for transport projects; he dismisses also the method of calculating the average cost of construction per mile.

[3] See R. Craig (pp. 131–48) about the 'pitfalls' of the shipping statistics, especially before 1786, the perturbations due to prizes, losses and recaptures in wartime, the difficulty of estimating shipbuilding costs, the special problems of steamships, etc.

without much certainty as to how representative the sample is; or it will refer to a more representative sample, but cover only a few years'. So aggregate capital formation figures will be available only for a few key years or groups of years, with the danger of the 'neglect of the cyclical nature, and possibly the cyclical switch of investment'.[1]

The methods which the Sheffield team will use for calculating capital formation in each sector belong either to a macro-economic or to a micro-economic approach – though on some occasions they will combine both. The macro-economic method starts with a statistical series of 'input' or 'output' for the whole sector (e.g. acreage of land enclosed, tonnage of ships built) and applies to it a coefficient of average capital requirements, calculated from the technical literature and other documents. Its drawback is the wide variation in effective inputs of capital within the sector under consideration. As for the micro-economic approach, it synthesizes totals for capital formation from data on firms or enterprises derived from their accounts, or other specific documents. It is more realistic for this reason, but depends upon the representative-ness of the available sample. A pioneer and highly suggestive example of this method has been given by S. D. Chapman in his study of fixed capital formation in the early cotton industry. It is based primarily upon the numerous insurance valuations of textile mills in the registers of the Sun Fire Office and the Royal Exchange, which, at the end of the eighteenth century, took the lion's share of this kind of insurance business. The valuation figures taken from the registers were extrapolated – with the help of a classification of cotton mills by 'types', and of the relationship between the investment of leading and of small firms in Stockport – to build up an estimate of total fixed capital formation in Britain's cotton industry *circa* 1795. Chapman admits that insurance valuations have to be inter-preted with some caution, but he asserts that they are realistic and 'approached a conservative estimate of what would now be recognized as net capital formation'.[2] At the Sheffield Conference, D. T. Jenkins, drawing on his own work on the

---

[1] Higgins and Pollard, op. cit., pp. 2, 8–9.

[2] Chapman, 'Fixed Capital Formation', pp. 235–56. Another estimate for 1811 was calculated on the basis of Crompton's mule census of that year.

West Riding, sided with Chapman to assert that there was a reasonable agreement between insurance values and real values (from firms' accounts). On the other hand M. M. Edwards suggested that insurance records might undervalue firms' assets, and J. Butt was still more critical, on the basis of his work on the Scottish cotton industry, where systematic and serious undervaluation seems to have been common. He also stressed that it was impossible to convert the insured values into investment figures. However, there was a consensus that insurance records could be used for calculating estimates of fixed capital formation not only for the textile industries but also for various industries such as brewing, paper, printing and for agriculture.[1]

One must mention finally another research project, which has been undertaken at the University of Liverpool, under J. R. Harris, on the supply of capital and the economic development of Merseyside from the late seventeenth to the late nineteenth century. It will be a regional study in depth, based on systematic analysis of local sources, such as wills and probate inventories, courts' and legal records, archives of insurance and transport companies, etc. The emphasis will be on the development of the capital market, the sources of investment funds, the changes in investment flows, the composition of capital and the spread of investment habits.[2]

IV

This new type of research in depth might eventually upset current ideas about capital formation during the industrial revolution. Presently, however, economic historians are sceptical about the unique role capital was formerly supposed to have played in the beginnings of modern economic growth.[3] They have given up the simple neo-classical models, in which increased capital accumulation led to the industrial revolution, which amounted more or less to an acceleration in the rate of capital formation. They see little evidence either of a shortage

[1] Higgins and Pollard, op. cit., pp. 108–13, 115–18, 194–5.

[2] Information supplied by J. R. Harris and B. L. Anderson.

[3] However, Pollard and Crossley, op. cit., pp. 158–9, maintain that, in agriculture, capital was the critical factor, which helped to break the Malthusian vicious cycle.

of capital or of a sharp increase in capital formation proportions, before and during the industrial revolution, which was achieved with a low average net investment and did not put a great strain on the supply of capital.[1] The relative abundance of capital in eighteenth-century England (and its increased availability, thanks to more sophisticated financial facilities) is undoubtedly not to be overlooked, but it is seen only as a permissive factor, a prerequisite of the acceleration in change and growth which occurred late in the century, and which was not a necessary and inevitable consequence of capital accumulation.[2] Several writers are indeed tempted to stress an inverse relation between the two phenomena: capital accumulation appears to them as a result rather than a pre-condition of industrialization, capital formation as the response to the growth of income rather than the creator of it, and a spurt of income as having preceded an acceleration of investment.[3]

Moreover, recent research and thinking have emphasized the demand rather than the supply side in the origins of the industrial revolution, which would have been called forth, in a large measure, by the pressure of demand (especially from the home market) on the traditional mode of production; and, as far as the capital market was concerned, accumulation is seen as having been stimulated by population growth and technical progress.[4] On the other hand a basic development during the industrial revolution was the increasing efficiency in the use of capital goods – this was more or less the crux of the factory system – and the continuous improvement in the quality of the capital stock, which at any moment during the eighteenth century had a higher productivity than at any previous time, as more new capital and an increasing proportion of replacement capital embodied new techniques.[5] The flow of technical,

[1] Substantial investment in breadth was needed to expand productive capacity in order to keep pace with the increasing needs of a growing population – and it made greater demands on resources than the deepening of investment; but it did not involve a rise in the capital formation ratio; Flinn, *Origins of Industrial Revolution*, p. 40; Mathias, op. cit., p. 196.

[2] Flinn, *Origins of Industrial Revolution*, pp. 54–5, 98.

[3] For instance, Cameron *et al.*, *Banking*, p. 64; Cairncross, 'Capital Formation', p. 245; Hartwell, *The Industrial Revolution*, pp. 10, 13.

[4] Landes, op. cit., pp. 38, 55, 77–8; Meier and Baldwin, op. cit., p. 175.

[5] Hartwell, *Causes of Industrial Revolution*, p. 19; Cameron, 'Some Lessons of History', pp. 314–15.

organizational, administrative and financial innovations (the latter permitting a more efficient allocation of savings to investment) is the crucial aspect of the industrial revolution, which was first and foremost a technical revolution. Recent thinking may have gone too far in its preference for 'balanced growth', and one must not overlook the decisive role of a small number of critical technological breakthroughs, nor the rapid increase in investment (especially in fixed capital which embodied technical progress) in a few areas of the economy. The discussion about the functional relations between capital formation, economic growth and technical progress is not over.

1 Recent Trends in the Accumulation of Capital

M. M. POSTAN

[This article was first published in the *Economic History Review*, vol. VI, no. 1, October 1935.]

Among the many things which have affected the position of socialists in the post-war world has been the loss of their exclusive rights in the 'decline of capitalism'. Nowadays the loudest lamentations at the deficient working of the system come from its most ardent defenders. The difference between them and the anti-capitalists is largely confined to the question of origins. Whereas the socialists still regard the illness of the system as something ancient and congenital, the individualists and the anti-socialists refer to it as an unfortunate accident of recent date. But however much they differ about the origin and the causation, they all agree about the reality of the disease and its symptoms. The dwindling of international trade, the cessation of international migrations, the strangulation of international credit recur in official speeches and in letters to the Press. The ossification of the system due to monopolies and price-fixing is now publicly reviled by all except the monopolists and the price-fixers themselves. In addition, the pure economists have been lamenting the 'rigidities' introduced by social legislation and trade union action, while the trend-artists among the statisticians have been trying to discover a general decline in the rate of industrial growth. One symptom of *Spätkapitalismus*, however, seems to have escaped the attention of the hypochondriacs. In enumerating the diseased members of the system they commonly leave out some of the morbid changes that have recently occurred in the most important member of all, in capital itself. The changes, like all the other symptoms, may yet turn out to be as superficial and easy to cure as some people fondly hope them to be. But their reality and their present effect cannot be in doubt, and should not be overlooked.

It will be an unforgivable truism to say that the chief reason why the economic system of the nineteenth century deserves the appellation of capitalism is the part which capital plays in it. But it will, perhaps, be less obvious to point out that until recently the use of capital, its accumulation and employment, was probably the only element of the system approaching the full perfection postulated and expected by economists. And to have made it so nearly perfect was one of the most important, though not, perhaps, the most spectacular, economic achievements of the nineteenth century.

At the beginning of the Industrial Revolution, capital, like the other factors of production, like land and labour, was not yet available in the form or the quantities required by the rapid rise of an industrial civilization. The response of savings to growth in demand was as yet too feeble to bring forth, when and where needed, new supplies of fresh capital. But on the whole the insufficiency of capital was local rather than general, and social rather than material. By the beginning of the eighteenth century there were enough rich people in the country to finance an economic effort far in excess of the modest activities of the leaders of the Industrial Revolution. It can, indeed, be doubted whether there had ever been a period in English history when the accumulated wealth of landlords and merchants, of religious and educational institutions would have been inadequate for this purpose. What was inadequate was not the quantity of stored-up wealth, but its behaviour. The reservoirs of savings were full enough, but conduits to connect them with the wheels of industry were few and meagre. To use the jargon of modern economics, much of the savings was hoarded, while much, even if available for some investments, was not available for all, and at any rate not for the investments which the new industry required most. In the last quarter of the eighteenth, and the first quarter of the nineteenth century the country banks and the City merchants succeeded, much to the surprise of foreigners, in employing the free resources of the rural classes for financing the sale of the new industrial products. But they never attempted, and would never have succeeded if they had attempted to finance the new production, and to divert the wealth of landlords and farmers into industrial investment. In spite of the fact that rural England had long been familiar with the new financial methods, surprisingly little of her wealth found its way into the new industrial enterprises, where the shortage of capital must have been acute, and the risks, even as they might appear to the investor, not immoderate.

In France and Germany the earliest privately established factories were not, and could not be financed by miscellaneous owners of capital seeking investment. Where capital did not come from abroad, and was not supplied by the governments, it had to be collected and maintained out of the personal resources and the family fortunes of the founders, or out of gifts from their friends and relatives. In France, both before and after the Revolution, state subsidies and foreign importation helped to provide the capital for a number of large enterprises at the beginning of their careers. But in French industry as a whole the small workshop, with its private supplies of capital, predominated throughout the nineteenth century. In east Germany, and especially in Silesia, the large-scale breweries, mines and foundries were originally established by the great feudal landlords as part of their estates. Elsewhere they grew from small enterprises financed out of the private resources of their owners. Most of the famous undertakings founded in the first half of the century were brought into existence in this way. The first of the Krupps established his foundry for cast steel with the 50,000 thalers which he had collected from family sources, and, in 1817, when these were exhausted, the whole enterprise was brought to the brink of ruin. The founder of the great engineering firm of Borsig started with 8,000 thalers of personal savings to which he later added 59,000 thalers, borrowed from friends. Richard Hartmann, the founder of the famous Chemnitz firm, built up his great business out of the profits of his repair shop. Perhaps the only important enterprise in the German metal industry before 1840 to be financed on a joint stock basis was the engineering firm of Emil Kessler. And what is true of metal industries is also true of the textiles and even of mining. Most of the early German coal mines belonged to coal merchants, who invested into the industry the profits of their trade. The Stinnes, of Mülheim, like the Haniels of Ruhrort, made their *début* as mine-owners in the twenties by diverting into mining some of their modest trading capital, and proceeded very far on the way to their immense mining concerns without calling upon a single important contribution from the general public.

In this country, the cradle of the new industrial order, the position was not much different, and the new enterprises, in their search for capital, were not much assisted by the fact that England happened to be at the time the richest land in Christendom. That in founding their enterprises the pioneers of the factory system had to draw almost entirely on their private savings, or on the assistance of friends, may not strike us as strange or 'non-modern'. But that throughout their subsequent operations, even after their ventures had proved successful, they should still have found it impossible to raise new capital, except among acquaintances and friends, is very significant. Arkwright obtained his first funds from a publican friend. For a time it looked as if he might draw in a firm of Nottingham bankers, but in the end the latter refused to be involved in his activities, and not until Need and Strutt joined him as partners did funds become sufficient. Cartwright financed his industrial venture out of his private means, which he soon proceeded to lose. Benjamin Gott drew his capital from his two friends and partners, Wormald and Fountaine. The Darbys and the Wilkinsons merely extended the operations of what had been family concerns, and for a long time continued to draw on family resources. Watt was financed by his friend Dr Black, a man of relatively modest means, while Boulton, who joined him as a partner in 1774, and was a man of substance, derived that substance in the first place from the profits of a family business and from other family sources, as well as from the support of his other partner Fothergill. These sources were very heavily drawn upon throughout the early life of the Soho works, and Boulton had to sink into the venture nearly the whole of his fortune, including £25,000 brought him by his wife and sums raised by the sale of his estate and the mortgage on his father's property. In the most critical period in the history of the firm, the bankers who financed him by short-term loans failed him, and more than once he had to depend, even for short-term accommodation, on the assistance of clients and friends, including Wilkinson and Wedgwood.

The financial history of most other industrial enterprises of the late eighteenth and the early nineteenth centuries is very similar. When the burdens were too heavy for the resources of a single man the financing could be undertaken by a partnership, which was usually a combination of a few friends or relatives. Even the most high-sounding companies of the time, such as the famous Carron Company, were composed of small and intimate groups of partners. Joint stock publicly subscribed was a very rare exception. Canal companies began to be floated on the public market during the canal mania of the nineties, and a few mining enterprises raised some capital in the same way. But for ordinary industrial activities the joint stock method was hardly ever invoked. In 1779 some preparations were made for starting a company for the manufacture of linens and printed calicoes, but the project was soon dropped, never to be revived again. Professor Clapham has recently demonstrated that it was only in the seventies or the late sixties that public flotations for industrial purposes became frequent and individual firms normally helped themselves out of the general reservoir of national savings. Fifty years earlier the single reservoir was not yet in existence; in its place there was a multiplicity of small disjointed pools. To use again the language of the economist, there were many special markets, instead of a single market of non-specific savings. Industry and agriculture each had a capital market of its own, and within industry almost every enterprise was restricted to its own private supplies. The Industrial Revolution got under way while capital was not yet capable of moving between its 'alternative employments'.

As is well known, the situation was in the end transformed, and the transformation was achieved by a combination of forces, some of which were subjective and psychological, and some objective and institutional. Capital, like all wealth and like most other things in the pre-Victorian era, was intimately bound up with human personality. It was a personal possession, not to be parted with easily for any length of time. A farmer might put his money into his farm, but he would do so because the farm was his own, and the investment remained under his physical control, a visible and tangible part of his personal belongings. Where capital is part of personal property it is as difficult to move and as difficult to distribute between available occupations as the bodily person of its owners. But even had the psychological obstacles been absent, the movement and the distribution of capital would still have remained difficult. Though far ahead of the banking system in most foreign countries, the English banks of the late eighteenth and the early nineteenth century did not act as suppliers of long credits, or as a contemporary writer, quoted by Professor Clapham, would call them, 'merchants of capital'. Above all, the new joint stock company and stock exchange were not yet there to provide an effective choice between investments, and to make the investments themselves divisible and mobile.

But in the end the economic development fashioned its own tools. The 'new man' may or may not have been one of them, and the importance of mental attitudes is only too easy to over-estimate. An economist shy of psychology and tired of too much Weber will probably doubt the reality or the novelty of the new economic mentality. He would doubtless recall (or would have recalled if he had deigned to use an historical argument) the innumerable speculators and speculations of the seventeenth and the early eighteenth century, of which the South Sea Bubble was merely the most spectacular and the best known. Yet in spite of all that can be said about the mentality-mongers, it remains true that, apart from the inner circle of merchants and financiers, the habit of investing has grown only in the course of the nineteenth century. An epidemic of investing speculation might break out at any period, but the chronic condition did not begin to develop until the revolutionary and Napoleonic wars. Whig finance called forth and nurtured the habitual bond-holder, the national debt of the revolutionary wars and the subsequent foreign flotation perpetuated him, while the financial crisis of the mid twenties drew him away from foreign bonds into industrial investment at home. By the middle of the century railway shares had been well established in the study and the drawing-room, and in the second half of the century newspapers began to publish, as a matter of daily routine, the prices of industrial stock for the benefit of their middle-class readers.

Equally recent was the related change in institutions. The country banks, essential as they were to the trade in the new industrial products, operated chiefly in the old agricultural areas. But by 1830 the new joint stock banks and the more substantial of the private banks situated in the industrial areas, were fully able to meet the needs of industry for short-term loans. By then these needs came to be provided for as well as, if not better than, they are now, and in the short-term market at least capital acquired its full measure of mobility. As for investment, the story of the joint stock company is too well known to require or to suffer any further explanation. Legal facilities for miscellaneous industrial investment were in existence long before the miscellaneous industrial investors appeared on the scene. Unsatisfactory as the legal position of the joint stock companies between 1825 and 1862 may appear to a modern speculator, it was far superior to those under which the professional traders and financiers had since Elizabeth's days been raising joint stock for exceptional ventures. Given a properly educated public, the law would have been quite adequate for the flotation of large industrial loans, and the necessary education came with the railway. After 1840 the public, matriculated in the school of Hudson, required little more than an occasional refresher course to keep on investing. By the time the acts of 1855 and 1862 gave the company law its present form, a single national market for long-term investment was functioning almost as smoothly as that for short-term loans, and the circulation of capital between the two was maintained by the activities of the brokers and discount houses, by the open-market operations of the banks and the marketing of the floating debt by the Treasury. At the height of the Victorian age in England, the Bismarckian era in Germany, and the generation of Pereira in France, the new industrial system can be said to have solved its problem of 'capital adaptation'. Capital very nearly became the perfect – one is tempted to say the ideal – factor of production envisaged by textbooks of economics: impersonal, divisible and capable of easy movement between places and occupations. Its mobility in time, i.e. the correspondence between its rate of growth and the secular changes in demand, may never have become perfect enough, and does not at present figure among the essential assumptions of theoretical economics. But in all its other movements it responded faithfully and truly to the indications of its market price. There emerged, indeed, a single market for capital, ruled and dominated by the rate of interest.

This peak of achievement has now unfortunately been abandoned. The descent has not yet gone very far, but it has gone far enough for us to be conscious of the 'malady of capital' in the modern world. Capital is no longer the perfect capitalist factor of production it must have been a generation or two ago; no longer as perfectly mobile, or as divisible, or as responsive to the dictation of the rate of interest. Some of this mobility it may have lost through force and under duress. The obstacles which government now put in the way of inter-national movement of capital are a *force majeure*, and so is the persistent cajoling of capital by governments into directions into which by itself it would not go. The resultant effect on the capital market should not be regarded as an organic change in the working of the economic system, for immobility due to chains is not the same thing as paralysis.

But it would be wrong to think that all, or even most, of the symptoms of the malady are due to the activities of government gaolers. Some of them go much deeper and have their root in the historical evolution of the system itself. And of these changes, none are more important than certain recent shifts in the social foundation of national saving. A social base to the capital market of the mid century was provided by the new class of 'pure' investors, the people who had learned to put their money into profitable use, and to decide that use by the sole criterion of interest, and whose expectations of income were very largely a matter of yields and quotations. It is their activities that imparted to the behaviour of capital all its characteristics of a perfect capitalist factor of production. Their rise accounts for the emergence of the new capital market a century or so ago, and it is their recent decline that lies at the back of the recent transformations of capital.

The decline has been relative, not absolute. In countries which have escaped serious inflation, the number of 'pure' investors, and the amount of new capital they supply, is probably as large as ever. What has changed is their relative share in the accumulation of capital, and their power of influencing the movement and behaviour of funds available for loans and investment.

In the modern world new capital comes from a variety of sources. In addition to the various forms of voluntary saving there are the agencies of compulsory savings, of which the state, with its capital expenditure out of taxation and its social legislation, is probably the most important. Within the field of voluntary saving, in addition to the conventional capital owner and investor, there are also the joint stock company with its saved-up reserves and the small-scale 'provident' investor saving (one is almost tempted to say hoarding) for the rainy day. Now the chief distinction between these different sources and the chief reason why they have been grouped as under, is that the supplies they are producing differ in their rate of growth, in their choice of employment, and in their response to the rate of interest. But different as they are from each other, they are alike in that they all impart to the market certain novel features, which confuse the theory of capitalism and obstruct its practice.

Thus, the so-called 'provident' savers, the countless millions of modest depositors in savings banks, friendly societies and insurance companies, add regularly and steadily to the total volume of saved-up capital, but do so at a rate and in a manner peculiarly their own. The total volume of their saving is almost uninfluenced by the rate of interest. Even among the richer rentiers, the 'pure' investors, the volume of savings has never been directly responsive to the changes in the rate of interest. Still some sort of response is produced automatically among them through changes in their income. But even this indirect connexion does not exist among the provident savers. While they go on saving the bulk of their income is not derived from their investments, and change in the yield of capital does not, therefore, affect their capacity to save. And where the object of saving is a fixed income at old age, the rise in the rate of interest is as likely as not to lead to the slackening of the saving effort, while the fall in the rate – according to Dr Cassel, until it reaches 3 per cent – is likely to stimulate the saving effort. As we all now know, a year of crisis, a prolonged strike, may eat up the poor man's savings, but as we also know, even a prolonged crisis cannot stop the bulk of the small men from saving. The factors determining the movement of these savings have not been studied by economists and are not yet properly understood. But even if this peculiarity of 'provident' savings can be neglected as immaterial to economic theory and not essential to the economic system, its other peculiarities cannot. And of the latter the most striking are the peculiarities of employment. The 'provident' savings form the timid fringe of the capital market, and are by their very nature driven into 'safe' forms of investment, mostly fixed-interest-bearing securities and the gilt-edged. In this they superficially resemble the non-capitalist, or pre-capitalist, hoardings, and the resemblance becomes more than superficial in times of crisis when, in the absence of safe investments, the 'provident' savings are prone to go out of investment altogether. But even in the best of times they disrupt the 'unity' of the capital market and create special supplies for special uses. Owing to them there is always a reservoir of savings available for the fixed-interest securities which is hardly ever available for equities. Where the provident savings are very large a situation is possible in which the market for fixed-interest securities and the gilt-edged, however small the yield, is chronically glutted with capital whereas industry is starved of funds. This actually was the situation in Germany before the war, and it is to that, as much as to better known causes, that Germany owes her magnificent municipal enterprises and her shaky industrial finance. The dependence of her industry on short-term loans, which in some mysterious way is supposed to have been produced by the Treaty of Versailles, was already the feature of German industry before inflation and even before the war, and was due to the fact that the main stream of popular savings flowed past the industrial field into the coffers of the state and the town government.

Still further away from the normal and the ideal are the savings of joint stock companies, or what the Americans describe as 'corporation' savings. Their volume, in theory, need not be influenced by the rate of interest, and it has not been so influenced in practice. It is only half true to say, as is sometimes said, that in so far as there is a connexion between high rate of interest and high industrial profits, the period of high interest happens also to provide large companies with larger income out of which to accumulate reserves. This only occurs when the rising profits of individual large companies are not accompanied by a rise of profits of trade and industry as a whole. When, however, the average profits of industry rise as well (and it is only then that a connexion between rising profits and the rising rate of interest can be established) individual companies may feel compelled to raise their distributed dividends up to the level of the average yield, which can at times only be done at the expense of the accumulated reserves.

But it is not here that a chief novelty of 'corporation' savings lies. Its chief 'novelty' is in its reactionary effects on the structure of the capital market. The self-financing of industrial enterprises restores in a new guise some of the financial conditions of the early Industrial Revolution. Specialized local supplies of capital are created, large blocks of capital are prevented from moving to alternative employment, the action of rate of interest as an impetus to the movement is neutralized. A century and a half ago the holding of capital turned out to be too personal, too closely associated with the individuality of its owner, to move away from his direct control. The turn of the wheel of history has restored again the personal connexions, this time with the collective and mammoth personality of 'the firm'. The difference is more one of scale than of essence.

What is true of the peculiarities of the different sources of voluntary savings is truer still of what can be described as 'compulsory' savings. That these in their movement through time pay no heed to market terms for capital, as expressed by the rate of interest, is obvious, and perhaps not important. As a matter of fact economic practice knows one form of truly involuntary saving, which is directly related to the rate of interest, namely the saving resulting from the compulsory repayment of bank advances out of profits. But of forced savings in the narrower sense of the word, those made by the state, or under its compulsion, the common supposition is more than true. With the possible exception of capital invested into the recent housing schemes in this country, most of the capital created by the government, through capital works financed out of taxation, or in different forms of social insurance, has been accumulating and moving in obedience to stimuli and forces which have little to do with the market terms for capital or with the optimum distribution of the available factors between the alternative uses. For capital thus saved there are no alternative uses. Even more than the savings of companies and certainly more than those of 'provident' investors, those of the state are earmarked before they are saved. The economists would be inclined to regard them as diverted from economic employment, sometimes as little better than waste. But whether approved or disapproved by economists, these are real savings, differing from the 'ordinary' supplies of new capital in little else except their refusal to conform to the ideal type of a mobile factor of production.

This classification does not yet by itself tell the whole morbid history of the patient. There is nothing new, and certainly nothing morbid, in the mere existence of the other sources of supply in addition to the conventional and orthodox saver. These sources were always there. Even in the most perfect days of Victorian capitalism the poor saved for a rainy day, companies accumulated reserves and governments turned some of their income into capital. And even before this age of war and inflation there were within the capital market timid fringes, monopoly pockets and earmarked revenues. What is new and morbid is the quantities. The provident savings always existed, but never have they been so great and never have they accounted for so large a share of capital accumulation. The play which was made in this country a few years ago with the figures illustrating the magnitude of popular savings is still fresh in our memory. In France the number of persons on the register of savers and investors grew more than twofold in the generation before the war, and reached 10 million in 1914. In Germany, on the eve of the crisis of 1930, out of 9·5 billion marks, which is the estimated total of annual savings, from 3 to 3·5 billion marks were supplied by the 'provident' savers. The average annual savings of the wage-earners rose from 18 marks in 1913 to 43 marks in 1929, whereas the average savings of the 'pure' investor seem to have remained almost stationary.

Similarly, the company reserves were always there, but it is only in the last twenty-five years or so that they have begun to form a very important proportion of new capital. In Germany, before the crisis, the savings of joint stock companies were estimated at about 2 billion marks as compared with the pre-war savings variously estimated at 220 and 550 million. In the United States 'corporation' savings are said to have grown between 1910 and 1919 from 1,185 to 5,190 million dollars, and to have reached between 1922 and 1929 about one-third of total annual savings. In this country the Inland Revenue estimate of undistributed profits of joint stock companies for 1924 was about 194 million, whereas for the total net savings of the nation estimates vary between 320 and 500 million. For the peak year of 1927 these profits are said to have reached 220 million pounds.

As for government savings, the savings of the German government in 1927, mostly through insurance schemes and capital works, were estimated at 1·8 billion marks (out of the total national savings of 9·5 billion). If we are to trust some recent estimates, the surplus realized by the government and local authorities in this country out of taxation and rates, together with net additions to insurance funds and capital outlay on roads not met by loans, amounted to 96 million in 1924 and reached 134 million in the peak year of 1927.

Crude and unsatisfactory as these figures are, they are sufficient to show that the supplies from the three sources have grown much faster than the general rate of saving, and that the relative importance of the other sources has been steadily diminishing. Of the remaining sources the most important are the savings of the 'pure' investor, the capital supplies of the 'capitalist' capitalist; and with the passing of the latter, there also comes an end to the golden age of the capital market.

The devoted students of our economic system find occasional consolation in the thought that the curious behaviour of the system as a whole, and of its capital supplies in particular, is a temporary reflection of a disordered world. The nationalist fever abroad and the socialist madness at home are the true causes of the irregular and unruly behaviour of capital, of its unpredictable migrations, its refusal to be tempted or repelled by the manipulations of the bank rate, its reluctance to go where the economic interests of individuals and the continued progress of society demand it most. The efficacy of this thought, as a consolation, cannot be doubted. It is pleasanter to think of one's hero perishing at the hand of a murderer, than dying in his own bed from senile decay. The only trouble about this consolation is that it is not altogether true. Our hero has suffered from violence, but he has also suffered from an organic complaint. Those very forces which have brought him to maturity – the rise in general prosperity, the growth of financial technique and the development of industrial organization – are also carrying him to senility. With prosperity come the provident savings and social services; with the banks and the joint stock companies come the big self-financing corporations. There is no failure like success.

2 Financing the Industrial Revolution[1]

HERBERT HEATON

[This article was first published in the *Bulletin of the Business Historical Society*, vol. XI, no. 1, February 1937.]

Until recently, students of the Industrial Revolution of the eighteenth and nineteenth centuries concentrated on technological changes or on labour and social problems but neglected capital and the capitalist. Mantoux gave 160 pages to technology, 100 to labour and only 34 to capital. Mrs Knowles devoted $8\frac{1}{2}$ pages out of 392 to capital, companies and combinations. The Hammonds have given us volumes on the town labourer, the skilled labourer and the village labourer, but we still lack the book Unwin once hoped they would write on the working life and ideals of the entrepreneur.

Within the last two decades the balance has begun to be redressed. The Manchester School has explored the business records of cotton, coal and iron firms;[2] the Boulton and Watt MSS have been combed for information concerning the organization of the great Soho firm;[3] Wedgwood's business history is now known, and the Yorkshire woollen industry has been painted in new colours.[4] Meanwhile the history of joint stock organization has been taken up at the point where Professor Scott dropped it – in 1720, and several writers have explored the 'risk factor' to investors, the high proportion of still births, the heavy infantile mortality, and the average

[1] The contents of this paper were presented at a joint meeting of the Business Historical Society and the American Historical Association, at Providence, R.I., 29 December 1936.

[2] e.g., G. Unwin, *Samuel Oldknow and the Arkwrights* (1923); T. S. Ashton, *Iron and Steel in the Industrial Revolution* (1924); A. P. Wadsworth and J. de L. Mann, *The Cotton Trade and Industrial Lancashire* (1931).

[3] E. Roll, *An Early Experiment in Industrial Organization* (1930).

[4] W. B. Crump, *The Leeds Woollen Industry, 1780–1820* (1931).

expectation of life among the first 20,000 British companies.[1] It is therefore possible to speak with a modicum of knowledge about (*a*) those private entrepreneurs who bore the burden of developing most manufactures, as well as much of the mining, metallurgy, shipping, wholesale trade and retail distribution during the nineteenth century, and (*b*) the joint stock companies which provided the canals and railroads, financed the new banks and stimulated foreign investment.

Since the industrial (as distinct from the transportation) developments of the eighteenth century and of much of the nineteenth were carried through by private firms, let us concentrate on them and ask 'Where did the money come from? How did it grow or diminish? What was its reward?' Well informed answers cannot readily be given; too few cases have been studied, and the necessary documents seem to be very scanty. As a contribution to the subject, or as an attempt to make the darkness more visible, I intend to answer these questions for a limited but not unimportant area and industry – the Yorkshire woollen manufacture.

Before seeking the source of the capital, it is worth asking 'How much was needed by those who built up enterprises with the new machines and power generators housed in mills or factories?' The erection and equipment of a factory large enough to house *all* the processes necessary to convert raw wool into finished cloth might cost £30,000 to £50,000 for land, buildings, engine or waterwheel and machinery. But such omnibus enterprises were rare. The textile industry was *the* land of opportunity for the energetic and ambitious man with little capital. 'Go textile, young man!' would have been a good bit of Georgian Greeleyesque advice to those whose courage was great but whose purse was light.

Several factors combined to smooth the path for these men. In the first place, they need sink little capital in buildings or equipment. An old flour or fulling mill, or even an old barn, could be adapted to scribbling, slubbing or spinning. If one must build, a small structure might suffice. Scores of mills were

[1] See the articles by B. C. Hunt in *Journal of Political Economy* (February and June 1935); by D. H. Macgregor, in *Economic Journal* (December 1929); by G. Todd in *Economic History Review* (October 1932); by H. A. Shannon in *Economic History Review* (October 1933). Also G. H. Evans, *British Corporation Finance, 1775–1850* (1936).

only 50 by 27 feet, and two or three storeys high; some were even smaller. The early machines were not expensive when new, and used ones could be obtained quite cheaply as factory discards or at an auction sale of some bankrupt's effects. One could get a 'forty-spindle jenny of the best sort' for £6 in 1792; a big scribbling or carding machine could be bought for £50, and in the 1830s a power-loom cost only £20, while a power-loom shed could be built and equipped with fifty looms for about £5,000. When fire destroyed a scribbling mill and all its contents in 1821, the total damage was only £1,500; and when an 'extensive corn and scribbling mill, with all the valuable machinery and stock' was gutted, the loss was only £5,000.

But the man with little capital need not sink *any* of it in plant. He could rent space – a single room, a floor or a whole mill; he could buy power from his landlord, and he might be able to rent the machinery as well. In depressed days assignees of bankrupt textile estates were eager to find tenants for part or the whole of the property, and might offer to advance 'the necessary sums of money for wages' or even to supply all the needed operating capital. In prosperous days the building of mills for lease to one or more tenants was a profitable way of investing capital. Large landlords were especially active, but merchants, manufacturers and others who had money to spare turned it into bricks, mortar and machinery, and then sought tenants among 'persons desirous of commencing the woollen or worsted business with a small outlay of capital'.

In the second place, a textile enterprise might be what we can call a service station. If the beginner needed to sink little capital in plant, he need not put any (or much) in raw material, since he could find full employment performing one process only on materials belonging to his patrons. Many corn or fulling millers, who ground grain or fulled cloth for their neighbours, installed the new carding and scribbling machines after 1775, and treated wool brought to the mill by local cloth-makers. Dyers and finishers might work on cloths belonging to merchants; worsted combers or spinners might take in wool and send back combings or yarn. The putting out system thus showed remarkable powers of adaptation, with a mill-operator rather than a domestic craftsman as the 'puttee'. Looked at from another angle, the man who put his capital into raw material need not put any into plant, but could draw on the services of others to carry his wool through the various processes. There was yet a third angle, since the operator of a one-process plant might buy material, carry it through one stage and then sell it. He might buy sorted wool, comb it and sell 'tops' to the spinner, who spun them and sold yarn to the weaving firm, which made it into cloth and sold raw pieces to merchants, who finished them and sold the final product.

In the third place a small factory with a few machines was not at a great disadvantage in competing with a larger rival. The raw material market and the method of selling cloth had for centuries been organized to cater to the small producer. Some tasks could not be done by machines. Further, apart from plain cottons and low grade or standard woollens, the product was one of great variety of patterns, weights and qualities, calling for a kindred variety of yarns, spinning and weaving standards, dyeing and finishing methods, as well as for ability to adjust production to rapid changes in fashion. A small firm could concentrate on one style, pattern, or quality, or market, process, or service. Hence, while some factories were born big and others grew big, specialization allowed the small or middle-sized firm to operate efficiently.

It should now be clear that fixed capital requirements need not be large. Yet they were frequently large enough to harass and perplex those who needed funds for building or equipping a plant of their own;[1] for they were often the last straw on a back that already bore a heavy load. That load was the need for large sums of operating capital, or 'floating capital' as the book-keepers called it. The service firm might confine its operating expenses to wages, rent, fuel, and cost of such necessary materials as dyestuffs; but business which bought raw materials, operated plants and sold semi-manufactured or finished goods usually were both debtor and creditor for sums far beyond the cost of their factories or even their total capital. They carried large stocks of raw materials and of goods in various stages of production. Three to six months might elapse before a bale of wool was converted into cloth, and another

---

[1] We know of Wedgwood's frantic call for £3,000 to meet one year's building costs at Etruria, and of the strain on Boulton's resources when he was erecting his Soho factory.

D

six or more months passed before sale and final payment had been effected. The man who consigned goods at his own risk and on his own account to transatlantic markets might have to wait still longer for his cash. Meanwhile wages must be paid when due, payments for services could not be long postponed, and providers of raw material did not grant indefinite credit. Bank loans might help to bridge the gap in time between outgo and income, but the firm must have some working capital of its own and must relate the scale of its operations to the amount of that capital. If it extended beyond a safe limit it sought disaster, for when some big merchant, manufacturer or banker in Leeds, London, Liverpool or America became a bad debtor, the overstretched rubber band snapped, with disastrous effects even on those who had tried to play the game as cautiously as was humanly possible.

So much for the demand for capital. Now, what of the supply? The landlords provided some by building mills. The merchants made a more important contribution; they supplied funds to some producer whose goods they were handling, or went into partnership, as in the case of Arkwright, Boulton and Wedgwood; or they went into the new form of production themselves, as in the case of Benjamin Gott and some of his fellow cloth merchants in Leeds, or of David Dale and his fellow Glasgow traders. Private bankers helped less. Like their joint stock descendants, they were commercial bankers, not investment houses; but the short-term credit they supplied liberated some of the entrepreneur's own funds for long-term use. The crash of more than 300 provincial banks in 1814–16 and in 1825–6 decimated or even obliterated local banking facilities, and deprived some areas of their main form of currency – the local banknote. Hence manufacturers and merchants eagerly undertook the establishment of joint stock banks after 1826, subscribed to their capital and supplied them with Scottish managers. Meanwhile the Bank of England established branches in the leading cities, and the modern banking system gradually took shape.

These external supplies of capital were, however, less important than the personal or family funds which the industrialists scraped together and ventured in the new productive equipment. The power of heredity and the vitality of the family as an economic group stand out whenever we examine the history of the pioneer manufacturers. Josiah Wedgwood was at least the fifth generation of potters; the Midlands ironmasters looked back on an ancestry of nail or lock makers, smelters or founders, brassworkers or ironmongers; and the builder of one of Yorkshire's early large factories was the eleventh generation of clothmakers. In each generation the business conscripted as many members of the family as it needed. Some ran the mill or warehouse, others were sent to New York, Lisbon or Rio de Janeiro, travelled round the British Isles, or slipped over to Germany to sell pieces and buy wool. If the family was cursed with too few sons and too many daughters, the sons-in-law might be drafted. While the firm swallowed everybody in the family, it might also swallow everything – even the latest dowry. Krupp's first cast steel plant absorbed 50,000 thalers taken from the family purse. Boulton sold a lot of the property he inherited, mortgaged most of the rest, and then did the same with the £28,000 worth of property his wife had brought with her. Yet rarely was the amount adequate, and if the family firm eventually survived, it did so after many years of grim abstinence, of pared family budgets, and of frantic efforts to find supplementary funds outside.

Closely related with the family firm was the partnership, which was usually a small group of relatives or friends, though even a stranger might be admitted as a sleeping partner. The biggest partnership groups were those which financed the 'company' or 'union' mills. These were erected to scribble, card wool or to full cloth, and the capital was provided by the clothiers who used the mill. The number of investors varied between sixteen and fifty-six; the shares, usually £25, were saleable, and a shareholder could hold two or more. One of these mills was at work by 1794, but after 1815 the number grew rapidly. Some of these experiments in producers' co-operation were small and unsuccessful, but others were large and flourishing. They never went beyond the two processing services of scribbling and fulling; spinning and weaving were still done in the clothier's home, and the gradual departure of the latter processes to the factory eventually destroyed the *raison d'être* of the company mills.

Few records survive to tell the financial history of the

enterprises of a century ago. The last chapter of many of them is a line in the bankruptcy list of the London *Gazette* and a few inches in the newspaper advertisements of auction sales. From these sources one soon concludes that while death and taxes alone were inevitable, bankruptcy was probable. The depressions that followed 1825 and 1836 were ancestors of whom 1929–33 might well be proud. Long-drawn out – four and six years respectively in duration, they quickly toppled over the heady boomsters and slowly pared away the capital and credit of the conservative. In 1836 there were 318 textile firms in Bradford; ten years later only 127 of them were still alive. The casualty lists contain the names of high and humble, of generals and corporals alike. The bigger the firm the greater the noise when it fell, and the longer the advertisement offering for sale its 'delightful villa', its 'capital large dwelling-house, pleasantly situated, with extensive plantations, pleasure grounds and gardens, trout stream, and picturesque views', and its accumulation of 'whatever is usually found in a well-furnished gentleman's house of the first respectability'. Failure leaves few other records, and even success is reticent. I have been able to find only two relics that are sufficiently detailed to tell a financial story. Each suffers by starting at a point where the business was well established; but by way of compensation, each covers the period when a large mill was being erected and equipped.

The first records begin in 1825, when William Brooke, merchant manufacturer, 62 years old, and blind as a result of being splashed with hot indigo, hands the management of his yarn-making and cloth-finishing mill near Huddersfield over to his two sons, John and Thomas. The firm is purely a family enterprise, but is organized as a formal partnership, for a fixed length of time and with a fixed initial investment by each partner. The father supplies the buildings, and charges £2,000 a year rent for them; he contributes the machinery and some cash, which combined, amount to £65,000; and on this sum he is to receive 5 per cent. The two active partner brothers have £18,000 and £9,000 respectively in the business; on these sums they are to receive 5 per cent, and in addition they are to share the profits on a 5 to 4 ratio, which is later changed to 50-50. A third brother, Edward, has £9,000 in the firm; but he has no love for textile work, prefers to be called 'squire', and likes to buy shares in the joint stock banks. Like his father therefore, he is a sleeping partner; he gets 5 per cent on his capital, and for six years receives £1,000 annually as a sort of goodbye gift.

The firm thus began operations with about £100,000 of capital stock, on which £5,000 interest must be paid, plus £2,000 for rent and £1,000 gift – £8,000 in all. It was overdrawn £10,000 at two banks, and owed £12,000 for materials. Against this it had book debts of £77,000 for goods sold, £43,000 of cloth in production, wool, and dyestuffs, and £665 in cash. The two young managers set out to modernize, mechanize and expand the plant, and by 1840 had spent £48,000 on new buildings and equipment. Yet they had been able to wipe out the overdraft and cross off an average of £1,000 of bad debts each year. They were ending each financial year almost entirely free of debt, but with book debts due to them for £40,000 to £80,000 of cloth sold, and with £80,000 to £170,000 worth of cloth in production or in the warehouse, of wool, dyestuffs and bank balance.

It has often been said that the early industrialists ploughed back their profits into their business. Mr Keynes said it more eloquently in his *Economic Consequences of the Peace*: 'The capitalist classes were allowed to call the best part of the cake theirs and were theoretically free to consume it, on the tacit underlying condition that they consumed very little of it in practice. The duty of saving became nine-tenths of virtue and the growth of the cake the object of true religion.' The Brooke family was in general ten-tenths virtuous, and its accounts show the zeal with which abstinence could be practised when necessary. Any partner could draw out in cash what was due to him as rent, interest, or profit; he could also draw out part or the whole of his capital. If however he left any part of his annual income in the business, it was added to his capital and earned interest. In the seven years of vigorous plant expansion (1830–6) the partners were entitled to take out £140,000, but they actually drew only £55,000. They thus left 61 per cent of their income in the firm, and increased their investment from £109,000 to over £190,000. In one Spartan year (1830) they ploughed back 85 per cent, and in 1831, 88 per cent.

This period of rigorous saving ended when the firm had a

good plant and adequate 'floating capital'. Then it became apparent that the members 'had religion' with different degrees of fervour. The father was fairly devout; true, at times, he took nearly all his due, and spent it on bank stock, but usually he left it almost untouched, and increased his holding by two-thirds in fifteen years. The squire also lusted after bank shares in all parts of the country; but he managed to let his capital more than double. Thomas, the younger son, was no doubter; in eleven years he drew only 17 per cent of what was due, and increased his capital eightfold in fifteen years. But John, the elder brother, was a backslider, who believed in diversified investment or in having a flutter when there was a bull market. In 1835 he drew out all his interest and profit, plus £4,000 of his capital. Two years later he took out so much cash that his capital was reduced from £42,000 to £17,000. A share of his father's holding when the old man died restored his capital to healthy dimensions; but when the railroad boom came in the mid forties he let family solidarity go with the wind. In 1846 he took £34,000 out of the firm, and thus abstracted all his capital and running £6,000 into debt; by rapid steps this debt rose to £22,000, hovered there for years, and only gradually was reduced to £16,000 in 1859. The total capital of the firm remained nearly stationary, since the other partners continued to leave part of their income untouched. It is probably true that the business could not continue to absorb new capital as easily as it had done in earlier days, and that John's policy of taking out while the others put in was sound. Yet his raids on the cash box must have been disturbing at times, and probably explain why the firm's bank account swung from a large credit balance to an equally large overdraft.

The second set of financial records is more obscure, but it tells much the same story as does the first. In 1785 two veteran Leeds cloth merchants took their ex-apprentice, Benjamin Gott, into partnership for five years. The 'neat stock and profits in trade' of the two elders were valued at £36,000, and were divided equally between them. Gott invested one-tenth of this sum (£3,600), and the total capital was thus nearly £40,000. The firm was purely mercantile; it bought raw cloth, put it out to be finished, and then sold it. But soon the old men died, two sons of one of them entered the firm, and young

Gott thus became senior partner at the age of thirty-one years. He knew nothing about making cloth, but felt it might be profitable to produce certain kinds, and as the firm had some spare capital he began in 1792 to erect a factory which eventually employed a thousand workers. Within ten years over £30,000 had been spent on land, buildings and machinery, and a second mill had been rented and equipped. The outlay on these two plants strained the firm's finances for a time, but the amount involved was small when compared with that of the 'floating capital'. The firm ended each year with large debts owed to others, but with far larger debts owed by others; the all-time high was reached in 1816, when the firm was a debtor for £320,000 and creditor for £540,000. The risks in such a situation were great, and in thirty years £150,000 of debts had to be labelled 'bad or suspicious', an average of £5,000 a year. The 'neat stock and profits in trade' rose from £40,000 in 1785 to nearly £400,000 in 1814; but when peace without prosperity came in 1815 the bad debts rose so much and the plant and goods in hand had to be written down so heavily that the value of the partner's interests fell from £400,000 to £240,000 in two years.

In Gott's firm, as in Brooke's, each partner received interest on his original capital and on any additions he made to it; but he was free to draw all his annual income out and dig into his capital as well. During the factory-building years the visits to the cash box were restrained; but when the years of fixed capital investment were ended, different attitudes became apparent. The younger men built up their holdings; the older man, Benjamin, drew out heavily, to build a mansion, to pay for portraits by Lawrence (the Sargent of the day), to buy railroad stock and consols, or to endow churches, schools and almshouses. The time had come for him to enjoy a more abundant life.

3 Capital Formation in Britain before the Railway Age [1]

PHYLLIS DEANE

[This article was first published in *Economic Development and Cultural Change*, vol. IX, no. 3, 1961.]

Over the past decade a great deal of analysis, formal model building and policy has been based on the evident association between capital formation and economic growth. Those concerned with problems of secular stagnation saw the level of investment as a crucial determinant of the rate of growth. Theorists have constructed models on this assumption. Arthur Lewis, in a now familiar passage, has defined an Industrial Revolution as a period in which the rate of annual net investment has moved from 5 per cent or less to 12 per cent or more.[2] Students of underdeveloped countries have started with Nurkse on the assumption that capital 'lies at the very centre of the problem of development in economically backward countries'.[3]

One consequence of this focus on capital has been an increase in the volume of empirical data on the subject. Much of it is highly approximate and inconclusive. It has been sufficient, however, to show that the relationship between capital formation and economic growth is neither simple nor direct. If there is a systematic relationship it is clearly a complex one. It no longer seems plausible to assume that the stock of capital and its rate of growth are the crucial determinants of a country's

---

[1] This paper is based on research undertaken in the course of an inquiry into long-term capital formation in the United Kingdom, now in progress at the University of Cambridge Department of Applied Economics.

[2] W. A. Lewis, *The Theory of Economic Growth* (London, 1955), p. 208.

[3] R. Nurkse, *Problems of Capital Formation in Underdeveloped Countries* (Oxford, 1953), p. 1.

rate of progress. In any particular instance, a variety of other factors, such as technological progress, the social and institutional heritage, the exploitation of external economies or changes in the industrial sector-mix may be as vital to the rate of growth as the rate of investment itself.

Comparative study of current international data (still regrettably incomplete and imprecise) suggests, for example, that there is an association between the level of industrialization and the level of investment.[1] Analysis of the historical record, as far as it goes, indicates that at some time during the pre-industrial phase, or perhaps in the early stages of the industrialization process itself, there must have been a significant rise – possibly a doubling – in the rate of investment. The search for empirical data which might establish or explain these hypotheses goes on. For Britain it is necessary to go back before the railway age to trace the transformation in the rate of investment. The data are sketchy and do not lend themselves readily to aggregative treatment. They are sufficient, however, to suggest orders of magnitude and rates of change. It is the purpose of this paper to review some of the published evidence on the character and volume of capital formation in pre-industrial Britain and consider the role of capital in early stages of British economic growth.

I *Capital Formation in the Seventeenth Century*

The political arithmeticians who wrote at the end of the seventeenth century were aware of the connexion between the nation's capital stock, broadly defined, and its economic growth. Gregory King, for example, illustrated 'this great Fundamental Truth, That the Trade and Wealth of England did mightily advance between the years 1600 and 1688' with estimates of the nation's capital stock for the years 1600, 1630, 1660 and 1688.[2] There is no reason to suppose that his figures – at any rate for the years before 1688 – were other than purely illustrative of his view of the rate of growth of capital. What

[1] S. Kuznets, 'Quantitative Aspects of the Economic Growth of Nations: V. Capital Formation Proportions: International Comparisons for Recent Years', *Economic Development and Cultural Change*, VIII, no. 4 (July 1960), part II.
[2] Gregory King, *Two Tracts*, ed. by G. E. Barnett (Baltimore, 1936), p. 61.

is interesting, however, is the estimate of a well-informed contemporary that what we might regard as an approximation to the 'reproducible capital' of England and Wales was growing at an average annual rate of between 1 and 1·5 per cent per annum during the whole of the seventeenth century.[1] Taken in conjunction with an estimated population increase of about 0·2 per cent this represents a distinct if slow advance in capital per head. By 1688, again according to King the reproducible natural capital amounted to a total of about £112 million made up as follows:[2]

		£ million
1	Producers' goods and inventories[3]	33
2	Livestock	25
3	Buildings[4]	54
		——
4	Total productive capital	112

This total of £112 million can be related to a national income of about £48 million to give an overall capital output ratio of about 2·3.[5]

For 1688 the rate of capital accumulation was put by King at £2·4 million[6] representing about 5 per cent of national income. This figure relates to what he called the 'actual stock', that is to say it includes plate, jewellery, coin, furniture, clothing, etc., and excludes buildings. After excluding household goods and including buildings on the assumption that the annual increase was of the same composition as the stock, we can deduce a rate of investment of about 6 per cent of national

[1] This includes 'plate, jewells and household goods' but excludes coin, lands and buildings.

[2] King, op. cit., p. 32.

[3] Shipping, military stores and equipment, stocks in trade, and instruments and materials held for trade and production.

[4] Yearly rents of housing and other heriditaments capitalized at 18 years purchase as for all lands and buildings. There is some doubt whether all the 'other heriditaments' come into the building and construction category and whether 18 is an appropriate capitalization coefficient. Petty used 12·5 for his 1665–7 calculations.

[5] For this national income estimate derived from King, see P. Deane, 'The Implications of Early National Income Estimates for the Measurement of Long-Term Economic Growth in the United Kingdom', *Economic Development and Cultural Change*, IV, no. 1 (November 1955), pp. 3–38.

[6] King, op. cit., p. 63.

income in relation to a productive national capital of about £112 million. However, 1688 was a prosperous year. King calculated that the annual increase in the actual stock had risen from about £1·3 million in 1670 (by which year he reckoned that the economy had largely recovered from the disasters of the 1660s) to its 1688 peak of £2·4 million.[1] In the following decade he estimated that the French wars had reduced the national stock of productive capital exclusive of buildings from £55 million to £46·5 million, which, even assuming no decline in the value of buildings, represents a fall of 10 per cent in the nation's capital in ten years. A fall of the same order of magnitude appears in King's national income figures.

All this is highly conjectural of course. At best it reflects an intelligent contemporary view of the economic situation at the end of the seventeenth century. If King's calculations were on the right lines we might conclude from them that in times of peace and prosperity the annual rate of capital formation towards the end of the seventeenth century may have averaged between 3 and 6 per cent of national income, but that the process of capital accumulation was readily reversed by wars and other temporary disasters. The long-term average for the seventeenth century does not seem to have exceeded 3 per cent. The broader concept of capital stock adopted by King is also significant. The unproductive elements which we have excluded from the above calculations – gold, silver, jewellery, furniture, apparel, etc. – bulked large in his total, with a value equivalent to more than 80 per cent of the fixed assets and inventories used in trade and industry.

In times of peace, therefore, the English economy tended to generate a surplus which was available for saving. The investor who did not want to hoard his wealth in gold and silver or in consumers' durables or stocks could find outlets in agricultural land and stock (there was still scope for opening up new land), in building (which may have accounted for half the nation's reproducible capital) and in trade and industry (which may have accounted for about a third). The most productive outlet in terms of its income yielding potential was undoubtedly trade

[1] Ibid., 'The Plague, the Fire of London and the Foreign Wars which happened between 1664 and 1670 did diminish or hinder the Increase of the Capital Stock of the Nation about 30 or 40 millions.'

and industry; but if it yielded quick and easy incomes in times of prosperity its dependence on overseas trade made it peculiarly vulnerable to the recurrent disasters of war. This was too risky and limited a channel to attract more than a fraction of the nation's savings.

Nevertheless, when the opportunities for investment presented themselves there seems to have been no lack of capital. This is evident first from the rapidity with which the losses incurred in the Plague and the Fire were made good and second from the ease with which joint stock companies were floated at the end of the century. There have been various estimates of the damage caused by the fire of London. Scott quoted an estimate of £10·7 million for buildings and their contents but of this St Paul's Cathedral accounted for £2·7 million.[1] Reddaway suggested a figure of about £8 million of which about half related to the houses and the remainder to their contents and to transport equipment.[2] King as we have seen put a global figure of £30 to £40 million on the whole of the losses incurred in the disasters of the 1660s.

Whatever the true extent of the loss there is no doubt that it was heavy and that recovery was rapid. As far as London was concerned 'the figures suggest that the bulk of private rebuilding was nearing completion by the end of 1670'.[3] In 1668–9 London's exports were above their 1662–3 level and when the Royal African company launched an appeal for £100,000 in 1671 the stock had been oversubscribed within a month.[4] Indeed it has been suggested that the building boom involved in the process of recovery from the Fire generated a favourable climate for new commercial ventures. 'Once the immediate dislocation had been overcome something nearer to full employment than was commonly to be found in Restoration London must have existed'.[5]

The last forty years of the seventeenth century seem to have

---

[1] W. R. Scott, *The Constitution and Finance of English, Scottish and Irish Joint-Stock Companies to 1720*, vol. I (Cambridge, 1911), p. 279.

[2] T. F. Reddaway, *The Rebuilding of London after the Great Fire* (London, 1940), pp. 270–1.

[3] Ibid., p. 281.

[4] K. G. Davies, 'Joint Stock Investment in the Later Seventeenth Century', *Economic History Review*, 2nd series, IV, no. 3 (1952), p. 288.

[5] K. G. Davies, *The Royal African Company* (New York, 1957), p. 55.

constituted a period of considerable entrepreneurial activity. 236 patents for invention were taken out: in the next forty years the number was only 204.[1] There was an extraordinary boom in the flotation in joint stock companies after the Revolution of 1688. An analysis of the data compiled by Scott indicates that in 1689 when the paid-up capital of the three foreign trading companies was nearly half a million pounds, the total paid-up capital of all British joint stock companies barely reached £630,000. By 1695 the total may have been near £3·5 million of which about £2 million was attributable to the Bank of England and the foreign trading companies taken together. According to Scott 'the majority of companies started in this period were designed to establish either an industry new to the country or to improve an existing one by a process not in ordinary use'.[2] About 38 per cent of the capital estimated to have been paid up *circa* 1695 was in foreign trade, about a quarter in banking, about 12 per cent in water supply undertakings and about 4 per cent in mining. Less than a fifth was in manufacturing industry – largely in textiles, paper, metal manufactures and glass.

By contrast later expansion in joint stock company capital was largely fictitious. Scott (using nominal rather than paid-up capital for the foreign trading companies) shows an increase in the total from £4·5 million to £8·5 million between 1695 and 1703 and again to £21 million in 1717. If this indicated anything at all it was the expansion of the national debt. Most of the increase was due to the inflation of the stocks of the foreign trading companies and the banks (which together accounted for about 85 per cent of Scott's 1703 total and about 95 per cent of his 1717 total) and these stocks in their turn were largely a reflection of government loans or market manipulations. This was the hey-day of the bubble companies. The most spectacular of them, the South Sea Company, had grown out of a modest and serious project set up in 1691 to manufacture grooved sword blades with the aid of nineteen or twenty immigrant craftsmen and their families. Mills and forges had been built and blades were sold in London over the period 1692 to 1704, but by the latter date the company had embarked on speculative activities in land, and by 1720 it and its imitators

[1] Davies, 'Joint Stock Investment', p. 285.   [2] Scott, op. cit., p. 328.

had brought the whole system of joint stock company finance into lasting ill repute.

In effect, by the beginning of the eighteenth century it was evident that the crucial bottleneck lay in the supply not of savings but of investment opportunities and, which may amount to the same thing, of skilful entrepreneurs. Whether a more efficient group of company managers could have made profitable use of the funds and opportunities open to them in the war-torn years of the early eighteenth century is dubious, however. Possibly they could have averted the débâcle of 1720 and preserved public confidence in the joint stock system. But by the time the crisis had passed into history another borrower had established a credit worthy claim to the nation's surplus – the State. In the second half of the eighteenth century the non-participant investor found a satisfactory outlet for his savings in the Funds.[1]

II *Capital Formation in the Eighteenth and Early Nineteenth Centuries*

During the eighteenth century there was surprisingly little contemporary interest in either the national income or the national capital. In the early decades of the nineteenth century, however, there were several serious attempts to compute its value. Three of them are well known. Beeke, in a pamphlet originally published in 1794, Colquhoun in a work first published in 1814 and Pebrer writing *circa* 1833 all produced estimates of capital stock and income, though none of them, unfortunately, sought to relate the two by estimating the annual rate of capital accumulation.[2] If we extract from each of these estimates a list of what might be regarded as the elements of reproducible productive capital and relate the resulting aggregates to relevant estimates of national income we find that they indicate capital output ratios of between 2·5 and 3.

---

[1] See Davies, 'Joint Stock Investment', where it is said that in the seventeenth century government borrowing 'limped along two or three or four per cent behind the private borrower'.

[2] H. Beeke, *Observations on the Produce of the Income Tax* (London, 1799); P. Colquhoun, *Treatise on the Wealth, Power and Resources of the British Empire* (London, 1814); P. Pebrer, *Taxation, Expenditure, Power, Statistics and Debt of the Whole British Empire* (London, 1833).

We are again in the realm of conjecture of course, and even were we confident of the reliability of the contemporary estimates we should still have difficulty either in excluding the non-reproducible elements or in ensuring that all classes of reproducible capital were adequately covered. The most that we can say about such calculations is that they suggest an increase in the nation's stock of capital (relative to income) since King was making his estimates at the end of the seventeenth century. To explore this hypothesis we must review the evidence on changes in the physical stock of capital in the intervening period.

(a) Investment in Agriculture

In considering the contemporary estimates we have focused on what is currently regarded as the reproducible element in tangible wealth. That is to say we have tried to exclude land and associated natural resources such as minerals and forests. It is evident that distinctions of this kind are not easy to make in any circumstances and that for countries at an early stage of development, when the agricultural sector bulks large, the problem is particularly important. If we include the value of land, for example, in the contemporary estimates of national capital we find that it accounts for about 64 per cent of the total at the end of the seventeenth century and about 54 or 55 per cent in the early nineteenth century.

In so far as investment in land and natural resources represents claims to a virtually static stock of assets it is appropriate enough to exclude it from a study of the growth of physical capital. In so far as it reflects extension or improvement of the cultivated area it is of considerable interest. Clearly there were important developments of this kind in eighteenth-century Britain. The problem is to form some kind of assessment of their importance in relation to the undoubted increase in agricultural output which took place during the century.

Most improvements in agricultural output seem to have taken place either through extension of the cultivated area or more efficient use of common or waste or new crops (clover, turnips and potatoes). There is no evidence of large-scale adoption of improved machinery and implements. Some advance there was but progress was slow and of limited extent. The first practical drilling machine, for example, was not widely adopted for many years after Tull's death in 1741 and even then its use was limited to large farms. The first effective threshing machine was patented in 1786, and the first successful reaper was brought out in 1826. These innovations effectively postdate the expansion of output which permitted population almost to double in the half century following 1770. The new crops, like the new implements, had generally to await enclosure before they could become effective on a wide scale. Everything, then, seems to point to enclosure as the forerunner of investment in agriculture. Estimates of the rate of expenditure on enclosures will not measure the expansion in the stock of agricultural capital but they should provide some indication of its relative importance and its distribution through time.

A definitive study of expenditure on enclosures must await full exploitation of the regional and parliamentary records relative to each act of enclosure.[1] Meanwhile, however, it is possible to make some rough calculations based on existing estimates of acreages enclosed and costs per acre in four counties.[2] These yield the following results:

	Acres enclosed in England and Wales 000	*Estimated cost* £000
1727–60	75	34
1761–92	478	459
1792–1801	274	477
1802–15	739	1,768

The movement reached its peak in the French wars when over a million acres were enclosed at an estimated annual cost of about £94,000. Thereafter the rate of enclosure dropped sharply. In the three decades from 1816 to 1845 the number of acres enclosed was under 200,000 and the total annual cost of enclosure probably did not exceed £15,000. Not all of the

[1] Not all enclosures required an Act of Parliament but it may be presumed that the majority of acres enclosed in the eighteenth century involved legislation.

[2] G. Slater, *The English Peasantry and the Enclosure of Common Fields* (London, 1907), appendix A, p. 267, for acreages enclosed by Act of Parliament. W. E. Tate, 'The Cost of Parliamentary Enclosure in England', *Economic History Review*, N.S., V, no. 3 (1952), pp. 258–65, draws examples from Cambridgeshire, Lincolnshire, Nottinghamshire and Oxford.

expenditure on enclosure represented net investment of course. About a third was estimated to have been spent on fencing. But much of the total was merely a transfer of capital from old to new owners and some went for lawyers' and surveyors' fees and various parliamentary expenses. On the other hand enclosure may often have been the preliminary step in a whole programme of new investment in ditching and drainage projects, farm buildings, carts, implements and so on. It may also have permitted improvements in the quality and turnover of the livestock population which are not adequately measured in the estimates of the stock but which involved heavier annual investment therein. These developments, most of which probably took place in the second half of the century, included improvements in the breed, earlier maturity of slaughter stock and substitution of horses for draught oxen.[1]

The evidence on the growth of capital in agriculture is incomplete. We know nothing about the changing levels of commodity stocks, though it is conceivable that improvements in bulk transport may have changed considerably the needs and opportunities of farmers to hold stocks. The evidence on forests suggests depletion rather than expansion of basic resources, but it is scanty. On balance, however, we can find nothing to suggest that there was a substantial increase in the stock of farm capital or in the rate of agricultural investment until towards the end of the eighteenth century; and even then the expansion appears to have been modest in relation to the growth of agricultural incomes at this period.[2]

(b) Investment in Building and Construction

One of the factors which must have contributed to an increase in the national capital in the eighteenth century was urbanization. An urban population requires (and is generally able to provide for) a larger social capital in buildings (both public and private), street paving and lighting, water supply and

[1] See, for example, G. E. Fussell, 'The Size of English Cattle in the Eighteenth Century', *Agricultural History*, III, no. 4 (October 1929), pp. 160–81.

[2] But see L. S. Pressnell, *Country Banking in the Industrial Revolution* (Oxford, 1956), p. 344: 'The far-reaching changes in agriculture which formed an essential feature of the Industrial Revolution required considerable investment for a prolonged period.'

sanitation.[1] An acceleration in the pace of urbanization, therefore, may be expected to imply a rise in the rate of capital
formation, particularly capital formation in building and construction projects.

The shifting character of urban boundaries makes it difficult
to measure the progress of urbanization even when the statistics
are reasonably complete. When, as is the case for the eighteenth
century, they are dubious and incomplete estimates it is not
possible to do more than take a tentative view of the orders of
magnitude involved in the process. The data available for this
purpose include: (1) the estimates derived by Gregory King
from the 1695 birth, death and marriage assessments and from
hearth tax returns and other administrative records available
at the end of the seventeenth century, (2) the returns of the
1801 and later censuses and (3) various estimates of town
populations, only a few of which seem to have been based on
actual counts.

In 1695 according to Gregory King about 26 per cent of the
population of England and Wales lived in the cities and market
towns – nearly 10 per cent in London itself.[2] Roughly a
century later, according to Colquhoun's analysis of the returns
of the 1801 census, the proportion in the cities and towns was
43 per cent – again including 10 per cent in the metropolis.[3]
Many of the towns which Colquhoun distinguished as such
had less than 1,000 inhabitants – some of them less than 500 –
so that they scarcely constituted urban areas in the modern
sense of the term, though they were probably comparable to
the cities and towns which underlay King's estimate. It seems
fair to conclude that there had been a substantial growth of
towns outside London.

Some of this growth had taken place before the middle of the
eighteenth century. At the beginning of the century there were
only two large towns outside the capitals of London and
Edinburgh. These were Norwich (with perhaps 29,000) and
Bristol (with perhaps 25,000). Birmingham and Glasgow were
already quite substantial – with between 10,000 and 15,000

[1] Urban corporations initiated and partly financed many of the large-scale
eighteenth-century developments in transport as well as their own town improvement schemes.

[2] King, op. cit., pp. 17–18.

[3] Colquhoun, op. cit., p. 48.

inhabitants each, but it does not seem that there were any other towns with a population exceeding 10,000. At most it is doubtful whether the population living in concentrations of 5,000 or more amounted to as much as 13 per cent of the population of Great Britain.

By the middle of the century this proportion may have risen to between 15 and 16 per cent of the national total. The large towns of some 25,000 inhabitants or more now included Liverpool, which had quadrupled its numbers, and Birmingham and Glasgow, which had rather more than doubled theirs. Manchester (excluding Salford) had roughly trebled in size, and Bristol had expanded by about 70 per cent. If anything the metropolis may have expanded slightly less than the total British population, but it still contained between 9 and 10 per cent of the total.

The striking transformation came in the second half of the century, however, as improved communications lifted some of the limitations on the growth of large centres of population. By 1801 about 19 per cent of the population was living in towns of more than 25,000 inhabitants and about 25 per cent in concentrations of 5,000 or more. This represented a considerable growth in urbanization since the 1750s.

Local records leave no doubt of the quickening in the rate of public building in the second half of the eighteenth century. Between 1750 and 1800, for example, the port of Hull, the population of which grew from under 20,000 to near 30,000, had built eight churches or chapels, a theatre, a jail, a new bridge and its first dock. Residential building must also have expanded as populations grew, though not proportionately. In the areas of most rapid expansion there is evidence of overcrowding. Gregory King's estimates, for example, show an average of 4·5 persons per house in the cities and towns (5·5 in London). Colquhoun's estimates for the comparable cities and towns in 1801 show an average of 5·5 with over 7 in the comparable area of London. For some of the more heavily populated areas – such as Manchester and Liverpool – the average was up to 6·5.[1]

[1] The 1773 and 1788 enumerations for Manchester suggest averages of 6·5 and 7 persons per house respectively. See Aiken, *Description of the Country round Manchester* (1795), p. 156.

In sum we may conclude that the process of urbanization involved a marked increase in the rate of public and private building in the second half of the eighteenth century, though it is doubtful whether this exceeded the increase of population or national income. The pace of urbanization accelerated further in the early decades of the nineteenth century. Between 1801 and 1811 the number of inhabited houses increased by an annual average of about 23,000 a year, between 1811 and 1821 by about 33,000 and between 1821 and 1831 by about 42,000. If we value the new houses at £100 each this represents an annual new investment rising from about 1 per cent of national income in the first decade to nearly 1·5 per cent in the 1820s.[1] From 1785 the brick statistics give some indication of the rate of new building. These do not distinguish between public or residential buildings and industrial or commercial constructions but they soar significantly in the canal mania of the 1790s and the industrial booms of the early 1820s and 1830s. Between the 1790s and the 1830s (comparing decade averages in each case) the output of bricks barely doubled, the population of Great Britain grew by about two-thirds and real national product expanded some 2·5 times. These figures give no reason to suppose then that capital formation in new building absorbed a larger proportion of national income in the 1830s than in the 1790s.

(c) Investment in Inland Navigation

The rivers of the British Isles offered an important source of power and one of the few means of cheap bulk transport available in the seventeenth and early eighteenth centuries. It is small wonder that projects to divert or control their courses were among the earliest capital works undertaken on any scale. The process of river improvement was the first stage in the British transport revolution. It was slow, it was not nearly so costly as the later stages but it was probably a very productive

---

[1] This is a token figure only. Colquhoun valued the houses existing in Britain *circa* 1812 at £133 each on the basis of an estimated annual rental of £6·65 capitalized at twenty years purchase (Colquhoun, op. cit., p. 56). But this seems high, even allowing for a wartime inflation of prices.

form of investment.[1] It has been estimated that 'by the end of the eighteenth century some 2,000 miles of navigable water existed in England, of which approximately one-third was in the form of canals built between 1760 and 1800; one-third was in the form of "open" rivers which were naturally navigable; and the remaining third had been created as the work of engineers, chiefly between about 1600 and 1760.'[2]

It is impossible to say how much was spent on river navigation before the canal age began. Willan has traced an expenditure of £376,650 during the period from 1600 to 1750.[3] This is admittedly not the whole improvement expenditure but it covers the major enterprises, and if we postulate an order of magnitude of about half a million pounds spread over a century and a half for all the major projects of this type, we may not be far wrong.

The pace and scale of investment in canals were altogether different. Only intensive research into the histories of the individual waterways could provide a reliable measure of the course and extent of these investments, but much has been written about them and a broad indication of the volume and timing of the expenditures involved can be estimated from the data already published.[4]

The first modern canal was the Sankey Brook which was authorized in 1755 with a capital of £18,600 and of which 10 miles were open by 1757. It was followed by the Duke of Bridgewater's Canal (authorized in 1759) and this inspired the first wave of investment in canals which lasted until the late

[1] W. T. Jackman, *The Development of Transportation in Modern England*, vol. I (Cambridge, 1916), p. 208, estimated that in the first half of the eighteenth century the cost of transport by land was three to eleven times that by water.

[2] By Skempton in Charles Singer *et al.* (eds.), *A History of Technology*, vol. III (New York, 1958), p. 456.

[3] T. S. Willan, *River Navigation in England, 1600–1750* (London, 1936), p. 78.

[4] J. Priestley, *A Historical Account of Navigable Rivers etc.* (1831), lists over 120 canal and river navigations in existence in 1830.

Among the other contemporary sources which yielded data for these rough estimates were J. Phillips, *A Treatise on Inland Navigation* (1785); J. Cary, *Inland Navigation* (1795); C. Fenn, *A Compendium of the English and Foreign Funds* (1837). The modern investigators whom we drew upon heavily are Jackman, op. cit., and C. Hadfield in *British Canals* (London, 1950) and *The Canals of Southern England* (London, 1955).

1770s.[1] By 1790 it is estimated from the published data on the canals then open that something like £2·5 million had been spent on them.[2] Then came the Canal Mania. In the nine years 1788–96 Parliament authorized the expenditure of nearly £10 million on canals and inland navigations. How much of this had been spent by the time the new century began it is impossible to say. Analysis of the accessible data suggests that at least £3 million had been spent on canals actually opened in the period 1790–1800 and perhaps another £3 million on work still in progress. A careful study by Porter of the Canal Acts passed between 1800 and the early 1840s yielded a total investment figure of £11 million of which about £4·5 million had been spent in constructing new canals and about £6·5 million in extending and improving existing ones.[3] Using these data as our basis of calculation, we might tentatively conclude that between the 1750s and the 1830s a total of not more than about £20 million had been spent on the construction and improvement of British inland navigation.[4] Of this perhaps £2·5 million to £3 million had been spent before 1790, perhaps £5 million or £6 million in the last decade of the century, and the remainder in the period 1801–35.

(d) Investment in Roads and Bridges

During the first half of the eighteenth century, when the majority of British roads were made and repaired by a grossly inefficient system of forced labour and ill-paid surveyors, there were few highways suitable for heavy traffic and most goods

[1] Like most enterprising activities of the period it was damped by the American War. See Pressnell, op. cit., p. 456: 'Only one canal was promoted between 1779 and 1787'.

[2] We were not able to find estimates of actual cost for all the canals concerned and were obliged to depend on figures of capital authorized as an indicator of cost in many cases. On balance it is likely that the use of capital authorized as a basis of estimate tends to overstate total new investment.

[3] G. R. Porter, *The Progress of the Nation* (London, 1847), p. 628.

[4] It should be noted that there are other estimates which suggest a much bigger total. Cf. U. A. Forbes and W. H. R. Ashford, *Our Waterways* (London, 1906), p. 136, which quotes an estimate by Rennie that, up to 1840, 2,236 miles of improved river navigation and 2,477 miles of canals had been constructed in Great Britain, at a cost of £6·269 million and £24·406 million respectively. S. Salt, *Statistics and Calculations* (1845), p. 87, gives a figure of £31 million for the cost of canal construction 1760–1824, but no source is given.

transported by road were carried by packhorse. If we assume
that all the able bodied males of the villages and hamlets were
performing their statutory week's work on the roads, and
evaluate their work at the average labourer's wage, we get a
total of about £50,000 per annum for the maintenance of roads
in the early years of the century in England and Wales. This
could hardly be called capital formation. For the most part it
represented no more than an attempt to keep the existing lines
of communication in operation. Not until interested parties
began to raise capital through turnpike trusts and to employ
road engineers could the nation's capital in roads be said to
have expanded appreciably.

Over four hundred Road Acts were passed in the first half
of the century, but although these resulted in additional
expenditure on certain stretches of road it is unlikely that the
annual aggregate for the country was much enlarged. There
was some expenditure on new bridges, especially in the growing townships. The most expensive and impressive of these
was Westminster Bridge, which took more than a decade to
build after nearly a century of agitation and obstruction by
vested interests and which cost (with its approaches) over
£400,000.

The beginning of serious development of the roads and
bridges of this country seems to have come in the 1750s when
there was a sharp acceleration in the number of turnpike trusts
in operation.[1] The first road engineer was Metcalfe who was
actively building roads from 1765 to 1792. The roads which he
and his successors constructed were classifiable as new capital
formation, not only because they yielded a direct income to
trusts but also because they were qualitatively of a different
kind from the seasonal tracks they often replaced. Nevertheless
their impact on the British road system was limited. As late as
1838 the mileage under the trusts amounted to only about a
sixth of the total length of highway and not all trusts employed
skilled engineers or built efficient roads.

It has been estimated that by 1809 expenditure by the turnpike

---

[1] 'Between 1748 and 1770 the number of separate Trusts in existence rose
from about 160 to about 530 whilst the mileage subject to toll was quadrupled.'
S. and B. Webb, *English Local Government: the Story of the King's Highway* (London,
1913), p. 124. See also Jackman, op. cit., vol. I, pp. 101 ff.

trusts amounted to over £2 million.[1] The first parliamentary returns of highway expenditure show an annual cost of about £1·4 million *circa* 1814. County expenditure on bridges during the first decade of the century amounted to less than £53,000 on the average and the programmes of expenditure on highland roads and bridges averaged under £20,000 per annum for the twenty-four years ending in 1827. In sum it appears that total expenditure on the roads and bridges of Great Britain may have reached an annual average of nearly £3·5 million by the first decade of the nineteenth century. Of this probably well under a half, or less than half of 1 per cent of national income, represented net capital formation in the shape of new roads and bridges, or roads of such improved quality that they permitted an appreciably heavier flow of traffic.

Beginning then in the second half of the eighteenth century there is evidence of a noticeable improvement in the nation's stock of capital in roads. The packhorse gave way to the wagon and the regular coaching service.[2] The seasonal interruptions to the flow of traffic along the main highways were steadily reduced. Vehicles moved faster and required fewer horses. The change was gradual overall but the effects were no doubt cumulative as the discontinuous patchwork of independent turnpikes extended along the main highways and began to link up with and feed each other. According to Jackman's avowedly conservative estimate: 'On the great highways of trade the time consumed on a journey between the termini of the longer routes was in 1830 only from one-third to one-fifth of what it was in 1750.'[3]

Nor did this achievement involve a heavy annual capital outlay. True the turnpike trusts were far from efficient and squandered much of the capital entrusted to their care. But even as late as 1848 their accumulated debt (gross of repayments) was only about £9 million. Even at their operational

---

[1] By R. J. Forbes in Singer *et al.* (eds), op. cit., vol. IV, p. 530. This seems high. The parliamentary returns which begin in 1834 show a maximum expenditure of £1·753 million (in 1835); on the other hand 1809 was a year of higher prices than 1835.

[2] The first mailcoach, for example, began to ply between London and Bristol in 1784.

[3] Jackman, op. cit., vol. I, p. 339.

peak at the end of the eighteenth and early years of the nineteenth century it is doubtful whether they accounted for new
capital formation of as much as half of 1 per cent of national
income. On the other hand the net effect of the road improvements must have been to free appreciable amounts of capital
tied up in horses, goods or travellers in transit.

(e) Investment in Docks and Harbours

Until towards the end of the eighteenth century there was little
substantial investment in dock and harbour works. There had
been some dock construction in London, Bristol and Liverpool
during the first quarter of the century – involving an expenditure estimated to have cost about £36,600 in all – but during
the whole of the first three-quarters less than 150 acres of dock
and basin accommodation were constructed.[1] During the last
quarter of the century this accommodation was doubled, and
in the first three decades of the nineteenth century the total
area of dockland expanded by over 4,700 acres, i.e. by more
than ten times its volume in 1799.

In Britain's biggest port, whose trade had doubled in the
course of the eighteenth century, nothing was done until the
French war made its improvement suddenly urgent and
precipitated the first London dock boom. Between 1799 and
1815 capital authorized by Parliament for the London docks
amounted to nearly £5·5 million; before the 1820s Liverpool
and Bristol had spent about £1·3 million and Hull and Grimsby
a further £0·3 million on dock construction; while the public
expenditure on the ports and harbours of the United Kingdom
was averaging over a million pounds per decade in the second
and third decades of the nineteenth century.[2] We may presume
that total new capital expenditure on British docks and

[1] See D. Swann, 'The Pace and Progress of Port Investment in England,
1660–1830', *Yorkshire Bulletin of Economic and Social Research*, XII, no. 1 (March
1960) for a chronology of the increase in dock and basin accommodation in
England 1700–1830 and for statistics of the cost of some of the major dock
and harbour projects.

[2] W. M. Stern, 'The First London Dock Boom and the Growth of the West
India Docks', *Economica*, N.S., XIX, no. 73 (1952), p. 70; Swann, op. cit., p. 39;
Sessional Papers 1876, LXV, for a parliamentary return giving public expenditure
on docks and harbours annually from 1800 to 1875.

harbours amounted to rather more than £8 million during the first two decades of the century. This represented an annual average of under half a million pounds, in relation to a national income which averaged between £250 million and £300 million.

The London dock system was largely completed in the 1820s but elsewhere construction was still accelerating. 'There was hardly a port of any size or a threatened part of the coast where improvements had not recently been undertaken or were not in hand during the middle twenties.'[1] Liverpool doubled its dock area between 1825 and 1846 and by the 1850s wet docks were being opened at the rate of nearly one a year.

(f) Other Channels of Investment

Investment in urban buildings and amenities, enclosures and means of communication took place on a large enough scale to leave their trace on the nation's administrative records. We may not be able to measure them satisfactorily at the national level but we can make a plausible assessment of their impact and timing. The conclusion which emerges from the preceding review, for example, is that there was little noticeable addition to the net stock of the return in the first few decades of the eighteenth century, that there was a distinct quickening of the tempo of capital formation in the 1760s and that (after the American War) the acceleration continued, or the level of advance was maintained, for most forms of investment except agriculture through the 1830s. For agriculture the evidence suggests a slowing down of new investment after the French wars, but by then capital was flowing into new channels. There had been expenditure of up to £7·5 million on railroads by 1835 for example, the annual average for the decade 1826–35 being near £0·7 million. Public gaslighting was installed for the first time in Westminster in 1814, and by 1825 there were twenty gas companies with a paid-up capital of over £2 million.

---

[1] J. Clapham, *Economic History of Modern Britain* (Cambridge, 1939), vol. I, p. 4. Southampton began its great tidal dock in 1839 and in the next half century spent over a million pounds on its dockland. See J. J. Davies, *History of Southampton* (London, 1883), p. 280.

At the same time there were sixteen water companies with nearly £3 million paid up.[1]

By then also there was an appreciable flow of capital abroad – for most of the eighteenth century the net flow may have been in the other direction.[2] Jenks traces an outflow of about £75 million in the period 1815–30.[3] Imlah's estimate of the accumulating balance of British credit abroad reached £143 million by 1835 and was averaging near 3 per cent of the national income in the decade 1816–25.[4]

We know little, however, about rates or levels of investment in industry or trade. If the export industries, for example, responded to expanding sales in the 1740s by adding to their capital we have no direct evidence of it. For the last quarter of the century, which saw a fresh acceleration in overseas trade and important innovations in steam, cotton and iron, some uncertain fragments of evidence exist which may give some indication of the orders of magnitude involved. Shipping figures, for example, available from the last decade of the century, show a merchant shipping fleet expanding at the rate of under 2 per cent per annum which may have reflected a net annual investment of near half a million pounds per annum. The expansion continued into the first two decades of the nineteenth century, when the annual net increase in British shipping may have been worth over a million pounds, slackened in the 1820s and did not grow strongly again until the 1840s.

Contemporary estimates for the cotton industry, which may well be exaggerated, suggest that between 1783 and 1802 its capital grew by about £8 million and there was another wave of investment in cotton mills in the early 1820s. It seems unlikely that the iron industry added more than £11 million

[1] See H. English, *Complete View of the Joint Stock Companies found in 1824 and 1825* (London, 1827) for figures of joint stock companies in gas and water in 1825.

[2] Sir J. Sinclair, *History of the Public Revenue*, vol. III (London, 1803), appendix p. 161, estimated that £15 million of the £89 million of stock managed by the Bank in 1762 was held by foreigners, and there are a number of contemporary estimates of the foreign share in the British National Debt. See A. Carter, 'Dutch Foreign Investment 1738–1800', *Economica*, N.S., XX, no. 80 (November 1953), pp. 322–40.

[3] L. Jenks, *The Migration of British Capital* (New York, 1927), p. 64.

[4] A. H. Imlah, *Economic Elements in the Pax Britannica* (Cambridge, Mass., 1954), p. 70.

to its capital in the two decades before 1806, and its level of capital formation was probably not above this again until the early 1830s.[1] The number of steam engines in existence at the end of the century probably did not exceed 1,000,[2] representing a total capital of less than half a million pounds. But by 1835 the number of steam engines operating in textiles factories alone was over 40,000.

The impression gained by piecing such fragments as these together is that at the end of the eighteenth century the annual flow of new capital into the leading commercial and industrial sectors (shipping, textiles and iron) was not more than about £2 million or perhaps 1 per cent of national income. At that stage the capital-saving characteristics of technological progress in manufacturing industry, as in some forms of transport, may well have predominated over its capital-using characteristics. The change-over from domestic to factory industry and possibly to day- and night-shift working must have involved a more effective and continuous use of machinery although it also involved the construction of new capital in buildings. The substitution of steam for water-power freed factories and forges from dependence on the seasonal flow of streams and rivers for their power supply, and thus permitted continuous activity in works which had been restricted to a forty-week year or less.[3] But by the early 1830s the flow of industrial and commercial capital had broadened, the share of the expanding industries in the national income had grown and the impact of their ploughed back profits was correspondingly larger. The evidence for a rise in the rate of capital formation in manufacturing and commerce (including overseas investment) is stronger for the 1820s and 1830s than for any preceding period.

[1] See P. Deane and H. J. Habakkuk, 'The Take-off in Britain', in W. W. Rostow (ed.), *The Economics of Take-off into Sustained Growth* (London and New York, 1963).

[2] See A. E. Musson and E. Robinson, 'The Early Growth of Steam Power', *Economic History Review*, 2nd series, XI, no. 3 (April 1959), pp. 418–39; and J. Lord, *Capital and Steampower 1750–1800* (London, 1923).

[3] See R. J. Forbes in Singer *et al.* (eds), op. cit., vol. IV, p. 161. See also his statement that: 'Steampower meant that the ironworks could be carried on with cheap mineral fuel so that there was no need for the separation of furnace, forge and mill that characterized the iron industry in the early years of the century.'

III *Conclusions*

In confining our attention to the accessible published material we have covered only a fraction of the total evidence which could be brought to bear on the problem of assessing changes in the level of capital formation before the railway age. The conclusions which can be drawn from these inadequate data are necessarily tentative. On the other hand, it does not seem likely that the most intensive research would permit firm estimates either of the total stock of capital or of the overall level of capital formation at this early period. The results of further first-hand study may be to strengthen the estimates of levels and rates of change for particular sectors, and it may confirm or destroy some of the interpretations which we have adopted here.

For the seventeenth century the conjectures of contemporaries and the experience of joint stock companies provide a starting point for speculation. If we accept Gregory King's quantitative assessment of the world in which he lived we can conclude that there was a slow secular growth in the national stock of capital. At best, however, the annual rate of capital formation probably did not exceed 5 per cent of national income and was so vulnerable to wars, epidemics and similar short-term disturbances that the long-term rate must have been well below this level. On the other hand the rapidity with which funds could be raised to repair the losses of the Fire and to finance the great foreign trading companies and the Bank of England suggests that there was no shortage of investible funds. The limiting factors to a higher role of accumulation came from the rate of investment rather than from the saving side.

It is not difficult to suggest reasons for a shortage of investment opportunities in late seventeenth- or early eighteenth-century England. In part it could be attributed to a shortage of entrepreneurial skill, in part to a primitive capital market and in part to the political uncertainties of the period. Innovations spread slowly – whether through ignorance or lack of enterprise or of warranted confidence is not clear. The usury laws discouraged investment in enterprises that were uncertain or slow to fructify. Economic activity was subject to a variety of crippling, if temporary, disasters – war, harvest failure, tempest, epidemic or fire. Most of the opportunities for economic expansion lay in the realm of overseas trade which was peculiarly vulnerable to circumstances outside the control of the individual entrepreneur. Nor was the domestic social and political environment as orderly and reliable as it gradually became during the eighteenth century.

Whatever the reason the shortage of investment opportunities seems to have persisted through the early decades of the eighteenth century. Certainly there is no evidence for a change in the level of capital accumulation in any major sector until mid century. Then there were signs that the traditional mould was breaking. The change had been preceded by a long period of relatively good harvests.[1] Population, relieved of what Professor Cipolla has called the 'dismal peaks' in the death rate, began to grow in the 1740s. There was a sudden expansion in the same decade in overseas trade. The opportunities and problems presented by concentrations of population in the growing townships seemed to be grasped and dealt with more efficiently and expeditiously in the 1750s and 1760s.[2] The order of change and causation is still obscure but there is unmistakable evidence for a rising rate of capital accumulation in roads, canals, buildings and agricultural enclosures.

Except during the period of the American War when all forms of economic activity seem to have faltered, the rate of new investment continued to accelerate. By the last quarter of the century, if we may judge by the difficulties encountered by some of the canal companies in calling up their authorized capital, the shortage of investment opportunities was less limiting than the shortage of capital. Perhaps this was partly because the would-be saver had other outlets for his savings – not least being the Funds.[3] But if government absorbed savings

[1] T. Tooke in *A History of Prices*, vol. I (London, 1838), pp. 39–40, refers to a period of half a century following 1715 when 'there appear to have been only five seasons which, whether by inference from prices or by historical notice could be considered as of a marked deficiency of produce in any way approaching to what could be designated as seasons of scarcity'.

[2] Pressnell, op. cit., p. 366. 'From about the middle of the eighteenth century there was a marked expansion of local investment carried out by public and semi-public bodies.'

[3] See A. J. Youngson, *Possibilities of Economic Progress* (Cambridge, 1959), p. 109: 'Near the beginning of the century the rate on the perpetual annuities

that might otherwise have flowed into private investment, its tax collections provided a basis of credit which the newly developing banking system could use to finance business enterprise.[1] The net effect of a more efficient public administration on the supply of capital to industry, commerce and agriculture was almost certainly favourable.

Clearly the nation's capital stock rose appreciably in the second half of the eighteenth century but so too did population and income. Considered in relation to national income the annual overall cost of the new investments was not heavy. Probably they brought the annual level of net capital formation in productive channels to a sustained average of more than 5 per cent. But given the possibility that much of the technological progress of the latter part of the eighteenth century was capital-saving in its effects, even this modest estimate of the rise in the annual level of capital formation may be exaggerated.

The end of the French wars removed another source of uncertainty in economic life, and from then on the evidence permits one to suppose that capital was growing fast – perhaps at times appreciably faster than income. The creation of new social capital in roads, railways, canals, harbours and cities accelerated in the two decades following 1815. There was a growing importance in the economy of industries such as textile and iron which were ploughing back a high proportion of their profits. Capital was also beginning to flow abroad in sizeable amounts. By the 1820s and early 1830s, in effect before the beginning of the main railway age, the economy had left behind its pre-industrial levels of capital formation. It is certain that average annual capital formation had risen above 5 per cent of national income, though it is difficult to see how it could have exceeded 10 per cent. Further research should make it possible to define the level of the 1820s and 1830s more precisely. Meanwhile, however, what is both interesting and reasonably well-established is the gradualness of the change. It had taken over a century for the average to rise from not much

---

was at least 7 per cent, but this rate fell through the first half of the century and in 1757 there came into existence the 3 per cent Consolidated Stock.'

[1] Pressnell, op. cit., pp. 56–77.

more than 3 per cent of national income to something less than 10 per cent.

By this time the economy was in full process of industrialization and was growing quite rapidly (at a long term rate of over 1 per cent per annum). The Industrial Revolution was by no means complete before the railway age, but it had got well into its stride with an average net investment of under 10 per cent per annum.

4 Capital Accounting in the Industrial Revolution

SIDNEY POLLARD

[This article was first published[1] in the *Yorkshire Bulletin of Economic and Social Research*, vol. XV, no. 2, November 1963.]

The notion of 'capital' has always lain at the centre of the concept of capitalism and of theories attempting to describe its evolution. It has generally been agreed that there has been a slow transformation from early 'personal' and 'specific' capital, mainly in its financial and commercial (circulating) forms, to capital as found in the advanced stages of 'high capitalism', by which time it had become typically general and anonymous, and included much fixed capital in industrial and public utility ventures. In this development, the industrial revolution in Britain is generally held to have formed a major step, and to have given rise to the first consistent theories of capital, as well as introducing the notion of fixed capital into accounting. The present article attempts to examine, in this light, actual accounts and other records, kept by British business firms in the period up to about 1830. It begins by reviewing briefly some of the literature on this subject, based (as nearly all existing accountancy history is based) mainly on textbooks of accountancy.[2]

I

It was Sombart who first placed accountancy practices at the centre of a theory of capitalist development. According to him,

[1] The article has also been reprinted, with a few minor changes, in S. Pollard, *The Genesis of Modern Management. A Study of the Industrial Revolution in Britain* (London, 1965), chap. 6, 'Accounting and Management', section V, pp. 233–45.

[2] The research on which this paper is based was made possible by a grant from the Houblon–Norman Fund of the Bank of England.

E

it is double-entry book-keeping which endows the economic world with accuracy, knowledge and system. It provided the idea of quantification, of maximizing incomes instead of providing a living, of increasing the value of a capital sum, irrespective of its material composition, and of separating the entrepreneur from the capital, creating the enterprise as an independent concern. '*It is only this way of looking at things which creates the very idea of capital* (his italics). It is therefore permissible to say that before double-entry book-keeping the category of "capital" did not exist, and it would not exist now but for it.'[1]

Capital could thus be defined as wealth-for-profit controlled by double-entry book-keeping, from which also sprang the finer distinctions of fixed and circulating capital, and others.

Weber extended the analysis, stressing the part played by accounting in creating rationality in business: 'A rational capitalist establishment is one with capital accounting,' he wrote,

> that is, an establishment which determines its income-yielding power by calculation according to the methods of modern book-keeping and the striking of a balance. . . .[2] The most general presupposition for the existence of this present-day capitalism is that of rational capital accounting as the norm for all industrial undertakings which are concerned with provision for everyday wants.[3]

The Sombart–Weber thesis was intended to fit into the framework of the accepted view of capitalist development, which, at the risk of gross over-simplification, may be described as having had two main stages: the early transformation from money-lending into commercial capitalism, beginning in Italy

---

[1] W. Sombart, *Der Moderne Kapitalismus*, 3rd ed. (Munich and Leipzig, 1919: 2 vols), vol. II/1, p. 120, also *passim*. See also B. S. Yamey, 'Accounting and the Rise of Capitalism', in *Studi in Onore di Amintore Fanfani* (Milan, 1962), vol. 6, p. 833.

[2] 'The device of a balance', he went on, erroneously, 'was first insisted upon by the Dutch theorist Simon Stevin in the year 1698'.

[3] Max Weber, *General Economic History* (Glencoe, 1950), pp. 275, 276, also p. 354.

in the thirteenth and fourteenth centuries, and the development from commercial into industrial capitalism, beginning in Britain in the eighteenth. While the earlier change created rational accounting, it was the latter which forced capitalists to fit fixed capital into their accounting, and led economists to evolve the modern concept of capital.

Within this historical scheme, to be henceforth called the 'classical', it is the first stage which is said to have led to the development of double-entry, for while the money-lender merely wanted a record of his sums outstanding, the merchant needed a check on his managerial performance and required a knowledge of the 'totals of his business investments'.[1] In practice, however, the books of the early merchants normally showed costs and returns separately for each trading venture, thus ignoring the merchant's stock of capital as a meaningful quantity. Even over most of the seventeenth century, 'the idea of a capital which is to be maintained, respectively increased, and consequently the idea of dividends is completely unknown to many of the . . . joint-stock companies':[2] costs were often calculated per individual share, and the profits of the trading companies divided in the form of goods. In the Dutch East India Company at the time, for example, 'dividends were paid out of the net balance in hand, and the strict notion of profit was never grasped or followed in keeping books'.[3] Lesser firms, without the mental stimulus of the calculation of share values and periodic profit distribution, were even more backward,[4] and Defoe's precepts, dating from the beginning of the eighteenth century, were a counsel of perfection rather than a reflection of current reality: 'The books are the register of (the tradesman's) estate, the index of his stock; all the tradesman has in the world must be found in . . . them; – Goods in the shop, money in cash, debts abroad.' If he casts up these three, 'and then examines his account to take the balance, which is a

[1] A. C. Littleton, *Essays in Accountancy* (Urbana, 1961), p. 66.

[2] Sombart, op. cit., p. 160, relying largely on Scott.

[3] A. B. Levy, *Private Corporations and their Control* (London, 1950: 2 vols), vol. I, p. 19.

[4] For an example of an eighteenth-century Portugal merchant keeping his accounts in a venture-by-venture way, see L. S. Sutherland, 'The Accounts of an Eighteenth-Century Merchant', *Economic History Review*, 2nd series, III (1932), p. 375.

real trying what he is worth in the world', he will, in fact, have a notion of his total trading capital.[1]

The date of the pervasion of commercial capitalism by rational views on capital, is thus by no means certain. Sombart, for example, appears to place it in the seventeenth to eighteenth centuries, while Weber favours the nineteenth century.[2]

The second step of the 'classical' scheme was the recognition of fixed capital.

> From the standpoint of the theorist the essential difference between industrial and commercial capitalism depends upon the nature of capitalist accumulation under both systems. Under mercantile capitalism, capital is largely a stock in trade or a revolving fund, which is used to buy raw materials and to pay wages and which is replenished by the sale of the finished product. Little is invested in productive equipment, with perhaps two notable exceptions: the shipping and the mining industries. Industrial capitalism, on the contrary, presupposes large investments in equipment before production can really start. Depreciation, maintenance, and overhead thus become important in figuring costs. An example will make this clear: depreciation in one of the sixteenth-century Medici partnerships for the manufacture of woollen cloth was less than one per cent of cost. In other words, depreciation was practically negligible. Overhead (sic) amounted to only ten per cent. Direct costs were consequently the determining factor.[3]

Even the greatest of the early capitalists whose accounts survive, like the Medici or the Fuggers, had too little fixed capital to make special forms of accounting or new concepts necessary,[4] while in Venice the major items of fixed capital, the galleys, were rented by the State to the partnerships or

[1] Daniel Defoe, *The Complete English Tradesman* (London, 1841 ed: 20 vols), vols 17 and 18, p. 310. The context makes it clear that Defoe was referring to large merchants, not to retail shopkeepers, who, according to him, needed books only if they gave credit.

[2] Sombart, op. cit., p. 126; Weber, op. cit., p. 167.

[3] R. de Roover, 'The Commercial Revolution of the Thirteenth Century', in F. C. Lane and J. C. Riemersma, *Enterprise and Secular Change* (London, 1953), p. 85.

[4] S. P. Garner, *Evolution of Cost Accounting to 1925* (Alabama, 1954), esp. pp. 5–13.

merchants and in this way turned into prime costs.[1] It was essentially only in the industrial revolution that 'the increase in the amount of fixed capital made investments permanent, and the regularity of the income derived from them became important'. With it, began the 'accountants' problems', 'problems which accountants and book-keepers had not previously needed to consider, except in a minor sort of way. These problems arose mainly in connexion with the large amounts of capital sunk in plant, equipment and transportation facilities'. The problems included the allocation of overheads, the question of whether to include interest as a cost, and the profits on unfinished contracts.[2] Weber appears to have come to a similar conclusion:

> A factory is a shop industry with free labour and fixed capital. The composition of the fixed capital is indifferent . . . the crucial fact is that the entrepreneur operates with fixed capital, in which connexion capital accounting is indispensable. Hence a factory in this sense signifies a capitalistic organization of the process of production, i.e. an organization of specialized and co-ordinated work with a workshop, with utilization of fixed capitalistic accounting. . . . As between the domestic system and the factory the volume of fixed capital was decisive.[3]

Lord's conclusion is even more uncompromising: 'The development of steam power and the accumulation of capital, are inextricably bound together, and their stories cannot be separated.'[4]

This 'classical' scheme has not been without its critics. First, it has been argued that the notion of a continuous capital and a continuous firm, was not necessarily more 'rational' than, for example, the older process of balancing each trade voyage

---

[1] Lane in *Enterprise and Secular Change*, p. 94.

[2] J. Lord, *Capital and Steam Power* (London, 1923), p. 231; R. S. Edwards, 'Some Notes on the Early Literature and Development of Cost Accounting in Great Britain', series in *The Accountant*, XCVII (1937), p. 193; Garner, op. cit., p. 28, also pp. 1, 29.

[3] Weber, op. cit., pp. 163, 173–4.

[4] Lord, op. cit., p. 62. Cf. also Garner, op. cit., p. 1 n. 1; and L. Urwick and E. F. L. Brech, *The Making of Scientific Management* (London, 1959 ed: 3 vols), vol. 2, p. 20.

separately. Not only was it less useful to merge all merchant activities and calculate profits on capital 'invested', rather than check the outcome of each major transaction separately; it was also less logical. With the industrial revolution,

> the use of fixed capital on a large scale increases incalculably the difficulty of determining the profits earned in any given year ... business is a continuum. Machinery serves for many years, the factory building stands for a generation, the railroad is built to last for ever. The industrial process is made up of a never-ending stream of raw materials, goods in process and finished commodities.

To arrive at the traditional figure of profits per annum, one has to chop up a lifetime of things.[1] At the same time it has been shown that double-entry does not necessarily ensure rationality.[2]

Secondly, doubts have been cast on the timing, on the grounds that a few early examples of double-entry book-keeping do not yet make a new ethos or a new economic system. 'Ideas the same in kind must produce very different results according to their social context. They may be isolated and socially insignificant, or they may be dominant and control their whole society.' The significance of the islands of early commercial capitalism in a non-capitalist environment has thus been exaggerated and the Weber–Sombart thesis had placed the rise of capitalistic attitudes too early in European history.[3]

But thirdly, as a matter of historic fact, a study of textbooks of accountancy and of some actual account books in the period 1494–1840 revealed remarkably little change, after methods had crystallized at the end of the sixteenth century, and little rationality relating to capital. Balances are struck, not at regular intervals, as checks and controls, but at the end of books, to save transfers to new folios; values of assets are rarely changed, as would have been necessary if merchants had really wanted to know their capital position; above all, the

[1] H. R. Hatfield, 'A Historic Defence of Book-keeping', in W. T. Baxter (ed.), *Studies in Accounting* (London, 1950), p. 11; also B. S. Yamey, 'Scientific Book-keeping and the Rise of Capitalism', ibid., esp. pp. 27–8.

[2] This point is developed at length by Yamey, 'Accounting', pp. 837 ff.

[3] P. C. Gordon Walker, 'Capitalism and the Reformation', *Economic History Review*, VIII (1937), pp. 1–4.

capital account, far from being the centre of rational calculation, had closed into it (as part of the profit-and-loss account)
a hotch-potch of items with only the single common quality
that they did not easily fit in elsewhere, such as dowries,
money lost, or claims for which there were no further dealings.[1]

The first textbook to propound the idea of capital as an
abstraction separate from the business, Hustcraft Stephens'
Italian Bookkeeping reduced into an Art (London, 1735), has been
described as one hundred years ahead of its time.[2] Even the
next two books to deal with capital in this way, J. W. Fulton's
British-Indian Bookkeeping of 1800 and F. W. Cronhelm's more
famous *Double Entry by Single*, of 1818,[3] were swallows of a
very distant summer.

Actual practice, in every age, lagged behind the ideal of the
textbooks.[4] Before turning to the practice of the industrial
revolution, it is worth noting that in the 1820s even banks
showed no awareness of the importance of distinguishing in
their accounts their own capital, or ranking their assets in
order of liquidity, and examples of primitive accounting may
be found late as the 1840s. The railways, also, despite their
joint stock structure, could not distinguish between capital
and revenue until well into the second half of the nineteenth
century, allowing men like George Hudson to batten on the
opportunities for fraud provided by such uncertainty. In turn,
the 'majority (of railways) were cavalier in their attitude to
railway finance and accounts' because 'there was little experience the companies could draw on'.[5] In the USA, right up to

---

[1] Yamey, 'Scientific Book-keeping', and 'Accounting', *passim*.

[2] J. G. C. Jackson, 'The History of Methods of Exposition of Double-entry
Book-keeping in England', in A. C. Littleton and B. S. Yamey (eds), *Studies in
the History of Accounting* (London, 1956), pp. 307–9.

[3] Ibid., pp. 309–10; also B. S. Yamey, 'Edward Jones and the Reform of
Book-keeping 1795–1810', ibid., p. 318.

[4] e.g. B. S. Yamey, 'The Development of Company Accounting Conventions',
Three Banks Review, 47 (1960); P. Ramsey, 'Some Tudor Merchants' Accounts',
in Littleton and Yamey, op. cit., p. 195.

[5] H. C. F. Holgate, *English Bank Accounting and its Historical Background* (Lon-
don, 1948), p. 13; H. Pollins, 'Aspects of Railway Accounting Before 1868' in
Littleton and Yamey, op. cit., esp. p. 339; H. Pollins, 'A Note on Railway
Constructional Costs, 1825–1850', *Economica*, XIX (1952), p. 401; N. A. H.
Stacey, *English Accountancy, a Study in Social and Economic History, 1800–1954*
(London, 1954), pp. 13–14.

the 1890s capitalists 'did not distinguish between fixed capital and working capital, at least not effectively', and in Britain also, the rise of modern cost accounting dates from the 1880s only.[1]

II

The industrial firms whose records have been drawn upon for the present study formed, inevitably, only a small sample of the firms in existence, and a sample biased by survival and accessibility of records, at that. Since, however, it is also heavily biased towards the large and go-ahead concerns of the day, we may be justified in assuming that it represents the most sophisticated practices currently in use; the general run of firms was likely to be more backward.

Very few of these advanced firms (to anticipate our conclusion at this point) showed, in their accounting practice, an understanding of the meaning or concept of capital, particularly fixed capital, as postulated by the 'classical' scheme. Their practices were characterized by two main heresies: the treatment of capital as an auxiliary to entrepreneurship instead of the central motive force behind the firm, and the confusion between capital and revenue.

For purposes of exposition, it will be easiest to begin with the fact that the typical firm was a partnership. Joint stock enterprises were rare, and often modelled on partnerships, while single proprietorships were perhaps rarer still among large firms. Normally a partnership would start with a round sum, divided in fixed proportions: in Cyfarthfa, for example, William Crawshay Sr was to have had a capital of £100,000 and his partner Benjamin Hall £60,000.[2] At the end of the year, each partner was first credited with interest on his capital, and the net surplus then remaining was divided in the fixed proportion, in this case 5 to 3, and also credited to the partners' accounts. Since, however, dividends and interest were not paid out, but allowed to accumulate except for irregular withdrawals by partners to meet their living expenses, actual capital

[1] N. S. B. Gras, 'Capitalism—Concept and History', in *Enterprise and Secular Change*, esp. p. 77; D. Solomons (ed.), *Studies in Costing* (London, 1952), pp. 18–19.

[2] *Cyfarthfa MSS* (National Library of Wales), vol. 1 and box 12.

holdings very quickly diverged from the original round sums, both in absolute terms and in the proportions of the partners' holdings to each other. Further, all partners did not necessarily contribute the full amounts of their nominal share; this was especially so when they were admitted into an existing partnership as managerial experts or sons of partners. The withdrawal of a partner, by death for example, requiring the paying off of the share to the executors, might also greatly distort the actual shareholdings from the nominal for many years.[1] Knight's Stourbridge partnership, according to the surviving accounts of 1726–36, made up their nominal capital to round sums whenever a new works was added to the group,[2] but normally actual holding tended to diverge increasingly from nominal capital, until partnership shares were adjusted at renewals and changes of the partnership. Throughout, however, partners continued to receive interest on the actual amounts held (an incentive to saving and the ploughing back of profits), while profits were shared out according to the original formula.

There was also a clear, and parallel distinction between interest and profits in cost accounting. Interest was treated as a cost, universally in computing the advisability of planned ventures, but frequently also in accounts of the past. This was natural where capital was borrowed,[3] or derived from an associated company, as in the case of the Soho Foundry, which drew its capital from Boulton and Watt,[4] or where payment was

[1] e.g. R. E. Wilson, *Two Hundred Precious Metal Years* (London, 1960), p. 39; W. G. Rimmer, *Marshalls of Leeds, Flax Spinners 1788–1886* (Cambridge, 1960), pp. 47, 68–9; H. Heaton, 'Financing the Industrial Revolution', *Bulletin of the Business Historical Society*, XI (1937), pp. 8–10; *Spencer-Stanhope Muniments* (MS, Sheffield City Library), no. 60458; J. R. Harris, *The Copper Industry in Lancashire and North Wales, 1760–1815* (Manchester Ph. D. thesis, n.d.), pp. 209, 246–8; R. H. Campbell, *Carron Company* (Edinburgh, 1961), p. 137.

[2] R. L. Downes, 'The Stour Partnership, 1726–36', *Economic History Review*, 2nd series, III (1950), pp. 90–1.

[3] e.g. *Herculaneum Pottery MSS* (Liverpool Central Library), Minute Book (no. 47), 5 February 1811, 27 February 1821; H. Malet, *The Canal Duke* (Dawlish and London, 1961), p. 145; British Transport Commission Archives (York), ACN/1/3, Minute Book, Aire and Calder Navigation, 9 March 1709.

[4] The old firm advanced £21,600, on which 5 per cent was paid regularly until its repayment in 1812. E. Roll, *An Early Experiment in Industrial Organization, being a History of the Firm of Boulton and Watt, 1775–1805* (London, 1930), esp. pp. 123, 164, 253–5, 260; J. R. Immer, *The Development of Production Methods in Birmingham 1760–1851* (Oxford D.Phil. thesis, 1954), p. 189.

in bills which had to be discounted.[1] But it was widespread also in other cases,[2] and there is much evidence to show that 'profits' in common parlance, were often understood to be the surplus *after* interest was paid.[3] Conversely, earnings *less* than the expected interest rate were termed 'losses'[4] – an echo of the present practice relating to the nationalized industries.

Normally, this interest as a cost was computed, year after year, on the original investment, but occasionally it was based on current capital values:[5] in the Mona Mine Co., for example,

[1] e.g. the allowance of 5 per cent claimed in 1814 on this account by the Walkers when submitting their costs to their landlord, the Earl Fitzwilliam, *Wentworth Woodhouse Muniments* (MS, Sheffield City Library), F. 106e.

[2] e.g. Cyfarthfa, Hirwain and Treforest, 1811–67: J. P. Addis, *The Crawshay Dynasty, a Study in Industrial Organization and Development, 1765–1867* (Cardiff, 1957), pp. 164–7. The Gadlis mines, 9 years ending 1790: A. Raistrick, *Two Centuries of Industrial Welfare, the London (Quaker) Lead Company, 1692–1905* (London, 1938), p. 127. Mona Mine 1818–30: *Mona Mine MSS* (University College of North Wales), nos. 159–64, 167, 1544–7, 2802, 3047. Gott mills, partnership accounts 1795–1814: *Gott Papers* (MS, Brotherton Library, Leeds), box 6.

[3] E. Hughes, *North Country Life in the Eighteenth Century* (London, 1952), p. 157; H. Heaton, 'Benjamin Gott and the Industrial Revolution in Yorkshire', *Economic History Review*, III (1931), p. 64; W. R. Scott (ed.), *The Records of a Scottish Cloth Manufactory at New Mills, Haddingtonshire, 1681–1713* (Edinburgh, 1905), p. xlix; *Factories Inquiry Commission, First Report*, PP 1833, XX, D. 2, R. H. Greg, p. 30 and appendix A; J. Horner, *The Linen Trade of Europe during the Spinning-Wheel Period* (Belfast, 1920), p. 105; *Nevill MSS* (National Library of Wales), no. 21, Minute Book, 24 June 1806; A. H. John (ed.), *The Walker Family, Ironfounders and Lead Manufacturers, 1741–1893* (London, 1951), p. 26, resolution of 1820; *Report of Committees on the Coal Trade* (1800), PP, Reports of Committees of House of Commons, 1785–1801, vol. X, ev. T. Ismay, p. 559; *Select Committee on Manufactures*, PP 1833, VI, ev. J. Dixon, Q. 4229, W. Graham, Q. 5547, J. Milne, QQ. 10995–11000.

[4] e.g. Boulton & Fothergill, J. E. Cule, *The Financial History of Matthew Boulton, 1759–1800* (Birmingham M. Com. thesis, 1935), pp. 18, 35–7, 63; for Sheffield Park Mines, 1780–4, in *Norfolk Muniments* (MS, Sheffield City Library), nos. S. 215–30; *Committee on South Wales Collieries*, PP 1810, IV, p. 3, ev. H. Smith; S. Pigott, *Hollins, a Study of Industry, 1784–1949* (Nottingham, 1949), p. 35. The Mona Mine called even a shortfall from a total desired profit rate of 10 per cent (£42,000) in 1794–1800 a 'loss' of nearly £30,000, though the net profits were £12,000: *Mona Mine MSS*, no. 3544; Harris, op. cit., p. 214.

[5] e.g. (wagonways), *Norfolk Muniments*, nos. S. 215–30; P. Mathias, *The Brewing Industry in England, 1700–1830* (Cambridge, 1959), p. 471; Rimmer, *Marshalls*, p. 85; *Mona Mine MSS*, nos. 166, 1333, 2633; A. and N. Clow, 'Lord Dundonald', *Economic History Review*, XII (1942), p. 50; *Factories Commission, 1833*, op. cit., p. 30 and appendix A; British Transport Commission Archives (York), SAD/1/6, Minutes 13 July 1830; *Spencer-Stanhope Muniments*, Furnace and Forge Accounts. For a deeper analysis of some of the concepts involved here, see Littleton, *Essays in Accountancy*, esp. pp. 66–7.

'upon the Estimated Value of Stocks, Debts, buildings, stores and implements on 31st December, 1810'.[1] In the case of the Carron Co., indeed, it was charged in full as a cost against revenue even after it had become clear that much of the original capital, on which it had been computed, had been lost.[2]

There are other clues to show the basic distinction made between interest and the remainder of the surplus. Thus Robert Owen, measuring his success at New Lanark, first allowed interest at 5 per cent and then included in the additional profit not only the increased capital value of the property but also the £7,000 paid out in wages relief during the cotton famine of 1808 – a notion of profits to mean any disposable surplus, however spent.[3] Again, John Curr, in presenting the Duke of Norfolk's coal accounts for 1781–90 in order to compare the returns of direct management with those of letting, called the surplus, 'profits and interest', to show that interest had to be earned before a venture became profitable. Alexander Mason, the Scots projector, offered investors their interest even before payment of his managerial salary, while Samuel Walker believed that his returns as an ironmaster should provide separately for interest on capital, risk and management.[4]

All these practices are linked by a common, though unspoken assumption: the assumption that profits are not directly related to the quantity of capital, and therefore not payment for capital or created by capital. Capital is adequately rewarded by interest at the current rate, at which, incidentally, the supply is clearly assumed to be highly elastic and limited by personal and specific shortages rather than by price. Profits are distinct and are rewards of entrepreneurship *per se*, depending on skill, the concrete business situation or sheer luck, the entrepreneur using capital merely as a tool for which he pays the market

---

[1] *Mona Mine MSS*, no. 3063, Sanderson to Paget, 2 October 1811.

[2] R. H. Campbell, 'The Financing of Carron Company', *Business History*, I (1958), p. 28.

[3] R. Owen, *Life of Owen, by himself* (London, 1920 ed.), p. 120; F. Podmore, *Robert Owen, a Biography* (London, 1923 ed.), p. 93.

[4] *Norfolk Muniments*, S. 196; (A. Mason), *An Appeal to the Common Sense of Scotsmen* (Edinburgh, 1747), p. 64, article VI; *SC on Manufactures*, 1833, ev. S. Walker, Q. 9561.

rate.[1] This contrasts directly with the classical economists' assumption that 'The sums received as "wages" by particular undertakers seemed to depend on the quantity of capital at their disposal, and not upon the amount of labour they performed'. Further, the accountants' pattern of thought is not consistent with a market-ordained distribution of capital according to its marginal return, or any bidding for it based on promised earnings: the price offered is the same everywhere – though the risk might differ. Conversely, no single instance has been found of a contemporary calculation of the profit rate on capital in the modern sense, though, significantly, many such have been made on the basis of surviving records by modern authors. Yet the contemporary economists' view was that 'the *rate* of profit . . . is always reckoned or estimated by the proportion or *ratio* which it bears to the stock or capital from which it arises. . . . The rate of profit was given by the ratio of the amount of profits obtained in a year to the amount of capital from which they were derived.'[2]

There is no space here for a discussion of the causes of this, our first, heresy, but three might be mentioned briefly. One was the method of partnership accounting mentioned above, which encouraged the distinction between interest on capital and profits of the partnership. The second was the legal limitation of interest. The third, *pace* the 'classical' doctrine, was the relatively small proportion of fixed capital (outside the public utilities) in relation to goods in process of production, stocks and debtors.[3] In many cases the two items of creditors

[1] Compare Sir James Steuart, describing 'ingenious workmen', who become large manufacturers: 'the interest they pay for the money borrowed is inconsiderable, when compared with the value created (as it were) by the employment of their time and talents'. Of course, he still uses the terms 'workman' and 'manufacturer' interchangeably, and calls their remuneration profits. Sir James Steuart, *Political Oeconomy* (London, 1767: 2 vols), vol. II, pp. 137, 490–1, 493.

[2] The best recent summary of contemporary economic doctrines of capital and profit will be found in G. S. L. Tucker, *Progress and Profit in British Economic Thought, 1650–1850* (Cambridge, 1960), chap. 5. The quotations are from pp. 78, 87 and 79. The nearest approaches to a modern notion of profit rates will be found in *Spencer-Stanhope Muniments*, 60478, no. 38; H. Hamilton, *The English Brass and Copper Industries to 1800* (London, 1926), appendix VII, pp. 359–60; Raistrick, *Two Centuries*, pp. 114, 127. For a recent calculation of profit rates in that period, see F. Crouzet, 'La formation du capital en Grande-Bretagne pendant la Révolution Industrielle', *Second International Conference of Economic History. Aix-en-Provence, 1962* (Paris–The Hague, 1965).

[3] I hope to deal with this problem elsewhere.

and debtors exceeded the partners' original capital several-fold, and since they tended to fluctuate wildly, they might leave the positive or negative residual of capital to be provided by the partners to fluctuate even more widely. Clearly, in these circumstances, it would be meaningless to speak in terms of profits on capital employed.

III

The second heresy was the confusion of capital and revenue. This may be viewed in two ways, from the point of view of ownership, i.e. as a liability, or from the point of view of actual equipment, i.e. as assets, though the two are connected. We shall take them in turn.

The partnership accounts, as described above, required the periodic determination of profits, to be credited to the partners in the firm's books, and this in turn required a valuation of the firm. Several methods were in use. The one found most commonly in our sample consisted of valuing the whole firm *de novo* at the date of a striking the balance. From the total assets, including debtors, all liabilities, except for the original partners' capital, were deducted and the difference, if positive, was capital-cum-profits. This sum, compared with the sum similarly arrived at at the last balancing date, might show how far the concern had been profitable in the interim, provided no funds had been withdrawn by the partners, though few firms seem to have made the comparison. Among the larger firms using this method of valuation were Truman's brewery, John Marshall, the Carron Co., Broadbent & Lockwood, the Mona Mine Co. and (doubtfully) its associated Stanley and Ravenhead copper works.[1]

While this approach has a certain internal logic, it is very far removed from the modern concept of profit maximization as

---

[1] *Mona Mine MSS*, nos. 3048 and 3544; Mathias, op. cit., pp. 556–8; Campbell, 'Financing of Carron Company', p. 28; R. M. Hartwell, *The Yorkshire Woollen and Worsted Industry, 1800–1850* (Oxford D.Phil. thesis, 1955), p. 626. In principle, this system had been in use since the fourteenth century and taught since at least the sixteenth: P. Kats, 'Early History of Book-keeping by Double Entry', *Journal of Accountancy* (1929), pp. 278–9, 284–5; Yamey, 'Accounting', n. 10; A. Simpson, 'Thomas Cullum, Draper', *Economic History Review*, 2nd series, XI (1958); Rimmer, *Marshalls*, p. 122.

the driving force of capitalism: indeed the notion of capital as a continuous, let alone autonomous factor, is virtually eliminated. Thus there might develop bewildering fluctuations of the 'capital' of a company from year to year, depending on trade, the valuation of assets, and the discount for bad debts. Kirkstall Forge, in a set of accounts for 1712–57, found its 'capital' fluctuating between £1,000 and £7,000. Again, some assets which could not easily be valued were left out of the calculation altogether: the Aire and Calder Navigation, valuing its 'clear and unencumbered surplus property' (a phrase much more realistic than 'capital') in 1817 at just under £30,000, including £20,000 in a round sum for the sloops, yet excluded completely some real estate bringing in about £3,000 a year. The Parys Mine Co. computed the increase in its 'capital' between March 1816 and March 1824 simply by comparing the two stock valuations, wholly ignoring such items as debtors or the value of leases, perhaps for reasons noted in some accounts of the associated Mona Mine in 1782–9: 'What the Mine capital may be worth no idea can be found as no Balance appears to have been struck'.[1]

Nothing, perhaps, shows up the resulting confusion in the notion of capital better than the terminology used. The Herculaneum Pottery, having found a 'surplus of capital arising from profits, more than sufficient to meet the current exigences (sic) for the current year', proposed a cash bonus of £30 per share, as well as a dividend of 8 per cent. The Coalbrookdale Co. described as 'profits' (divisible by shares) the whole net surplus remaining after 'dividends' (also divisible by shares, but in round sums) had been paid out, while in the next century, William Matthews, the ironmaster, considered 'the profits of the iron trade as part of the interest of capital'.[2]

---

[1] A. Raistrick and E. Allen, 'The South Yorkshire Ironmasters (1690–1750)', *Economic History Review*, IX (1939), p. 185; BTC Archives (York), ACN/1/32; *Mona Mine MSS*, nos. 2635, 1280. As a contrast, it may be noted that some of the best contemporary farm accounts ignored stocks at the beginning and the end of their periods, cf. R. A. C. Parker, *Financial and Economic Affairs of the Cokes of Holkham, Norfolk, 1707–1842* (Oxford D.Phil. thesis, 1956), p. 57.

[2] *Herculaneum Pottery MSS*, no. 47, minute for 23 November 1815; A. Raistrick, *Dynasty of Ironfounders, the Darbys and Coalbrookdale* (London, 1953), pp. 277–8, e.g. period ending 28 September 1740. Notions were no clearer at the end of the century, e.g. pp. 244–6; *SC on Manufactures*, 1833, ev. W. Matthews, Q. 9647.

In the partnership later to become the Sheffield Smelting Co., 'Debts owing by Read and Lucas were deducted from the total value of stock plus the money owing to them. This was the gross profit. From it was deducted the capital of the partners. The difference was then divided in the agreed proportions and entered as the net profit.'[1] In other words, here capital becomes part of gross profit.

A second method was to value the firm's capital by its earning capacity. Sometimes this took the form of valuing the assets by conventional means and then adjusting values so arrived at, at other times the total valuation seems to have been built up on earning capacity alone. The Walkers of Masbro' entered a £14,000 increase in capital on 1 May 1778, 'As the works have answered very well this year (except the Fire Engine) it is hop'd it is not laid too high.' Two years later, the entry runs: 'I suppose (£120,000) is a moderate estimate. N.B. on the last acco'ts, settled May-Day 1780, turning out so well, think £2,000 should be added, the Capital is £122,000.' By contrast, in 1816, 'In consequence of the general stagnation of trade, and the depreciation of every kind of property . . . this valuation may be considered as nominal rather than real.'[2] Similarly, Benjamin Gott wrote down the fixed capital of the Bean Ing mill, from its long-standing book value of £26,500 to £10,000 in 1817 and £5,000 in 1818 because of bad trade conditions.[3]

When the Albion Mill was planned for London, the 500 existing mills were 'valued at' £200 per annum each, and the Albion Mill itself was 'valued' at £3,000 per annum, arrived at by calculating 5 per cent on a planned investment of £60,000.[4] The former appears to be a valuation purely by earning capacity; it is difficult to assign a meaning to the 'valuation' of the latter. On a more sophisticated level, Thomas

---

[1] Wilson, op. cit., p. 39, referring to 1787. Benjamin Gott began manufacturing, after paying out £34,000 for the share of a deceased partner, with £20,000 'Net Stock and Profit in Trade': W. B. Crump (ed.), *The Leeds Woollen Industry, 1780–1820* (Leeds, 1931), p. 255.

[2] John, *Walker Family*, pp. 14, 16, 25.

[3] Crump, op. cit., p. 258. For Crawshay, cf. *Cyfarthfa MSS*, vol. 1, W. Crawshay to B. Hall, 26 August 1813.

[4] A. D. Insull, *The Albion Mill Story* (Nottingham B.A. dissertation, 1955), p. 18; O. A. Westworth, 'The Albion Steam Flour Mill', *Economic History*, II (1932), p. 383.

Fenwick, the famous northern coal viewer, wrote in 1818: 'The mode of valuing coal in Northumberland is according to the system of valuing Annuities – the Duration of the colliery being considered as the term of the Payment of the Annuity – the annual Rent of the Colliery is considered as the Annuity itself, and the p'centage is fixed according to the Hazard attending the coal property', being 8 per cent normally, 10 per cent if risky.[1]

IV

In considering capital in the sense of working assets, most manufacturers of the industrial revolution were apt to confuse fixed investments and current expenditure[2] as frequently as they confused capital and profits. Indeed, influenced by the historical fact that industrial accounting evolved from commercial accounting or, concretely, that the accountants in the works had been trained in, or with textbooks written for, merchants' counting houses, there was a common tendency to ignore the fixed equipment altogether, except for the annual interest in some firms, as noted above.

Whether or no interest charges on the initial capital were included, any additions and improvements to the capital equipment were normally entered in the current accounts. The identification of capital and current accounts was, perhaps, most complete in the Cornish 'cost book' system, in which the adventurers contributed capital or drew dividends during the whole lifetime of the mine in proportion to their shareholding, according to the balance available, irrespective of whether the balances were due to capital or current items.[3] Though the

---

[1] *Spencer-Stanhope Muniments*, 60579, no. 24, note dated 14 December 1818.

[2] Even when they were kept apart, confusion might reign: Wyatt, in 1744, proposed that the cotton-spinning firm's capital be divided into 'two portions pretty nearly equal. . . . That the first portion be called a dead or quiescent stock for which an interest or annual profit (!) be allowed at the rate of between 10 and 15 per cent. . . . That the second portion being employed in trade shall have a profit of not less than 20 per cent per annum.' A. P. Wadsworth and J. de L. Mann, *The Cotton Trade and Industrial Lancashire: 1600–1780* (Manchester, 1931), p. 439.

[3] Descriptions will be found in J. Rowe, *Cornwall in the Age of the Industrial Revolution* (Liverpool, 1953), pp. 22–4; H. W. Dickinson and A. Titley, *Richard Trevithick* (Cambridge, 1934), p. 9; G. R. Lewis, *The Stannaries, a Study of the*

system was considered anachronistic at the time,[1] it was in truth more so in the freedom of the Stannaries from the obstructions of contemporary law and lawyers than in its attitude to capital.

A high rate of profit and a relatively low ratio of fixed capital, as well as technical considerations, made it easy to enter capital additions in the revenue accounts. In mining, for example, where occasionally the cost of sinking a pit could be recovered in three months' working,[2] the larger companies were constantly sinking new pits while working out the old ones. It then became normal practice to absorb capital costs in the current working of the whole enterprise:[3] the Larwood colliery account for 1789, for example, included an expenditure of some £25 for sinking pits, £3 for boring to draw the water off the sinkings, and £6 for 11,000 pit bricks, with the note: 'N.B. These (3 items) are charg'd as the annual average expence, none of these expences having occurr'd in 1789.' As late as 1872, at the Dalcoath mine employing 1,000 men, 'invested capital is only nominal, outlay for machinery being paid for as a working expense'. The occasional fluctuations in the apparent annual costs of the enterprise, owing to such discontinuous investment, then required explanation: 'The present Compt'g Ho., Carpt'rs Shop & Storehouse was built

---

Medieval Tin Miners of Cornwall and Devon (London, 1907), pp. 205–6 and 'Tin Mining', in *V. C. H. Cornwall*, I (London, 1906), pp. 554–5; F. Trevithick, *Life of Richard Trevithick* (London, 1872), p. 38; *Report of the Copper Committee*, PP, 7 May 1799, p. 39; A. Titley, 'Cornish Mining: Notes from the Account Books of Richard Trevithick, Senior', *Transactions of the Newcomen Society*, XI (1930–1), pp. 27–8.

[1] Rowe, op. cit., pp. 133–4.

[2] P. L. Payne, 'The Govan Collieries, 1804–1805', *Business History*, III (1961), pp. 87–8.

[3] e.g. F. J. Monkhouse, 'An Eighteenth-Century Company Promoter', *Transactions of the Cumberland and Westmorland Antiquarian and Archaeological Society*, N.S., XL (1940), pp. 148–9; G. Rimmer, 'Middleton Colliery, near Leeds (1770–1830)', *Yorkshire Bulletin of Economic and Social Research*, VII (1955), p. 43; O. Wood, *The Development of the Coal, Iron and Shipbuilding Industries of West Cumberland, 1750–1914* (London Ph.D. thesis, 1952), pp. 46, 149; *Middleton of Wollaton Muniments* (MS, Nottingham University Library), Mi Ac 120; A. Raistrick, 'London Lead Company, 1692–1905', *Transactions of the Newcomen Society*, XIV (1933–4), p. 130; Malet, *The Canal Duke*, p. 139; G. G. Hopkinson, *The Development of the Lead Mining and the Coal and Iron Industries of North Derbyshire and South Yorkshire, 1700–1850* (Sheffield Ph.D. thesis, 1958), p. 245; *Shipley Colliery MSS* (lent by courtesy of Dr J. E. Williams), accounts for 1824, 1835.

in this quarter & a considerable part of the cost included (in this quarter's current account).'[1]

In the ironworks, the fixed capital consisted largely of furnaces, bellows and hammers which required regular relining and repair and appeared as running costs even in such sophisticated accounts as those of the South Yorkshire ironmasters;[2] even the cost of erecting a large cotton mill might appear largely as an item in the weekly wages bill, as at Mellor.[3] It was for the same reason that the equipment of the Duke of Norfolk's collieries was valued according to the weight of iron and timber in the various engines and machines, showing the nature of the original outlay.[4] Elsewhere, large profits were simply ploughed back in generous annual extensions of capital.[5]

Even the public utilities, however, with their heavy fixed capital investment, found the distinction between it and the current costs difficult to maintain. The Stockton and Darlington Railway Co., conscious of a decade of this confusion, reported to the shareholders on 10 July 1830 that 'The statement presented of the Company's affairs is the result of constant care to keep the Accounts so as to distinguish between the current expenses of the concern, and the charges consequent upon the Works now in hand, and incompleted', yet the following accounts were as confused as ever. Similarly the Aire and Calder Navigation went to great trouble to recast its accounts in 1817, in a form to show real income and expenditure, profit and loss, as well as 'the increased or decreased value of your Property from year to year', but by 1822 had still not succeeded in separating capital and revenue. Again, the Birmingham Canal Co. attempted a rigorous separation when it opened a new set of books in 1795, but in the half year

---

[1] *Wentworth-Woodhouse Muniments*, F. 96; Trevithick, op. cit., p. 38; *Nevill MSS*, no. 49, quarter ending 31 March 1808.

[2] A. Raistrick, 'The South Yorkshire Iron Industry', *Transactions of the Newcomen Society*, XIX (1938–9), p. 52. Also cf. *Spencer-Stanhope Muniments*, Accounts; Campbell, *Carron Company*, p. 62; B. L. C. Johnson, *The Charcoal Iron Trade in the Midlands, 1690–1720* (Birmingham M.A. thesis, 1950), appendix 3 and 4.

[3] G. Unwin *et al.*, *Samuel Oldknow and the Arkwrights* (Manchester, 1924), p. 151.

[4] e.g. for 1773–1805, see *Norfolk Muniments*, S. 205, S. 215–30.

[5] For the West India Dock Co., R. A. H. Page, *The Dock Companies in London, 1796–1864* (Sheffield M.A. thesis, 1959), p. 94.

to March 1797 timber was still shown under new work, while in the next half year it was entered under current expenditure.[1]

There were, indeed, examples of greater sophistication, to the extent not only of entering such capital costs as interest and depreciation, but collecting them in the central (as distinct from the branch) accounts with the other 'general' or overhead expenses, as in the varied enterprises of the Fitzwilliam estate near Sheffield or at the Cyfarthfa and Hirwain works.[2] This method, however, invited the error of using the incomplete departmental accounts for comparative cost calculations and thus again failing to take capital costs into account.[3]

Capital depreciation was by no means the rule even in the larger firms. Apart from the examples enumerated above of firms entering maintenance costs of capital in revenue instead, and such well known concerns as Crowley's ironworks, there was, for example, the Imperial Continental Gas Association, established in 1824:

> In common with the generally accepted practice among the public utility companies operating in this country, the Association made no provision for depreciation in its accounts. Expenditure for renewals was charged against revenue as it was incurred and since substantial sums were involved when the periodic renewal of major items of gas-work equipment took place, there were quite serious fluctuations in profit for particular half-years and also . . . serious financial stringency was experienced at times because down to 1850 the association used to distribute in dividend almost all its profits and had no fund of retained profits with which to finance capital expenditure.[4]

The absence of reserve funds or depreciation charges was, in fact, typical of joint stock firms at the end of the eighteenth

[1] BTC Archives (York), e.g. SAD/23/21, Treasurer's account to July 1825, SAD/1/6, Minute Book 10 July 1827, 13 July 1830, ACN/1/32; BTC Archives (London), BCN/4/364 and 4/365.

[2] e.g. *Wentworth-Woodhouse Muniments*, F. 100 (Elsecar Colliery), F. 701 (Elsecar Furnace), G. 44 (Elsecar Ironworks, Milton Ironworks), G. 94 (Collieries), A. 61; *Cyfarthfa MSS*, vol. 2, box 12, Profit and Loss Accounts, Balance Sheets for 1810, 1811. The Quaker Lead Co. may have done the same: Raistrick, 'London Lead Company', p. 150, appendix III.

[3] e.g. *Cyfarthfa MSS*, vol. 2, fol. 7; *Mona Mine MSS*, no. 1281, 30 January 1816.

[4] N. K. Hill, 'Accountancy Developments in a Public Utility Company in the Nineteenth Century', *Accounting Research*, VI (1955), p. 384.

century,[1] a failing, it has been said, which meant that a 'complex business was no better than a blind man's buff'.[2] In 1793, the valuation of one of the largest and most advanced firms in Britain, the Ketley ironworks, 'was examined and subjected to the same objection as the Coalbrookdale one, that little or no allowance for depreciation of materials and tools had been made, so a revaluation was called for and lengthy rules for the valuation of different kinds of property were laid down'.[3] Pleasley Mills was running for six years before its buildings, and sixteen years before its machinery began to be written off. The Stockton and Darlington Railway Co., in its early comparative cost calculations, omitted to take into account any depreciation on locomotives, though by 1836 it had evolved a capital account, in which engines and coaches were written off separately. The Midland Railway operated a depreciation fund for the permanent way between 1848 and 1857, in order to even out large changes in expenditure, but at other times it followed the general practice of simply charging capital repair and replacement costs to revenue: in the 'manias' any potential depreciation funds were raided for new building; in slumps they were raided for dividends.[4] As late as 1884, a standard accounting textbook could state that '. . . the capital accounts are not always deemed to be of such pressing importance; and variations in the value of plant, arising from the wear and tear and other causes, may be left unnoted'.[5]

It will be evident that to some extent the errors in accounting

[1] A. B. Dubois, *The English Business Company after the Bubble Act, 1720–1800* (New York, 1938), p. 364; also J. H. Soltow, 'Scottish Traders in Virginia, 1750–1775', *Economic History Review*, 2nd series, XII (1959), p. 89.

[2] W. T. Baxter, *The House of Hancock: Business in Boston 1724–1775* (Cambridge, Mass., 1945), p. 243.

[3] Raistrick, *Dynasty of Ironfounders*, pp. 214–15. The property was written down from some £138,000 to some £105,000.

[4] Pigott, *Hollins*, p. 38; BTC Archives (York), SAD/1/145, Report 1836. Cf. also *Herculaneum Pottery MSS*, no. 47, Minute Book, 2 November 1819; Pollins, 'Aspects of Railway Accounting', pp. 347–8; S. Everard, *The History of the Gas Light and Coke Company, 1812–1949* (London, 1949), p. 111.

[5] E. Matheson, *The Depreciation of Factories*, 4th ed. (London, 1910), preface to 1884 ed. The author went on to state that the extension of fixed capital and joint stock enterprise had necessitated the introduction of the practice of depreciation. Cf. also Edwards, 'Early Development of Cost Accounting', p. 193. The first textbooks dealing with depreciation were French: Payen (1817), De Cazaux (1824) and Godard (1827); Garner, op. cit., pp. 44, 53–4; Solomons (ed.), *Studies in Costing*, p. 10.

cancelled out, a fact which allowed them to continue for so long, without punishing the companies concerned by failure. Thus the absence of depreciation might, at a certain stage of growth, be neatly compensated by additions to capital *not* entered in the capital account, so that book values and real assets continued to correspond. Similarly, sharing out surpluses to the hilt would be neutralized by letting them accumulate, as book entries – until the revaluation of the next partnership change rectified the position. The example of the Gas Association above, however, shows that this fortunate complementarity did not always occur, and several companies had to take more drastic steps to protect their funds. Some of the large breweries, Benjamin Gott & Partners, and the Llangavelach copper works divided partners' holdings into two parts, only one of which was withdrawable; the Carron partners agreed formally to reinvest all their surplus beyond the 5 per cent interest; and some joint stock companies explicitly prohibited the payment of dividends out of capital.[1]

Even where the practice of depreciation had been introduced, it did not necessarily derive from a 'rational' view of capital. In some cases, it was to get tax allowances: 'It is best to *write off* & not uphold all Accounts of the sort I point out,' ordered William Crawshay in 1814, 'more particularly while there is still property tax to pay,'[2] not before making certain, of course, of the *real* state of the property before writing-off. In other cases, depreciation had fraudulent objectives: the machinations of the Stanton family within the Carron Company have recently been described in some detail by Mr R. H. Campbell.[3]

Generally, however, the objects of depreciation ranged from the wish for a true valuation to the more practical need to allow for replacement, repair and maintenance without upsetting

---

[1] Mathias, op. cit., p. 315; R. M. Hartwell, *The Yorkshire Woollen and Worsted Industry*, p. 657; G. G. Francis, *The Smelting of Copper in the Swansea District*, 2nd ed. (London, 1881), pp. 106–8; Campbell, 'Financing of Carron Company', p. 23; G. H. Evans, Jr, *British Corporation Finance* (Baltimore, 1936), pp. 4, 76, 116–19.

[2] *Cyfarthfa MSS*, vol. 1, W. Crawshay to B. Hall, 6 May 1814. It is significant that in this period of the French wars no depreciation allowance, properly speaking, was granted at all on schedule D tax. P. K. O'Brien, 'British Incomes in the Early Nineteenth Century', *Economic History Review*, 2nd series, XII (1959), p. 261.

[3] Campbell, *Carron Company*, pp. 137, 165 ff.

the balance of any one accounting period or permitting an over-distribution of dividends.[1] An attempt at a true valuation, however, could be made as easily by the mercantile practice of annual stock valuation as by writing-off, which presupposes the more advanced notion of a continuous, fixed capital. Here, for example, are the fixed capital items in the 'Stock Account' of the Mona Mine for 1829 and 1830 (shillings and pence omitted) :[2]

	£		
	1829	*1830*	*Notes*
Steam engine, 'valued at'	400	350	
Whimseys & appurtenances	629	663	Additional items in 1830
Schooner 'Hero', per valuation	1,500	1,500	
Furnaces	1,600	1,540	18 in 1829, 17 in 1830.

Despite first appearances, all items here are simple valuations, extracted, in point of fact, from a long list in which they were indiscriminately mixed with stores and stocks and from which the notion of a permanent capital was clearly absent. Similar examples may be found in large porter breweries, at Crawshay's ironworks and at the Herculaneum Pottery.[3] Even where percentage depreciation had been introduced, it was often derived from merchant's practice of reducing the book value of stocks in hand to allow for discounts, obsolescence and lower manufacturing costs.[4] 'True' percentage depreciation for the sake of valuation was rare; among the best-known examples were Boulton & Fothergill, the Soho Foundry and the Carron Co. after Gascoigne's reforms of 1769.[5]

---

[1] Cf. Pollins, 'Aspects of Railway Accounting', p. 343.

[2] *Mona Mine MSS*, no. 166.

[3] Mathias, op. cit., pp. 553, 556; *Cyfarthfa MSS*, box 12, Balance Sheets 1810–34; *Herculaneum Pottery MSS*, no. 47, 1 November 1814.

[4] Good examples showing this derivation will be found in *Herculaneum Pottery MSS*, n.d. cited; Wedgwood, in V. W. Bladen, 'The Potteries in the Industrial Revolution', *Economic History*, I (1926), pp. 126–7; also Mathias, op. cit., p. 566; Campbell, 'Financing of Carron Company', p. 27; and, doubtfully, Raistrick and Allen, op. cit., p. 180. Crowley's general manager alleged in 1744 that their stocks were over-valued by 20 per cent, M. W. Flinn, *Men of Iron, the Crowleys in the Early Iron Industry* (Edinburgh, 1962), p. 177, also footnote on pp. 174–5.

[5] *Boulton and Watt MSS*, Accounts (Birmingham Assay Office), 'M. Boulton, Inventory, 22 June 1782'; *Boulton and Watt MSS* (Birmingham City Library), Soho Foundry Inventory Book, 1797–1800; Campbell, 'Financing of Carron Company', p. 27.

Depreciation to account for the practical needs of repair and replacement was much more common.[1] Inevitably, these two were often confused, as were physical deterioration and technological obsolescence. Joshua Milne, for example, the well-known Oldham cotton spinner, justified his practice of depreciation by the need to provide for wear and tear, replacement, annual upkeep, the 'fall in value' and, in reply to a leading question, that without it he would soon have a 'fictitious capital', all at the same time. R. H. Greg, another cotton spinner, more thoughtfully explained his depreciation on 'sunk' capital, i.e. 'the amount spent on buildings and machinery', as 'not only for actual wear and tear, but also for its deterioration arising out of new inventions'. The Albion Mill's boilers were depreciated for 'repair and fund for renewing'.[2]

With its rapid obsolescence (Heathcoat's patent bobbin net machine, reducing hand machines from £1,200 to £60 in value was often quoted),[3] textile machinery was usually depreciated very rapidly. Elsewhere, 'wear and tear' tended to mean repair: this was true also of Wyatt and Paul, pioneers of industrial cost accounting as well as roller spinning.[4]

Replacement came up against the problem of 'betterment', i.e. replacement by a superior piece of equipment of which the addition should be charged to capital.[5] Where the additions were large in relation to the original capital, accountants found it hard to ignore the difference between capital and revenue, and the inability of the latter to provide for the former. The Birmingham Canal Company offers a useful illustration. In 1800 it opened a 'Sinking Fund' fed by irregular surpluses, for the repayment of borrowed funds. In 1820, the repayment completed, this was renamed a 'Surplus Fund', but its income virtually ceased. It was rescued in 1824, renamed 'Improvement Fund', given the income from thirteen shares held by the

---

[1] Yamey, 'Company Accounting Conventions', p. 29.

[2] *SC on Manufactures*, 1833, ev. Milne, QQ. 10998–11006; *Factories Inquiry Commission*, 1833, D. 2, ev. Greg, p. 30; Insull, op. cit., appendix B, pp. 82–4.

[3] E. Baines, Jr, *History of the Cotton Manufacture in Great Britain* (London, 1835), p. 341; C. Babbage, *On the Economy of Machinery and Manufactures*, 3rd ed. (London, 1833), pp. 283–9.

[4] Wadsworth and Mann, op. cit., pp. 435, 438.

[5] Pollins, 'Aspects of Railway Accounting', pp. 352–3.

Company itself and debited with expenditure on improvements, the whole being balanced independently and the balance being carried forward from period to period. Almost at once, however, in 1825 heavy expenditure on new vast capital projects completely swamped the original modest sums, yet the borrowings and expenditure were still being passed through this fund, though the interest alone, payable on the borrowings, quickly exceeded the total original outgoings on 'improvements'. It was at this stage that the company was slowly forced to consider a separate capital account.[1]

There were other examples of 'funds', established originally as security against losses or to even out cash flows, which drew the attention of their originators towards depreciation and separate capital accounts. In 1829, having just paid off a large liability arising out of some bad debts, Nevill & Co. 'resolved that it will be expedient henceforward to divide a moiety only of the annual Profits, and to transfer the other moiety to the Sinking Fund accounts, till the same be sufficient to protect the concern against any loss which may occur upon any of the accounts in our ledgers'. The Gas Light & Coke Co. also in 1821–9 made provision for a 'reserve fund' over and above 'wear and tear'.[2]

Finally, perhaps the differences in actual rates of depreciation may also be taken as an indication of the uncertain philosophy behind them[3] (see table opposite).

---

[1] BTC Archives (London), BCN/4/365 and 366, also BCN/4/375, showing summaries and significant comparative statements. Cf. also the method adopted by J. Grout, *Report of Select Committee on the Silk Trade*, PP 1831–2, XIX, ev. Q. 10300; and J. Massey & Co., *SC on Manufactures*, 1833, ev. G. Smith, Q. 9144.

[2] *Nevill MSS*, no. 21, Minute Book, 30 June 1829; Everard, op. cit., p. 111; also Aire and Calder Navigation in 1819, BTC Archives (York), ACN/1/32.

[3] Babbage, op. cit., pp. 283, 285; J. P. Muirhead, *The Life of James Watt* (London, 1859), p. 123; *Boulton and Watt MSS* (Birmingham City Library), Inventory Books, 1797–1800, 1822–31; *Factories Inquiry Commission*, 1833, D. 2, ev. Greg, p. 30, also *Supplementary Report*, PP 1834, XIX, p. 119T; Campbell, 'Financing of Carron Company', p. 27, and *Carron Company*, p. 128; M. Blaug, 'The Productivity of Capital in the Lancashire Cotton Industry During the Nineteenth Century', *Economic History Review*, 2nd series, XIII (1961), p. 361; Rimmer, *Marshalls*, p. 195; *Nevill MSS*, no. 21, Minute Book, 24 June 1806; *Pontrhydyrun (Tinplate) Works MSS* (Cardiff Public Library), Account Book for 1831–72; *SC on Manufactures*, 1833, ev. W. Graham, QQ. 5547–8, G. Smith, Q. 9139, A. Hill, QQ. 10399–401, J. Milne, QQ. 10998–11006; *Committee of*

Date	Firm or industry	Annual Rate of Depreciation (%) on:		
		Buildings	Steam engines	Machinery
1769	Carron Iron Works	8	8	8
1780s	Soho	5 (a)	—	—
1797–1800	Soho Foundry	5	8	—
1822–31	Soho Foundry	10	15	—
1806	Copper Works	5	—	—
1814	Herculaneum Pottery	10	—	—
1825	Locomotives	—	15	—
1827	Marshall Flax Co.	—	—	7·5
1831–72	Tinplate Works	5	—	—
1832	Greg Cotton Mill (b)	5	5	10
1832	Ashworth Cotton Mill	—	5 (c)	5 (c)
1833	Cotton Industry	—	10	—
1833	Cotton Mill		6	
1833	Cotton Mill	—	—	10–33·3
1833	Ironworks	2·5	—	—
1833	Ironworks	—	10 (d)	—
1830–80	Textile Mills	2·5	2·5	7·5

Notes:
(a) 'The same as the rate of interest'
(b) Not straight line, but on value remaining
(c) Expects to get: 5 per cent interest
                        5 per cent depreciation
                      15 per cent clear profit
(d) 15 per cent, but that includes interest on capital

V

The conclusion must be that the growth of fixed capital in the industrial revolution, the speed of which has, itself, been often exaggerated, did not lead to a general 'rationalization' of accounting as postulated by the 'classical' scheme, though the sixty years after 1770 saw some advances towards it. Surviving accounts may not tell the whole story, but it seems unlikely that they were notably less advanced than those which have perished.

Perhaps the outstanding fact to emerge from this brief survey is the enormous variety and range of practices in the counting houses in this period, and the variety of assumptions on which they seem to have been based. The differences may be largely derived from the different practical demands which the accounts were designed to meet, but in all the variety found, there was no clear-cut attempt to adapt accounting practice to the notion of capital as generalized, depersonalized property, seeking the highest returns irrespective of its concrete embodiment, as postulated by economic theory.

5 Fixed Capital in the Industrial Revolution in Britain[1]

SIDNEY POLLARD

[This article was first published in the *Journal of Economic History*, vol. XXIV, no. 3, September 1964.]

The provision of capital is generally recognized to be one of the main problems of countries undergoing the process of industrialization. This is true also of the special case of Great Britain, the first country to experience an industrial revolution. In the British case, however, it is important to note that much capital had been accumulated even before the 1760s, the decade when industrial growth began to accelerate and to change its direction. Most of this earlier capital was invested in commerce, in finance, in farming, and in stocks of manufactured goods and raw materials,[2] and what was noteworthy in the next two generations was, not so much the absolute (and probably also relative) growth in the quantity of capital, but a change in its composition: the emergence, for the first time, of large concentrations of fixed capital.

The large resources sunk in factories, machinery or mines have often been taken to epitomize the new age of industrialism.[3] Some historians and philosophers of history, indeed, have not only laid great stress on the importance of the new element, the fixed capital, in the industrial revolution,[4] but have attempted to prove that it was a major factor in altering

---

[1] Research on which this paper is based has been made possible by a grant from the Houblon–Norman Fund.

[2] P. Deane and W. A. Cole, *British Economic Growth 1688–1959* (New York, 1962), pp. 259–63.

[3] For example, Max Weber, *General Economic History* (Glencoe, 1950), pp. 163, 173–4; J. Lord, *Capital and Steam Power* (London, 1923), p. 62.

[4] See my 'Capital Accounting in the Industrial Revolution', *Yorkshire Bulletin of Economic and Social Research*, XV, no. 2 (November 1963), pp. 75–91.

the shape and direction of movement of the whole economy. Yet, curiously, actual historical investigations have usually found that the provision of fixed capital in industry appears to have presented no great problem in this period.[1]

Part of the explanation of this paradox lies in the nature of the investments made. To understand it, we must divide the fixed investments of that period into two groups: those made in the public utilities which swallowed up a large proportion of the fixed capital, and those made in private manufacturing, mining and transport companies. Contemporaries were well aware, for example, of the differences between – on the one hand – Turnpike Trusts and Canal Companies which could tap the savings of potential rentiers most of whom had accumulated them outside the industrial field and – on the other hand – the cotton mills or ironworks which had to rely on savings of a more narrowly circumscribed class and of individuals committed more closely to the firms in which they invested.[2] Our main concern, in this paper, will be with the latter form of enterprise in the period from 1760 to 1830, with some backward glances to the years 1690–1760.

I

The fact that much of the fixed investment which historians of capitalism associate with the industrial revolution took place outside the sector of 'private' – that is, partnership – industry, forms part of the explanation of the absence of the expected capital shortage in that sector, but it is not the whole explanation.

As a result of recent work which has accumulated much new evidence on the financing of industry by the first generation of entrepreneurs, the variety of their sources of capital is coming to be more widely appreciated. Those who entered factory industry from a background of putting-out, or merchanting, generally disposed of sufficient resources to raise their indus-

[1] For example, C. Wilson, 'The Entrepreneur in the Industrial Revolution in Britain', *History*, XLII (June 1957), p. 115.

[2] Adam Smith's belief that joint stock organization was suitable only for canals, waterworks, banks, and insurance companies, and his reasons for it, are well known. A. Smith, *Wealth of Nations* (Cannan ed., 1904), book V, chap. I, part III, article I.

trial capital, both fixed and circulating, without recourse to outside help: they formed a group to which we shall return later. Other budding entrepreneurs found it possible to rent fixed-capital equipment, like buildings, power, or mines; or, alternatively, to 'take in' work on materials not belonging to them and thus to shift the burden of accumulation onto other and broader shoulders: this practice is so well known[1] that it will not be considered here any further. But thirdly, the new entrant to an industry could hope to survive by relying on certain technological and financial factors which are commonly underrated and which this paper will seek to elucidate further.

To begin with, the amount of fixed capital involved in industry, compared with circulating capital, has often been exaggerated. The eye is caught by the new industries; but even in the early cotton mills, coal mines, and iron furnaces, the fixed-capital equipment was relatively simple and cheap. Moreover, not every industry had as yet gone through a technological revolution, and even many of those which played a major part in the industrial transformations of the age did not necessarily do so by installing much costly machinery: firms like Soho or Etruria achieved their increases in output, and their predominance, by methods described fully in Adam Smith's pin manufactory, that is, by order and organization rather than by costly mechanical devices. Others, again, were still in the stage of the putting-out system, employing domestic workers.

Between the days of the earliest large-scale industrial enterprises of which details exist (the mines and metallurgical concerns of the Elizabethan age),[2] and the first half of the

[1] Examples are A. P. Wadsworth and J. de L. Mann, *The Cotton Trade and Industrial Lancashire* (Manchester, 1931), p. 489; H. Heaton, 'Financing the Industrial Revolution', *Bulletin of the Business Historical Society*, XI (February 1937), p. 2; *Select Committee on Manufactures, Commerce and Shipping*, Parliamentary Papers 1833, VI, ev. H. Houldsworth, QQ. 5303-4; H. A. Wooster, 'Manufacturer and Artisan, 1790-1840', *Journal of Political Economy*, XXXIV (February 1926), pp. 61-2; G. Unwin, *Samual Oldknow and the Arkwrights* (Manchester, 1924), pp. 147-9; S. Pigott, *Hollins, a Study of Industry, 1784-1949* (Nottingham, 1949), p. 63.

[2] See M. B. Donald, *Elizabethan Copper, The History of the Company of the Mines Royal 1568-1605* (London, 1955), p. 244; also his *Elizabethan Monopolies. The History of the Company of Mineral and Battery Works from 1565 to 1604* (Edinburgh and London, 1961), p. 75; C. M. C. Bouch and G. P. Jones, *A Short Economic and Social History of the Lake Counties, 1500-1830* (Manchester, 1961), p. 126; D. Glyn John, *Contributions to the Economic History of South Wales,* part I (unpublished University of Wales D.Sc. thesis, 1930), p. 4 and appendix.

eighteenth century, the ratio of fixed to circulating capital had altered hardly at all. Crowley's ironworks, in 1728, had a total fixed capital of under £12,000 compared with stocks of nearly £93,000; at the Backbarrow furnace, in 1713, the ratio was £733 to £6,246; the Bersham valuation of 1735 showed a ratio of £170 to £1,254; in 1745, at the Llangavelach copper works, Swansea, the ratio was £5,400 to £37,700; in textiles in a Stockport silk mill in 1762, it was £2,800 to over £13,800; and at J. & N. Philips', a Manchester smallware manufacturer, £400 to £4,800 in 1755, with half of the fixed capital, £200, representing the 'investment' in a Dutchman brought over to teach the trade to the local workers. Among the large London porter breweries, fixed stock amounted to well below 10 per cent of the net assets over the whole of the eighteenth century.[1]

With the coming of the industrial revolution, these ratios increased substantially in the key industries as each, in turn, began to be transformed by factory or other capital-intensive methods. The timing of this transformation differed from industry to industry and, indeed, from firm to firm; but the new pattern, once established (whether at one swoop, as with the creation of a new steam-driven cotton-spinning mill, or progressively, as in the building-out of a large colliery), was not significantly changed thereafter, until the end of our period, at least as far as the fixed-capital ratio was concerned. Thus the period to 1830 saw an increase in the proportion of firms with higher fixed-capital ratios within each industry, rather than any marked changes in the fixed-capital ratios within advanced firms themselves.

Only in cotton did the fixed capital ever become the major component. Even here, the proportions were often exaggerated

---

[1] M. W. Flinn, *Men of Iron, the Crowleys in the Early Iron Industry* (Edinburgh, 1962), pp. 174–5; A. Raistrick, *Quakers in Science and Industry* (London, 1950), p. 98; also *Dynasty of Ironfounders, the Darbys and Coalbrookdale* (London, 1953), p. 61; Unwin, op. cit., p. 24; W. H. Chaloner, 'Charles Roe of Macclesfield (1715–81): An Eighteenth-Century Industrialist', part I, *Transactions of the Lancashire and Cheshire Antiquarian Society*, LXII (1950–1), p. 138; Wadsworth and Mann, op. cit., p. 290; P. Mathias, *The Brewing Industry in England, 1700–1830* (Cambridge, 1959), especially pp. 63, 77, 79, 474, 556–8. To arrive at these figures, all doubtful items were included in 'fixed capital'. J. Steuart and A. Smith both assumed the capital needs of the 'manufacturer' (as distinct from the merchant) to be small: *Wealth of Nations*, vol. I, p. 325; Sir J. Steuart, *An Inquiry into the Principles of Political Oeconomy* (1767), vol. II, p. 137.

in public discussion:[1] in the typical up-to-date mill in the period 1780–1830, fixed capital represented only just a little more than one half of the capital invested.[2] In other textile industries it was much less. At Gott's, the first large integrated woollen mill, fixed capital was valued at £28,000, circulating capital at £65,400, in 1801; while at Marshall & Benyon's, the giant flax-spinning firm, the ratio fluctuated wildly in wartime because of speculation in stocks, but always left the fixed capital at well below the 50 per cent mark.[3]

It is the iron industry which is usually held to have had the highest ratio of fixed capital to turnover or circulating capital. Ashton's example of a firm in which one quarter of the cost of bar-iron was accounted for by interest on capital invested, is often quoted in support of this view.[4] Unfortunately, no source for Ashton's figure was given; it might have been true in some exceptional case or might derive from a misunderstanding.[5] In any case, Ashton's figure included royalties, and it is not known what proportion of the 25 per cent of cost these represented. More normally, fixed capital was comparable in size with the annual turnover and smaller than the circulating capital employed. It is true that at Carron, at an early stage, fixed capital exceeded circulating capital by a wide margin – £79,500 compared with £46,000, in 1769 – but this was an

[1] H. D. Fong, *Triumph of the Factory System in England* (Tientsin, 1930), pp. 40, 41; *Factories Inquiry Commission, First Report*, PP 1833, XX, ev. Pooley; *SC on Manufactures*, PP 1833, ev. H. Houldsworth, QQ. 5303–4.

[2] E. Baines, Jr, *History of the Cotton Manufacture in Great Britain* (1835), pp. 401, 412–14; Fong, op. cit., p. 42; *Factories Inquiry Commission, First Report*, D 2, appendix A, p. 34, R. H. Greg; M. Blaug, 'The Productivity of Capital in the Lancashire Cotton Industry during the Nineteenth Century', *Economic History Review*, 2nd series, XIII (April 1961), p. 359; J. Montgomery, *The Theory and Practice of Cotton Spinning* (Glasgow, 1833), p. 281; *SC on Manufactures*, PP 1833, ev. J. Milne, Q. 11070.

[3] W. B. Crump (ed.), *The Leeds Woollen Industry, 1780–1820* (Leeds, 1931), p. 257; W. G. Rimmer, *Marshall of Leeds, Flax Spinners 1788–1886* (Cambridge, 1960), pp. 39, 43–4, 313; *Marshall Papers* (MS, Brotherton Library, Leeds), book 2 ('Leeds Mill, 1804'), book 3 ('Shrewsbury Accounts, 1806').

[4] T. S. Ashton, *Iron and Steel in the Industrial Revolution* (Manchester, 1924), p. 163; S. P. Garner, *Evolution of Cost Accounting to 1925* (Alabama, 1954), p. 28; R. S. Edwards, 'Some Notes on the Early Literature and Development of Cost Accounting in Great Britain', *The Accountant*, XCVII (June–December 1937), p. 193.

[5] Possibly based on Anthony Hill's statement that invested capital (of all kinds) in the iron trade amounted to four times the annual turnover. *SC on Manufactures*, PP 1833, ev. Hill, Q. 10402.

exceptional case of a firm built up greatly ahead of its actual market and turnover.[1] Cyfarthfa, in 1812, showed the more usual distribution: £68,900 sunk in fixed capital on the most generous interpretation, compared with £95,000 in stocks and stores.[2] Some examples of other large firms in the metallurgical industries compared as follows:[3]

TABLE I

Firm	Year	Fixed capital (buildings, machinery, etc.) £	Circulating capital (stocks, stores, etc.) £	Fixed capital as percentage of inventory valuation
Mona Mine Co. (Copper)	1788	6,729	30,643	18·0
Mona Mine Co.	1829–30	4,129 *	43,000	8·8
M. Boulton (Buttons, Toys)	1782	2,800	6,700	29·5
Soho Foundry	1822	3,200	33,300	8·8
Soho Foundry	1830	10,700	21,500	33·2
Nevill Copper Works	1806	3,785	10,250	27·0
Pontrhydyrun Tin Mill	1832	3,186	15,923	16·7

* Not complete.

The technical reasons for this are not difficult to find. The furnaces, buildings, even the hammers or boilers, were not normally bought from or installed by outside firms but were built, maintained, renovated or altered by the firm's own workers in the course of their normal duties. Their book values were thus often set at the cost of cheap raw materials such as stone or iron, plus, possibly, wages. Their sale values were even lower. Their actual costs to the firms concerned could easily be absorbed in annual revenue accounts without appearing in the books as 'capital' costs at all – a practice by no means unknown even among larger firms. This was true also

[1] R. H. Campbell, 'The Financing of Carron Company', *Business History*, I (December 1958), pp. 26, 27. Compare below, pp. 159–60.

[2] *Cyfarthfa MSS* (National Library of Wales), box 12, Balance Sheet, 30 June 1812.

[3] *Mona Mine MSS* (University College of North Wales), nos. 166, 3039, 3048; *Boulton and Watt MSS*, Accounts (Birmingham Assay Office), 'M. Boulton, Inventory', 22 June 1782; *Boulton and Watt MSS*, Accounts etc. (Birmingham Central Library), Inventory Books, 1822–31; *Nevill MSS* (National Library of Wales), no. 20; *Pontrhydyrun [Tin] Works MSS* (Cardiff Public Libary), Account Book.

of mining, when the costs of sinking a pit might be recouped in four months of working, and a colliery with equipment worth £1,000 in 1804 was sold, in 1813, for £30,000.[1] Equipment which had to be bought in, wholly or in part, like steam engines, therefore tended to occupy a disproportionate share of the fixed capital shown in the balance sheet, as well as weighing correspondingly heavily on the minds of entrepreneurs, and it required a correspondingly large expenditure on the part of the firm. Even so, the Albion Mill, the most highly mechanized unit of its kind, was estimated to require £20,000 of fixed capital only, compared with £24,000 in stocks and other circulating capital.[2]

Thus the problem of finding capital was largely a problem of finding circulating capital, for stocks of raw materials, work in progress and finished commodities, and for rents, interest and wage payments, and the like; and this was a problem not unknown to merchants and to employers of the 'putting-out' type, before the birth of the factory system. In consequence, the new industrialists took over from the older types of industry and commerce, with little change, the methods both of providing capital and of making payments. These methods were based on an elaborate and delicately balanced system of credit.

II

The figures for 'capital' given in the examples above represent only the inventory values of the balance sheets. In addition, the typical firm also showed debtors and creditors, and these items were not only very large in relation to the 'fixed' and 'circulating' capital, but shaded imperceptibly into (debenture-type) loans and partners' capital at one extreme, and into running costs, such as wages, at the other, both in the practices of businessmen and in the minds of the accountants, as shown in their books.[3]

The amounts standing under the headings of 'debtors' and 'creditors' – that is to say, the share played by trade credit in

[1] P. L. Payne, 'The Govan Collieries, 1804–1805', *Business History*, III (June 1961), pp. 87–9.

[2] O. A. Westworth, 'The Albion Steam Flour Mill', *Economic History*, II (January 1932), p. 383.

[3] Compare my paper on 'Capital Accounting'.

F

the transactions of a firm – tended to be largest where the firm was on the point of emerging from the stage of merchanting and putting-out into that of an integrated manufacturing firm. Thus Benjamin Gott, when he was about to launch into factory industry, possessed a net capital of around £20,000; but his debtors (remaining from his merchant days) stood at £174,000 and his creditors at £172,000. Even by 1796, his debtors still stood at £146,100 and his creditors at £120,000, compared with the partnership capital of £69,500. Similarly, Crowley's in 1728 had £87,000 owing by debtors (£15,400 of this in bad debts) and owed £26,000 to creditors.[1]

For firms somewhat further removed from the putting-out system, the following may be taken as typical valuations:[2]

TABLE 2

Firm	Year	Fixed capital £	Debtors £	Creditors £
Llangavelach Copper Works	1745	5,400	9,700	16,000
Eccleston Cotton Mill	1784–92	2,340	5,000	13,000
Mona Mine Co.	1788	6,729	24,462	33,167
Pontrhydyrun Tin Mill	1832	3,186	3,445	1,924
		Total inventory capital		
Coalbrookdale Ironworks	1740	7,553	9,224	796
Glasgow Glass Bottle House Co.	1798	16,600	12,000	8,800

Again, in 1810, Wedgwood's 'net worth' was put at £35,383; accounts outstanding amounted to over £41,000. For Coalbrookdale, in 1793, the 'net value' of the company was £39,856, while debts owing by the company amounted to £50,549.[3]

[1] Crump, op. cit., p. 255; *Gott Papers* (MS, Brotherton Library, Leeds), box 6, Annual Statements of Partnership Accounts, 1 January 1796; Flinn, op. cit., pp. 174–5.

[2] G. G. Francis, *The Smelting of Copper in the Swansea District*, 2nd ed. (1881), pp. 106–8; T. C. Barker and J. R. Harris, *A Merseyside Town in the Industrial Revolution: St Helens, 1750–1900* (Liverpool, 1954), p. 121; Pontrhydyrun Account Book; *Mona Mine MSS*, nos. 3039, 3048; Raistrick, *Dynasty*, pp. 277–8; A. and N. L. Clow, *The Chemical Revolution, A Contribution to Social Technology* (London, 1952), p. 288.

[3] R. M. Hower, 'The Wedgwoods, Ten Generations of Potters', *Journal of Economic and Business History*, IV (February 1932), pp. 672–3; Raistrick, *Dynasty*, pp. 214–15.

It will be seen that these items are so large in relation to the fixed, or even to the total inventory capital, that normal variations in them, especially if in opposite directions, could easily be of an order of magnitude equivalent to the total capital that was tied up in the firm as a productive unit. It was thus possible for firms beginning in a small way and with greatly inadequate capital resources of their own to insert themselves into the circulation of credit and, in this way, to acquire working capital by a process of running creditor balances of much larger amounts than debtors'. Conversely, firms of merchant origins, or otherwise well provided with capital, could find themselves, even in the factory age, using it to finance other firms' current needs rather than their own productive base.

This process, as it developed in the Yorkshire woollen industry, was first described by Heaton in a stimulating article published before the war.[1] It was based largely on Benjamin Gott's experience, which first drew attention to this mechanism of credit finance in the industrial revolution, and it has been confirmed in a more recent study of the woollen industry of the first half of the nineteenth century:[2] 'Up to 1830,' R. M. Hartwell writes, 'variable costs were probably more important than fixed costs. . . . The variable costs were spread in a network of credit which eased the burden of the manufacturer: he bought his raw materials on credit, and although he sold his cloths on credit he could get advances on consignments.'[3] Heaton appeared to incline to the view that this method of credit financing was exceptional and quoted some well-known large firms which showed a different history of credit shortage and difficulty. The weight of the evidence which has come to light since then, however, points to the opposite conclusion: namely, that trade-credit financing was the rule, and the experience of the well-known large firms was the exception.

[1] Heaton, op. cit., esp. pp. 2–5, 10.
[2] R. M. Hartwell, *The Yorkshire Woollen and Worsted Industry, 1800–1850* (unpublished Oxford D.Phil. thesis, 1955), esp. pp. 371, 373, 623, 660.
[3] Ibid., p. 11.

III

The hypothesis that credit finance within the mercantile–industrial field played a major part in most firms, both those with surpluses and those with deficits of capital of their own, and that this web of credit should be placed near the centre of the exposition of the accumulation of capital, should be subjected to the usual tests, such as whether it explains some of the more puzzling features of its period better than other hypotheses and whether it opens up new and profitable avenues of inquiry. The remainder of the paper will attempt to apply some of these tests.

First, the role of the British banks during the industrial revolution suggests itself for re-examination. In the established view, they did not, like those of other countries in similar stages of development, contribute share 'capital' to British industrial firms, but provided short-term credit only, by discounting bills and by other means. Several recent writers have had to admit some exceptions to this generalization, and it is well known that firms such as Boulton and Watt, the Carron Company and some South Wales iron works obtained substantial bank credits in effect for considerable periods, but in the main the traditional view may be accepted as correct. With it, there is the clear implication that this selectivity of the banks, and their lending patterns as a whole, were developed by them according to their own needs and experience and, in particular, because of their insistence on liquidity.[1] In view of the very different practices of banks in other countries at a similar stage of rapid industrialization, banks which showed no greater instability than the English country banks, this explanation

---

[1] For example, T. S. Ashton, *The Industrial Revolution 1760–1830* (London, 1946), pp. 105–6, and *An Eighteenth-Century Industrialist, Peter Stubbs of Warrington 1756–1806* (Manchester, 1939), p. 116; W. H. B. Court, *Concise Economic History of Britain from 1750 to Recent Times* (Cambridge, 1954), pp. 91–2; L. S. Pressnell, *Country Banking in the Industrial Revolution* (Oxford, 1956), chap. 10. The best recent discussion of this and some related points touched upon in this paper will be found in an essay by F. Crouzet, 'La Formation du Capital en Grande-Bretagne pendant la Révolution Industrielle', *Second International Conference of Economic History, Aix-en-Provence, 1962* (Paris – The Hague, 1965).

has never been entirely satisfactory. 'It can be argued,' H. J. Habakkuk wrote recently,

> ... that financial institutions adapt themselves to meet the principal economic needs of their period and that English banks concentrated on the provision of working-capital because that was what industry needed; if there had been a large unsatisfied demand from industry to finance fixed capital, financial institutions would, with relative ease, have adapted themselves to meet this need, or new institutions would have arisen for the purpose.[1]

Our new emphasis, based on the actual experience of firms, would in fact allow us to say that the banks provided little long-term capital because little long-term capital was demanded. What was needed was a sufficient injection of short-term credit into the system to allow the mutual extension of credit to be developed. For the rest, banks merely had to provide a smooth transfer mechanism. By this means, firms short of capital were enabled to use it all on fixed investment, relying on the credit circulation provided by their market for the remainder of their capital. Hence, also, the sources of capital were felt to be interchangeable. The Hawkesbury colliery, for example, forced by its bankers to repay £4,000 of its overdraft during the banking crisis of 1793-4, made this repayment out of the partners' pockets and considered it equivalent to adding so much capital. An instance of an opposite flow is provided by Cyfarthfa, which invested, in the 1790s, its surplus funds in easily saleable securities or lent them to discount houses, to be used in discounting bills, when it could not use them for the works itself.[2]

Thus in effect the banks mobilized the country's savings, not merely for commodity sales and merchanting but also for commodity production. It was as true of the end of the eighteenth century as of its beginning, that 'trade credit facilities could contribute to variable capital. When the balance of

[1] H. J. Habakkuk, *American and British Technology in the Nineteenth Century* (Cambridge, 1962), p. 175.
[2] W. H. B. Court, 'A Warwickshire Colliery in the Eighteenth Century', *Economic History Review*, VII (May 1937), p. 227; J. P. Addis, *The Crawshay Dynasty, a Study in Industrial Organization and Development, 1765-1867* (Cardiff, 1957), p. 156.

capital was so heavily weighted in favour of variable capital, the problems of capital accumulation would clearly differ from those associated with heavy fixed capital investment.'[1]

Of course, the forms of institutions and their methods matter. While it might be true that 'in general, businessmen formalized in a considerable degree the credit they granted among themselves' in this period,[2] this might vary as to usance and rate of interest, while the ease of borrowing would also vary according to the state of the market[3] and the fortunes of the individual firm. Further, it would make a large difference to a firm's solvency and its rate of capital accumulation whether it was, on balance, a lender or borrower of capital. In times of stringency especially, when the very existence of an elaborate credit system led to innumerable failures,[4] a firm relying largely on credit was *ipso facto* more vulnerable.

Yet, when all these reservations are made, it remains true that the existence of this credit system allowed the smaller firm, in particular, to enter the production circle with only a small fraction of the capital it ultimately used and in this way to accumulate enough to enlarge the base of its operations, until perhaps in due course it had sufficient to become, in turn, a net lender. Robert Owen's story was in many ways untypical; but his beginnings as a mule manufacturer, employing forty men, on a capital of £100, the rest being supplied by credit,[5] was not at all unusual for firms which later grew to considerable size.

Apart from the banks, the main suppliers of this type of credit were mercantile firms whose investment, in effect, in the stocks and stores of manufacturers was but an extension of their long-established investments in commodities. Some of these houses were overseas merchants, importers or exporters, or wholesalers for the home trade; others had, before the rise of the factory system, acted as the central figures and financiers

[1] Flinn, op. cit., p. 175.

[2] 'The Rate of Interest in the Eighteenth Century', in L. S. Pressnell (ed.), *Studies in the Industrial Revolution* (London, 1960), p. 199.

[3] T. S. Ashton, *An Economic History of England: The Eighteenth Century* (London, 1955), pp. 26–9; J. R. T. Hughes, *Fluctuations in Trade, Industry and Finance* (Oxford, 1960), pp. 266–8.

[4] Heaton, op. cit., p. 5.

[5] Robert Owen, *Life of Owen, by Himself* (London, 1920 ed.), p. 31.

of putting-out manufacture. Together, they supplied a large part of the circulating capital to industry. But while the existence of this source of capital is generally recognized, its importance is sometimes underrated, simply because the capital appearing as 'bills' or 'creditors' is not as easily recognized as such, as a shareholding or a bank overdraft.

In this way the existence of a wealthy and enterprising mercantile community was both a cause and a consequence of the industrial revolution. Its wealth, throughout this period, compared well with that of even the largest industrialists. In cotton, the Drinkwaters and David Dales could launch the largest mills of their day while scarcely diminishing the merchanting business from which the sums establishing these enterprises were drawn; it took many years before Arkwright approached the original wealth of the Strutts. In wool, Benjamin Gott completely overshadowed the early West Riding machine wool-spinning industry with a mere fraction of the capital he had used as a trader. In 1817, Walker, Parker & Co. had over £450,000 locked up in stocks of lead, while the Cornish Mining Company had over £500,000 of traders' and smelters' capital locked up in copper in 1787. In South Wales, ironworks, coal mines and tin mills had to be financed by Bristol, even by London, merchants.[1]

The supplying merchant or trader was paid in bills, or he gave credit in other ways, so that fuel, raw materials, machinery and components need not be paid for by the factory owner until the finished article had long since been sold. Interest and even dividends were paid out by book entries, in the normal expectation that they would not be withdrawn. Royalties were commonly calculated as a proportion of the value of the mineral, paid *after* sales. Rent alone might have to be found out of the current returns. There remain wages, but they also could be based on credit. For not only were wages in arrears always, but they were often 'paid' in the form of book entries or paper credits for rent, coal, purchases at the truck shop or

---

[1] A. H. John (ed.), *The Walker Family, Ironfounders and Lead Manufacturers, 1741–1893* (London, 1951), p. v; L. J. Williams, 'The Welsh Tinplate Trade in the Mid Eighteenth Century', *Economic History Review*, 2nd series, XIII (April 1961), p. 447; G. C. Allen, 'An Eighteenth Century Combination in the Copper-Mining Industry', *Economic Journal*, XXXIII (March 1923), p. 80.

other supplies provided by the firm. These, in turn, where they were not produced by men within the factory village itself, were paid for in bills, and the circle of credit was thus complete.[1] It is hardly necessary to stress that at *some* stage the ultimate supplier, perhaps the foreign planter or home farmer, had to be paid out of real resources saved; but it was precisely along the extended lines of communication reaching out to them that the surpluses of non-industrialist savers could be inserted.

In the accepted view, the most significant feature of the widespread system of paying wages in credit instead of cash was the national shortage of actual coin and small banknotes, so that even firms which had the resources simply did not have the gold, silver and copper in small change to pay out to their 'hands'. In the light of the foregoing considerations, it would in many cases be more correct to say that some firms survived while having so few resources of their own that they could not even raise enough cash to pay their wages. For once again, following Habakkuk's logic above, a simple shortage of token coins or paper would have been met by the ingenuity of financial institutions. In some cases of genuine shortage, they were so met; but typically, the firm paying wages in truck, in book entries and in arrears, had no financial resources of any kind: it lived by borrowing in the course of trade, and it borrowed, in effect, also from its own wage-earners.

There was another noteworthy consequence of the relatively large share of capital used in business which came from bankers and outside creditors. This credit helped to blur the notion of 'capital' as a separate entity on which profit is earned. The confusion between a firm's own capital and credit granted to it, and indeed between capital and income, to which contemporary accountants were prone, was made worse by the necessarily violent fluctuations of the residual credit or debit balance left from the debtor–creditor entries. It was also encouraged by the current practice of charging a rate of interest

[1] For example, M. Dunn, *View of the Coal Trade of the North of England* (Newcastle upon Tyne, 1844), p. 151. Credit by bills became so regular that manufacturers and traders were wont to pay at irregular intervals by bills covering only approximately the outstanding debts, thus carrying debits and credits in their ledgers for years without ever exactly balancing their accounts with customers and suppliers: Ashton, *Peter Stubbs*, p. 111.

as 'cost' both on the capital borrowed and on the firm's own capital.[1]

Finally, our new emphasis may allow us to throw fresh light on the problem raised by Heaton[2] and others, that some of the strongest firms, and firms most generously provided with funds, were in acute difficulties over long periods because of capital shortage. Why should they have fared so much worse than many small and ill-provided concerns?

The two Soho partnerships of Boulton & Fothergill and Boulton and Watt, and the Carron Company, are probably the best-documented cases, though Josiah Wedgwood's firm was, at times, also in the same quandary. The problems of all these concerns showed much similarity. Boulton, for example, was time and again near bankruptcy in 1765–8 and in later years, having locked up too much capital in unsaleable stocks and uncollectable debts, so that he was desperately short of means to provide for other necessary circulating capital. He was saved on several occasions only in the nick of time by windfall incomes and loans, and his position did not really improve permanently until the high tide of profits from the steam engine partnership so flooded the concern with funds that even Boulton's thirst for capital was satisfied. Carron Company also quickly outgrew the resources of its original and its second set of partners. With needs of circulating capital always well ahead of its own resources or its powers to borrow from bankers or partners, the firm had to go bankrupt before the success of the carronades pulled it out of danger.[3]

To be sure, there were special factors operating in the case of both these firms, but it is worth nothing that they had two important features in common (besides their inability to foresee the large demands for circulating capital in relation to their

[1] This problem is treated at length in my article quoted above, and therefore only touched upon here.

[2] Heaton, op. cit., p. 4.

[3] J. E. Cule, *The Financial History of Matthew Boulton, 1759–1800* (unpublished Birmingham M.Com. thesis, 1935), esp. pp. 8–9, 21–2, 44, 63; and 'Finance and Industry in the Eighteenth Century: The Firm of Boulton and Watt', *Economic History*, IV (February 1940), pp. 320–2; *Boulton and Watt MSS* (Birmingham Assay Office), Boulton to J. H. Ebbinghaus, 18 November 1767, 2 March 1768; Campbell, 'Financing of Carron Co.', pp. 22 ff. and *Carron Company* (Edinburgh and London, 1961), pp. 123 ff.; H. W. Dickinson, *Matthew Boulton* (Cambridge, 1937), p. 109.

investment):[1] they were both immensely large in relation to their market and intensely ambitious in their initial scale.[2] Not only did their sudden arrival on the industrial scene make it impossible for them to accumulate favourable credit balances in proportion to their turnover, as firms growing piecemeal could do, but they were also too large for the existing credit base in their industries to support or, in other words, too large to insert themselves into the circulation of credit. They failed to see that in appearing, fully grown, as whales among the minnows, they would cut themselves off from the mutual support of more equally matched units that was the rule elsewhere. As new arrivals on that scale, they would have, by themselves, to prime the pump of their customers and to pour untold thousands into a seemingly bottomless pit of stocks, consignments and credits granted, without receiving credits on the other side of the ledger in anything like the same proportion. Inasmuch as they relied on sales to Government departments, the notorious tardiness of the latter in paying their suppliers aggravated the imbalance of these firms. In the given conditions, firms like Boulton & Fothergill or Carron Company required very much more capital to sustain a given level of turnover than would a number of smaller firms which had grown slowly with the market. It is evident that the entrepreneurs concerned failed to see this danger, and not only were they lamentably unprepared to meet it, but they were loath to recognize it after it had appeared, as it involved the admission that their elaborate calculation had been based on wrong premises. It requires the hindsight of later historians to point out the inevitable.

IV

The sources of capital in the industrial revolution were many and varied. This paper did not so much attempt to reassess their relative importance as try to suggest that in some respects the need for fresh capital, especially for fixed assets, has been less than is often supposed, since much capital could be generated

[1] For an earlier example, see A. Moller, 'Coal Mining in the Seventeenth Century', *Transactions of the Royal Historical Society*, 4th series, VIII (1925), p. 87.

[2] Wedgwood was subject to the same factors with similar consequences.

from within the existing domestic manufacturing and associated credit systems. It has, further, tried to show that many institutional factors within the credit market were such as to ease the provision of the (relatively more important) circulating capital from banks, merchants, wage-earners and others, during the industrial revolution.

However, it is necessary to stress that this is not the whole story. We must return to our initial division between the large public utilities like canals, turnpikes or docks, and the ordinary industrial firm. To the extent that our new emphasis is right, it allows us to conclude that there was a further important difference between them, beyond that of mere size or regularity of management, to account for the great difference in organization. Because the public utilities had such a high proportion of fixed capital, and because they were so large in relation to their markets, they found it even less possible than Soho or Carron to insert themselves into a credit circle, and thus their need for capital was relatively even greater than might at first sight appear. In the industrialization process, the pressure for capital stems to a very large extent indeed from the needs of public utilities, rather than from the factories or the mines.

6 Capital Formation in Great Britain during the Industrial Revolution [1]

FRANÇOIS CROUZET

[A preliminary version of this article was first published in *Second International Conference of Economic History. Aix-en-Provence, 1962*, vol. II, Paris – The Hague, 1965.]

I

The Industrial Revolution meant an acceleration of technological progress but also of capital formation, the two phenomena being moreover closely linked. The effects of the technical discoveries which were achieved in eighteenth-century England would have been very limited if considerable capital resources had not been invested to develop and exploit them.[2] This is self-evident – and the point is made only to show the importance of the problem discussed in this paper – inasmuch as England, as the pioneer country, industrialized without any outside help. Unfortunately this problem remains obscure owing to the scarcity of sources. The eighteenth and early nineteenth centuries are pre-statistical periods for anything connected with savings, capital flows or investment aggregates, and the available quantitative data are of doubtful value. Historians have to rely mainly on individual cases drawn from monographs in business history, but these are relatively few

[1] Helpful comments on this paper were made by D. S. Landes, M. Gillet and J. R. Harris, to whom I would like to express my sincere thanks, but they have no responsibility for the opinions expressed. Slight modifications have been made in the light of the discussion at the Aix-en-Provence conference.

N.B. The passages between brackets [. . .] have been added to the footnotes for re-edition in the present book, especially in order to take recent research into account.
[2] T. S. Ashton, *The Industrial Revolution, 1760–1830* (London, 1948), p. 94; S. Kuznets, *Capital in the American Economy. Its Formation and Financing* (Princeton, 1961), p. 391.

and the value of the available sample uncertain. In this paper, therefore, I can only present a provisional and defective progress report, which attempts to synthesize existing works, with no claim to originality.

I must add that I shall deal solely with the formation of capital in industry and have excluded investment in agriculture, transport and building, although, in the eighteenth and even at the beginning of the nineteenth centuries, these sectors certainly absorbed much more capital than was invested in British industry.[1] The emphasis has been put on the textile and metal industries, but I have frequently drawn on the excellent studies recently published on the glass, paper and brewing industries. For convenience sake I have taken as the limits of the Industrial Revolution in England the currently accepted dates of 1760–1830, with occasional forays on either side.[2] The breadth and complexity of the problem have prevented me from considering it in its entirety and I have concentrated on the three less obscure aspects: the origin of the capital used to finance the Industrial Revolution; the accumulation of capital during the growth of industrial concerns, and lastly, the fluctuations of investment.

II

Our first task is therefore to look at the sources of capital which were tapped for the setting up and development of the business enterprises which put into practice the new technical inventions; this means effectively an analysis of the financing of the 'factories' – the cotton-spinning mills, the woollen mills, the coke-using ironworks, etc. – the appearance of which is an essential feature of the Industrial Revolution. Admittedly some eminent historians have suggested that this problem is an artificial, or at any rate an insoluble one. They contend that,

[1] T. S. Ashton, *An Economic History of England. The Eighteenth Century* (London, 1955), pp. 75, 83; from 1758 to 1802 £13 million was subscribed for canal shares; Phyllis Deane, 'Capital Formation in Britain before the Railway Age', *Economic Development and Cultural Change*, IX (1961), p. 362, puts the total amount of investment in river and canal navigation between 1750 and 1830 at £20 million.

[2] The choice of 1830 as *terminus ad quem* has the disadvantage of concealing some changes that were becoming apparent at about this time, such as the bigger part played by banks in financing industry, and the growing number of joint stock companies. There seems to be a turning point which could be clarified by an analysis pursued beyond 1830.

the available data being too contradictory, all that emerges is that the capital which financed the Industrial Revolution came from very varied sources, nay, from all sectors of the economy.[1] Their objection is valid, but it seems that these different sources are by no means of equal importance and that it is not impossible to establish a hierarchy. We can also learn from such an analysis a great deal about the nature of the Industrial Revolution and of capital formation in that period. A distinction must, however, be made between two significantly different aspects of the problem: on the one hand, the origin of the 'initial outlay' which allowed new firms to build up their factories out of nothing, or existing ones (which had started in a small way) to enter large-scale manufacturing; and, on the other hand, the financing of the later expansion of these enterprises.

In both cases we shall distinguish between 'internal' and 'external' sources of capital; on the one hand, capital which came from within industry itself, which was already present there as the Industrial Revolution got under way (it will appear to have played a preponderant part) and on the other hand, capital which had accumulated in other sectors of the economy. Among the former are the capitals which were supplied by artisans or small manufacturers.

Their contribution seems to have been substantial, allowing for the fact that, at the beginning of the Industrial Revolution, the threshold of entry into 'factory' production was relatively low, especially in the textile industry, where even the largest production units were small, the plant rudimentary and inexpensive; consequently the initial outlay involved in setting up a factory was modest – at the end of the eighteenth century a few thousand pounds would finance a substantial cotton mill.[2] In circumstances such as these a large number of indus-

[1] Ashton, *The Industrial Revolution*, pp. 94–5; C. Wilson, 'The Entrepreneur in the Industrial Revolution in Britain', *History*, XLII (1957), p. 112. Compare M. Abramovitz, in *Capital Formation and Economic Growth. A Conference of the Universities – National Bureau Committee for Economic Research* (Princeton, 1955), pp. 3–5, where he insists that a study of savings and the origin of capital is essential to that of capital formation.

[2] For example, see H. Heaton, 'Financing the Industrial Revolution', *Bulletin of the Business Historical Society*, XI (1937), pp. 2–3. This concept of a threshold of entry into 'factory' industry needs to be clarified. Data on the cost of building and tooling textile mills and ironworks should be systematically gathered and an attempt made to calculate the unit cost of installing a cotton-spinning spindle at

trial enterprises of the second half of the eighteenth century were founded on a small initial capital, provided by profits from production at the artisan level,[1] and thanks to the rapidity of accumulation – a topic we shall consider later – many of them subsequently experienced a phenomenal expansion. Examples abound, especially in the textile industry. James McConnel came to Lancashire from Scotland in 1781 to be apprenticed to a manufacturer of textile machinery; after working as a journeyman-spinner and having built machines himself, he entered into partnership in 1791 with John Kennedy – whose background and beginnings were the same as his – and two Manchester fustian warehousemen; it was their activities on what was in fact an artisan level that enabled McConnel and Kennedy to save a capital of £1,770 with which they set up on their own account in 1795 – the starting point of their meteoric rise that, twenty years later, made them the largest cotton-spinning firm in Britain. Several other young Scotsmen who came to Lancashire at the same time and also became prominent cotton-spinners – James Kennedy, Adam and George Murray, Thomas Houldsworth and the Welshman, Robert Owen – had parallel careers; working as artisan machine-makers and mule-spinners, they amassed within a few years the capital to set up proper factories. Thanks to the profits resulting from the strong demand for cotton yarn, many Lancashire artisans, who had installed some of the new spinning machines in their workshops, were able to follow suit during the last twenty years of the eighteenth century.[2]

---

different periods, or the capacity needed to produce 1,000 tons of pig-iron. This might perhaps also enable us to evaluate the capital invested in those industries where we have a rough idea of the volume of machinery at a given time.

For the paper industry, see D. C. Coleman, *The British Paper Industry, 1495–1860. A Study in Industrial Growth* (Oxford, 1958), pp. 232–3. For the metal industry, see below, p. 167, n. 6.

[1] And usually by 'self-made' men of humble origin who raised themselves firstly from wage-earners to the level of artisans, or small merchant-manufacturers and thus acquired a little capital. But the question of the social background of industrialists is different from the problem of capital formation, although somewhat connected with it. One must also remember that it was not at all easy for a workman or even an artisan, to acquire a small amount of capital – a few pounds or a few dozen pounds.

[2] *A Century of Fine Cotton Spinning. 1790–1906. McConnel and Co. Ltd. Ancoats, Manchester* (Manchester, 1906), pp. 8–9; G. W. Daniels, 'The Early Records of a

The same pattern can be seen, but at a later date, in the West Riding woollen industry, which retained its essentially artisan structure until the beginning of the nineteenth century. A fair number of woollen mills were established by master-clothiers, who started with scribbling mills to card their own wool and do jobwork for their neighbours, then added some spinning jennies and a few looms. Later on, in the mid nineteenth century, wealthy clothiers set up the first large factories for power-loom weaving. In two or three generations, according to Crump, more than one enterprising family transformed its clothier's warehouse into a huge mill.[1]

Although the iron industry needed much more capital than the textile industry, some large enterprises were also established with funds accumulated in 'artisan' activities. The most striking example is that of the three Walker brothers who set up a small foundry near Sheffield in 1741 and rose gradually from 'workshop' (in 1746 their capital was only £600) to large-scale manufacturing. One could also cite Abraham Darby I who started as an artisan making equipment for malt mills, became a partner in an iron and brass foundry in Bristol and, by selling his share in this business (already a large one), was able to set himself up at Coalbrookdale in 1709; Isaac Wilkinson, who saved enough money as a foundry worker and foreman to set up as an ironmaster in 1740. T. S. Ashton estimates that many of the eighteenth-century ironmasters were former artisans of the secondary metal trades, who had made good. And one stage higher, it was some small iron-masters who supplied the capital for the establishment of several

---

Great Manchester Cotton-Spinning Firm', *Economic Journal*, XXV (1915), pp. 175–7; also his *The Early English Cotton Industry* (Manchester, 1920), pp. 122, 126–8, 141–2; P. Mantoux, *The Industrial Revolution in the Eighteenth Century*, rev. ed. (London, 1928: trans. from the French), p. 383.

[In the Midlands cotton-spinning industry, the artisan or mechanic with a small capital played a negligible part; however, in marginal areas, like the Peak District, a number of 'small men', who had started with jennies workshops, were able to keep pace with technical progress, and eventually to turn to mules and steam-power; S. D. Chapman, *The Early Factory Masters. The Transition to the Factory System in the Midlands Textile Industry* (Newton Abbot, 1967), pp. 56, 59–60, 92, 216.]

[1] W. B. Crump, *The Leeds Woollen Industry, 1780–1820* (Leeds, 1931), p. 26; W. B. Crump and G. Ghorbal, *History of the Huddersfield Woollen Industry* (Huddersfield, 1935), pp. 69, 71, 74, 82, 84, 89, 90.

large ironworks – e.g., those of Clyde and Muirkirk in Scotland.[1]

There is also the case of Josiah Wedgwood, who began with no capital at all, worked as a journeyman, then, after two short-lived partnerships, set up on his own in 1759; he amassed a small capital and expanded his business, which enabled him to build the Etruria factory in 1769.[2] In the paper industry one can also find some large enterprises – e.g. the Crompton firm – growing out of small family concerns.[3]

The role of 'artisan' capital was thus quite important,[4] but possibly its importance tended to decrease as technical progress and concentration inevitably raised the threshold of entry into 'factory' industry. However, this happened with significant time-lags between the various branches of industry; in a highly capitalistic industry, like the brewing of porter in London,[5] the threshold may have been beyond the reach of the small entrepreneur by the beginning of the eighteenth century, and, by the end of the century, tens of thousands of pounds were needed to set up an ironworks;[6] nevertheless, this still

[1] T. S. Ashton, *Iron and Steel in the Industrial Revolution*, 2nd ed. (Manchester, 1951), pp. 25–7, 46-8, 209–10; A. Raistrick, *Dynasty of Iron Founders, The Darbys and Coalbrookdale* (London, 1953), pp. 17, 19–20, 23, 26, 50; W. H. Chaloner, 'Isaac Wilkinson, Potfounder', in L. S. Pressnell (ed.), *Studies in the Industrial Revolution. Essays presented to T. S. Ashton* (London, 1960), p. 25; B. Hoselitz, 'Entrepreneurship and Capital Formation in France and Britain since 1700', in *Capital Formation and Economic Growth*, p. 316; H. Hamilton, *The Industrial Revolution in Scotland* (Oxford, 1932), pp. 165–6. The question of A. Darby's capital resources remains obscure.

[A. Birch, *The Economic History of the British Iron and Steel Industry, 1784–1879* (London, 1967), pp. 196–7, points out that mineral leases – with very low rents in many cases – allowed ironmasters with a small capital to start a concern.]

[2] R. M. Hower, 'The Wedgwoods: Ten Generations of Potters', *Journal of Economic and Business History*, IV (1932), pp. 285–8, 291; N. McKendrick, 'Josiah Wedgwood: An Eighteenth Century Entrepreneur in Salesmanship and Marketing Techniques', *Economic History Review*, 2nd series, XII (1960), p. 408.

[3] Coleman, op. cit., pp. 161, 238, 245.

[4] With 'artisan' capital, one can connect that of the 'managers', the highest grade employees of large industrialists, who often retired when they had accumulated enough capital to set up on their own. G. Unwin, *Samuel Oldknow and the Arkwrights. The Industrial Revolution at Stockport and Marple* (Manchester, 1924), p. 51, stresses their importance in the cotton industry; T. C. Barker and J. R. Harris, *A Merseyside Town in the Industrial Revolution: St Helens 1750–1900* (Liverpool, 1954), p. 68, in the coal industry.

[5] P. Mathias, *The Brewing Industry in England, 1700–1830* (Cambridge, 1959), p. 23.

[6] Ashton, *Iron and Steel*, pp. 100, 163; A. H. John, *The Industrial Development of South Wales, 1750–1850. An Essay* (Cardiff, 1950), pp. 35–6.

left a wide field of action open to 'artisan' capital, e.g. such industries as the secondary metal trades. Also, small entrepreneurs could often obtain outside help in order to found large factories.[1] Some of this capital was supplied by wealthier people – the merchant-manufacturers – who were also considerable investors of their own.

As early as the middle of the eighteenth century several branches of British industry were organized on a commercial capitalism basis – the putting-out system – and dominated by powerful merchant-manufacturers. Naturally, these men, who were used to organizing and financing production and who provided 'the historical transition', as P. Mantoux wrote, 'between the master-craftsman of the Middle Ages and the modern industrialist',[2] did not hesitate to encourage the rise of the factory system by investing in it the abundant capital at their disposal.[3] The main stimuli for these investments came from the high profitability of mechanized production, and from the desire to ensure a regular supply of semi-finished goods (e.g. cotton yarn) or to control the quality of the products.[4] It is typical that Richard Arkwright should have been

[1] [P. Mathias, *The First Industrial Nation. An Economic History of Britain 1700–1914* (London, 1969), pp. 156–7, stresses that very few first generation entrepreneurs sprang from labouring groups; most came from families with some savings, even if modest, and enjoyed positions of respectability in local society, which enabled them to borrow money or get credit.]

[2] Mantoux, op. cit., p. 487.

[3] The rates of profits and capital accumulation seem to have been high for the merchant-manufacturers during the last quarter of the eighteenth century. S. Oldknow made a fortune in a few years by manufacturing muslins (Unwin, op. cit., pp. 16, 42, 45). J. de L. Mann mentions the case of a Wiltshire clothier whose capital increased by an average of 7 to 8 per cent a year between 1767 and 1805; 'Clothiers and Weavers in Wiltshire during the Eighteenth Century', in Pressnell (ed.), *Studies in the Industrial Revolution*, pp. 86–7.

[4] D. S. Landes, 'Encore le Problème de la Révolution industrielle en Angleterre', *Bulletin de la Société d'Histoire moderne*, 12th series, no. 18 (1961), pp. 6–7.

Moreover, before the Industrial Revolution proper, some prototypes of 'factories' – the silk-spinning mills of the first half of the eighteenth century – had been largely financed by merchant-manufacturers of silks and by silk merchants. Cf. W. H. Chaloner, 'Charles Roe of Macclesfield (1715–81): An Eighteenth-Century Industrialist', *Transactions of the Lancashire and Cheshire Antiquarian Society*, LXII (1950–1), pp. 134–5; A. P. Wadsworth and J. de Lacy Mann, *The Cotton Trade and Industrial Lancashire, 1600–1780* (Manchester, 1931), p. 305; Unwin, op. cit., pp. 23–5, 27.

Johnson and Touchet, who tried to set up cotton-spinning mills using Lewis Paul's machines were also merchant-manufacturers (Wadsworth and Mann, op. cit., p. 447).

given financial backing by two rich merchant-hosiers, Jedediah Strutt of Derby and Samuel Need of Nottingham, who went into partnership with him; they probably provided the greater part of the £13,000 he invested before 1774 to perfect his invention and build his first two mills. A few years later J. Strutt built the spinning mills of Belper and Midford. His cash-book for the years 1780–9 shows the transfer of large sums from his hosiery business to his expanding cotton mills, which his sons made into one of the biggest cotton firms in the country.[1]

A number of merchant-manufacturers of Manchester and the surrounding area followed this example after 1780 by investing in the building of mechanized spinning mills the capital they had acquired as middlemen. Peter Drinkwater was one such, a wealthy manufacturer and exporter of fustians, who built two spinning mills at Northwich and Manchester.[2] Samuel Old-know was another example; around 1790 he was the first manufacturer of muslins in England – but he operated on the putting-out system. In 1786 he decided to embark on mechanized spinning and he was able to put his idea into practice from 1790 thanks to the huge profits he had made; he built a steam-mill in Stockport and a large water-mill in Mellor. At the same time most of his fellow calico manufacturers in Stockport turned over to spinning.[3]

Capital supplied by merchant-manufacturers played also a crucial part in the creation of the first Scottish cotton-spinning mills; they were the work of such men as David Dale, founder of New Lanark and two other mills, James Monteith and the Buchanan brothers, who had started as weavers of fine linen in Glasgow or Paisley and then became importers of linen yarn which they put out to domestic weavers.[4]

[1] R. S. Fitton and A. P. Wadsworth, *The Strutts and the Arkwrights, 1758–1830. A Study of the Early Factory System* (Manchester, 1958), pp. 1, 47, 50, 60, 63–4, 77–8, 81.

[2] W. H. Chaloner, 'Manchester in the Latter Half of the Eighteenth Century', *Bulletin of the John Rylands Library*, vol. 42 (1959), p. 48; also, 'Robert Owen, Peter Drinkwater and the Early Factory System in Manchester, 1788–1800', ibid., vol. 37 (1954), pp. 85–7.

[3] Unwin, op. cit., pp. 39, 72, 85, 103, 123–5.

[4] Hamilton, *Industrial Revolution in Scotland*, pp. 124, 126–9, 136–7; M. L. Robertson, 'Scottish Commerce and the American War of Independence', *Economic History Review*, 2nd series, IX (1956), p. 130.

D. Dale founded the New Lanark (1786), Blantyre and Catrine mills (1787);

In the woollen industry the first large mills were nearly all established by wealthy merchant-manufacturers, such as Benjamin Gott, who built the great Bean Ing mill in 1792, again financed by profits he had made as a woollen cloth merchant and as a putter-out. In the next few years several merchants from Leeds, Halifax and Huddersfield followed his example in setting up mills.[1] In the worsted industry the trend was much the same; it was highly capitalistic and had been dominated by rich merchant-manufacturers since the early eighteenth century. A recent and excellent monograph describes the typical case of John Foster: he set up as a putter-out in Queensberry in 1819; his business rapidly prospered and in 1834 he had a capital of £11,185; he began spinning and weaving for himself, at first in a small rented mill, then at Black Dyke Mills which he started to build in 1835.[2]

In the light metal industries, where commercial capitalism was likewise well developed, merchant-manufacturers set up also their own factories, like the one Peter Stubbs established in Warrington in 1802.[3]

The capital provided by merchant-manufacturers thus appears as a very important factor in the birth of the factory textile industries; moreover, they were able to invest on a much larger scale than the artisans, and their intervention partially explains the upsurge of investment (which we shall discuss later) that resulted in the founding of numerous cotton mills in the years following 1783.[4]

---

the Buchanans those at Deanston and Ballindalloch; after this they went into partnership with Kirkman Finlay, a dealer in linen, cotton fabrics and yarns.

[1] Crump, op. cit., pp. vii, 2, 13, 255; H. Heaton, 'Benjamin Gott and the Industrial Revolution in Yorkshire', *Economic History Review*, III (1931), pp. 45–8, 51.

Mantoux (op. cit., p. 66) draws attention to the same phenomenon in the West Country.

[2] E. M. Sigsworth, *Black Dyke Mills. A History of John Foster and Son* (Liverpool, 1958), pp. 137–41, 155, 159, 165, 172–4, 176–7, 218.

[3] T. S. Ashton, *An Eighteenth Century Industrialist. Peter Stubbs of Warrington. 1756–1806* (Manchester, 1939), pp. 1, 9, 20, 26–7.

[4] [An important contribution to this problem has been made by S. D. Chapman, op. cit., especially pp. 17, 19–20, 23–6, 77, 216, and also his 'Fixed Capital Formation in the British Cotton Industry, 1770–1815', *Economic History Review*, 2nd series, XXIII, no. 2 (August 1970), pp. 248–9; investment in cotton-spinning mills on Arkwright's techniques was characterized by a preponderance of merchant capital; in the Midlands, from 1769 to 1800, the principal partners of

Up to now we have been analysing the financial contributions from traditional forms of industry – the artisans and commercial capitalism – at the outset of the Industrial Revolution, but as it gathered momentum, factory industry, not content with financing its own expansion, was soon providing capital for the creation of new enterprises and this transfusion helped the Industrial Revolution to go from strength to strength.[1] Thus Richard Arkwright lent considerable sums to Samuel Oldknow,[2] and the great ironmasters – such as the Darbys, Reynolds and Crawshays – built new ironworks or lent money to their less wealthy colleagues.[3] They also played an important part in financing the first tinplate factories.[4] In other cases, a shift of capital from one industry to another took place: thus the development of coal-mining at the end of the eighteenth century was largely financed by the coal-using industries – the ironmasters, but also in South Wales the copper-smelting industry and, around St Helens, the owners of the Cheshire salt-works.[5]

---

42 out of 75 firms came from other textile occupations, and most of them were merchant-hosiers or other kinds of merchant-manufacturers; in the 'northern region' (i.e. Lancashire), 12 out of 43 leading cotton-spinning firms in 1795 were headed by established Manchester fustian merchants, 10 by middlemen-manufacturers of various 'country' centres, 4 by the Peel family and their partners, who were in fact Manchester merchants. In 'The Peels in the Early English Cotton Industry', *Business History*, XI, no. 2 (July 1969), p. 62, Chapman points out that nearly all the manufacturers of the Blackburn area (especially the calico-printers) were former middlemen, chapmen or dealers in linen and cotton cloth.]

[1] See J. R. Harris' interesting remarks on the subject in 'Michael Hughes of Sutton. The Influence of Welsh Copper on Lancashire Business, 1780–1815', *Transactions of the Historic Society of Lancashire and Cheshire*, vol. 101 (1949), p. 162.

[2] Unwin, op. cit., pp. 85, 140, 156.

[3] John, *Industrial Development of S. Wales*, pp. 31–2; Ashton, *Iron and Steel*, p. 53; Raistrick, op. cit., pp. 13, 70; J. P. Addis, *The Crawshay Dynasty. A Study in Industrial Organization and Development, 1765–1867* (Cardiff, 1957), p. 158. Between 1753 and 1757, the Coalbrookdale Company founded ironworks at Horsehay and Ketley; later it received large loans from R. Reynolds. By contrast the Midlands ironmasters, who moved into South Wales, brought very little capital with them; John, *Industrial Development of S. Wales*, pp. 25–6.

[4] W. E. Minchinton, *The British Tinplate Industry* (London, 1959), pp. 17, 95. It was one way of securing a regular outlet for their products.

[5] T. S. Ashton and J. Sykes, *The Coal Industry of the Eighteenth Century* (Manchester, 1929), pp. 5–6; A. Redford, *The Economic History of England, 1760–1860*, 2nd ed. (London, 1960), p. 36; E. D. Lewis, *The Rhondda Valley. A Study in Industrial Development from 1800 to the Present Day* (London, 1959), p. 37; John,

But in some cases there was no direct link between the industry providing the capital and the one in which it was invested. Thus a large part of the money which Samuel Garbett and John Roebuck invested in the Carron Company came from the profits made by the sulphuric acid factory they had founded at Prestonpans in 1749.[1] As for the St Helens Crown Glass Company, founded in 1826 (now Pilkington Brothers), it was mainly financed by Peter Greenall, a member of a rich brewing family, in conjunction with the Pilkington brothers; the latter invested (for £13,000 in three years) the profits of their family distilling business.[2]

The capital, which made possible the creation of large-scale 'factory' industries, came, then, mainly from industry itself. This conclusion is supported by some relevant remarks by Ashton who noted that the technical innovations of the eighteenth century tended – by accelerating not only production but also transport – to free funds which were formerly used as circulating capital (its circulation was, however, very slow) and which could be thus transformed into fixed capital.[3]

The Industrial Revolution was not, however, entirely self-

Industrial Development of S. Wales, pp. 36, 38; Barker and Harris, op. cit., pp. 58–61; the copper-smelters also invested in the Cornish copper mines, which moreover received much capital from the copper-using industries; cf. J. Rowe, *Cornwall in the Age of the Industrial Revolution* (Liverpool, 1953), p. 19.

[1] R. H. Campbell, *Carron Company* (London and Edinburgh, 1961), pp. 7–10; also 'The Financing of Carron Company', *Business History*, I (1958), pp. 21–3. On the other hand, the ironmaster S. Walker undertook in 1778 the manufacture of white lead; cf. A. H. John (ed.), *The Walker Family. Iron Founders and Lead Manufacturers. 1741–1893* (London, 1951), p. iv.

[2] T. C. Barker, *Pilkington Brothers and the Glass Industry* (London, 1960), pp. 30–2, 58–62, 78. This author thinks that the Pilkingtons entered the glass industry by accident; their distilling business itself grew out of the wines and spirits trade that their father had combined with his surgeon's and apothecary's profession.

[3] Ashton, *An Economic History*, pp. 90, 100, 110–12, according to whom the main innovations that freed capital by reducing the proportion of funds invested in stocks of raw materials, work in progress and goods being transported, were canals, the steam engine, the substitution of metal for wood and chlorine bleaching.

[On this point, Mathias, *First Industrial Nation*, p. 143, who points out that 'it is accurate to call the main innovations capital-saving and cost-reducing, if by this one is referring to the costs of a unit of output. By themselves they vastly increased the capital behind production.' The capital-saving characteristics of technological progress must not be overestimated.]

financed, and capital from external sources also made an important contribution in the initial stages. The most important – indeed perhaps the only important – supply of such capital came from commerce, especially from merchants who invested large sums in the industries producing the goods they sold. The most spectacular example is that of the iron merchants and wholesale ironmongers in Bristol and London who played a decisive part in establishing the South Wales iron industry. This region had no industrial tradition and its expansion was due solely to the arrival of entrepreneurs and capital from England; the capital was principally of mercantile origin.[1] Thus, the Cyfarthfa works was built in 1765 by Anthony Bacon who had made his fortune in a variety of enterprises, including iron trading. After his death the works was taken over in 1786–7 by Richard Crawshay, a self-made man who had become a prosperous iron merchant in London, and he was to make it the largest ironworks in Britain.[2] Other works were built by partnerships of ironmasters and merchants, but it was the latter who supplied the greater part of the capital, and often went on to take an active part in the management; the Ebbw Vale and Nantyglo ironworks are examples, as they were financed by the Harford brothers, who were wealthy Bristol Quakers, and likewise the works of Penydarren, Tredegar and Abernant.[3] Iron merchants and ironmasters were also joint financers of the tinplate industry.[4]

In other industries 'merchant' capital, usually from an associated trade, played a much less important, although by

[1] Bristol iron merchants had, at an earlier date, already financed the charcoal iron industry of South Wales (John, *Industrial Development of S. Wales*, pp. 31–2); some of them had sponsored Abraham Darby I; and Richard Reynolds was the son of one of them (Raistrick, op. cit., p. 12). The Caddells, who were among the founders of Carron, included the importing of wood and iron among their activities.

[2] Addis, op. cit., pp. 1–12; John, *Industrial Development of S. Wales*, pp. 24–5. During the American War of Independence three smaller ironworks were built or taken over by iron merchants. Hoselitz (op. cit., p. 324) points out that in 1788 nine out of twenty-five people occupying an 'entrepreneurial position' in the South Wales iron industry were merchants.

[3] John, *Industrial Development of S. Wales*, pp. 32–5, 116, points out that these merchants, thanks to their contacts with the financial centres of London and Bristol, were later well placed to procure the considerable capital needed to expand these large works. The Harfords also invested in copper-smelting.

[4] Minchinton, op. cit., pp. 17, 20, 97–8.

no means negligible part. It seems that London coal merchants invested in the Northumberland and Durham coalfields,[1] London and Bristol merchants in the South Wales coal mines;[2] in 1750 the coal magnate in the St Helens area was Sarah Clayton, the daughter of a wealthy Liverpool merchant.[3]

In the textile industries, purely commercial capital was probably of secondary importance compared with that supplied by merchant-manufacturers. However, the foundation of the largest mechanized flax-spinning firm in Britain was largely financed by merchant capital. It was set up by John Marshall, who financed in part the building of his first mill in 1791 by disposing of the modest linen-draper's business left to him by his father. He subsequently expanded his spinning mill in 1793 by forming a partnership with Thomas and Benjamin Benyon, two rich woollen merchants from Shrewsbury, who subsequently financed the construction of a second mill there by selling their draper's business.[4]

D. C. Coleman points out that in the paper industry a number of businesses were created or taken over and developed with the help of capital provided by stationers – wholesale paper merchants. He mentions particularly the two London stationers, H. and S. Fourdrinier, who used capital from their trading business to finance the development of the 'Fourdrinier' machine (derived from an invention by the Frenchman Robert) which was the starting point of mechanization within the paper industry.[5]

In the brewing trade, there was a different pattern of capital movement from commerce to industry; a fair number of enter-

[1] E. Hughes, *North Country Life in the Eighteenth Century. The North-East, 1700–1750* (London, 1952), p. 163.

[2] John, *Industrial Development of S. Wales*, pp. 26–7. Much later on, coal merchants like George Insole invested capital for developing the Rhondda Valley coalfield (Lewis, op. cit., pp. 46–7).

[3] Barker and Harris, op. cit., pp. 25–7, 46, 50, 53. A lot of mercantile capital was also invested in the Cornish copper mines (Rowe, op. cit., p. 22).

[4] W. G. Rimmer, *Marshalls of Leeds, Flax-spinners, 1788–1886* (Cambridge, 1960), pp. 10–14, 22–3, 26–7, 36–41, 44, 55. [See also Chapman, *Early Factory Masters*, pp. 17, 77, on investment by drapers and mercers in the Midlands cotton industry.]

[5] Coleman, op. cit., pp. 163–9, 179–83, 235–6. In 1807 the Fourdriniers withdrew £60,228 from their trading business; these massive withdrawals brought about their bankruptcy in 1810. Printers and publishers also put capital into the paper industry.

prises were established or taken over by merchants who dealt in the raw materials of brewing, especially malt merchants.[1]

There were also cases – but one gains the impression that they were relatively scarce – where merchants invested their capital in industries unconnected with their former businesses. The Pleasley cotton-spinning mill in Derbyshire was founded in 1785 by five partners, of whom one was a Nottingham brass merchant and three were drapers.[2] In 1803 three Bristol linen-drapers went into partnership with J. Homfray to operate the Hirwaun ironworks.[3]

It may seem surprising that there has so far been, in this discussion of 'merchant' capital, no mention of capital accumulated in the colonial trade. Some writers (e.g. Eric Williams) maintain that the huge profits made in colonial trade were used to finance the Industrial Revolution, which was thus based on colonial exploitation and the slave trade. A. P. Wadsworth asserts also that Liverpool 'fertilized' Lancashire, where 'new branches of capitalist enterprise' were created with the profits of the trade in slaves and colonial produce. H. Hamilton, for his part, claims that the Glasgow tobacco lords financed the beginnings of the Scottish Industrial Revolution, after the American War of Independence had destroyed the tobacco trade, and diverted their capital into the cotton industry.[4] These are attractive theses, but their authors have been unable to provide supporting evidence.[5]

---

[1] Mathias, *The Brewing Industry*, pp. 255–6, points out that commerce was, in the eighteenth century, the most important 'external' source of entrepreneurs and capital in this industry. [Also his *First Industrial Nation*, p. 157.]

[2] S. Piggott, *Hollins. A Study of Industry. 1748–1949* (Nottingham, 1949), pp. 21–4.

[3] John, *Industrial Development of S. Wales*, pp. 31–2, 34. John and Thomas Butler, who founded Kirkstall Forge in 1779, were merchants (R. Butler, *The History of Kirkstall Forge through Seven Centuries, A.D. 1200–1954*, 2nd ed., York, 1954, p. 22); Charles Roe of Macclesfield left the silk industry between 1762 and 1764 to invest all his capital in the copper industry (Chaloner, 'Charles Roe', p. 138).

[4] Wadsworth and Mann, op. cit., pp. 212, 224; Hamilton, op. cit., pp. 3–5, 120.

[5] In this connection, see M. L. Robertson (op. cit., p. 130), who writes: 'It is possible, though there is little evidence to support the assumption, that there may have been some financial connection between the one-time tobacco merchants and the new industrial developments. . . . It is, however, impossible to estimate to what extent capital thrown idle by the failure of the tobacco trade was behind these new developments.'

[R. Cameron *et al.*, *Banking in the Early Stages of Industrialization. A Study in*

As a matter of fact, the fortunes amassed by West India planters and merchants, or by East India nabobs, were used to buy landed estates in Britain or Government stocks, and to make mortgage loans to planters, but not for investment in industry. As R. Pares neatly remarked, the West India merchants built 'more Fonthills than factories'.[1]

In fact one can find only a very few cases – and these seem exceptional – of direct investment of 'colonial' capital in the new 'factory' industries. Anthony Bacon admittedly had important colonial interests; it is also worth noting that some Bristol West India merchants set up a copper-smelting works near Swansea in 1737 and that in 1778 the Sirhowy ironworks was established by a group of London tea and spices merchants.[2] There were also important 'East India investors' among the sponsors of the British Cast Plate Glass Manufacturers (1773);[3] and R. Dunmore who, with the Buchanans, set up the Ballindalloch spinning mill, was a former Virginia merchant.[4]

Comparative Economic History (London, 1967), p. 65; recent research has failed to reveal massive direct transfers of capital from the tobacco trade to the cotton industry; some tobacco merchants shifted to the West Indies sugar trade, others invested in a variety of industrial and mercantile ventures or purchased landed estates; a favourite investment was in banking. However, Cameron thinks that Scotland benefited from the American War, as it released large quantities of capital from an employment that had few linkages either backward or forward, and made it available for domestic investment generally.

R. Ford, 'Tobacco and Coal: A Note on the Economic History of White-haven', *Economica*, IX, no. 26 (June 1929), pp. 192–6, does not really prove his point that the profits of the Whitehaven tobacco trade were used to develop coal mining.]

[1] K. G. Davies, 'Empire and Capital', *Economic History Review*, 2nd series, XIII (1960), p. 110. Moreover, at the end of the eighteenth century the West Indies, far from being a source of capital for English industry, consumed enormous capital sums for their own development; cf. S. G. Checkland, 'Finance for the West Indies, 1780–1815', *Economic History Review*, 2nd series, X (1958), pp. 461–3.

[W. E. Minchinton, in H. G. J. Aitken (ed.), *Explorations in Enterprise* (Cambridge, Mass., 1965), pp. 283–4, stresses that merchants wanted to become country gentlemen rather than to perpetuate their business, and founded very few mercantile dynasties.]

[2] John, *Industrial Development of S. Wales*, pp. 8, 25.

[3] Barker and Harris, op. cit., p. 113.

[4] M. L. Robertson, op. cit., p. 130. The Caddells (see above, p. 173 n. 1) had colonial interests, and the Dunlops, founders of the Clyde ironworks, had been American merchants.

All this does not amount to much, but, on the other hand, there is no doubt that the rise of colonial trade influenced indirectly British industry and stimulated its growth by widening its markets and enriching the country.[1] However, as Ashton points out, the Industrial Revolution gathered momentum after 1783, by which time England had lost the thirteen colonies and the sugar islands were on the decline.[2]

As for 'landed' capital, i.e. that of the great landowners, it seems to have played an altogether minor part in financing the Industrial Revolution, with the exception of coal-mining; its contribution was much less important in the eighteenth than in the seventeenth century, when landowners had supplied large funds to industry, and it tended to decline.[3] This withdrawal of landed capital can be explained mainly by competition from other outlets for investment which seemed both safer and equally profitable: agriculture (enclosure and technological progress absorbed vast sums, attracted by the increase in grain prices during the second half of the eighteenth century),[4] turnpike trusts and canal shares,[5] Government stocks. Moreover, technological progress raised the costs of investing in mining or in the metal industries and placed them beyond the reach of the mere gentry, inasmuch as at the same time its consumption expenditures were increasing.[6] It is also possible

[1] It was not by accident that the merchants of a great 'colonial' port like Bristol supplied industry with a lot of capital; admittedly it was the iron merchants who invested in the Welsh iron industry and not the West India merchants, but the former supplied the latter with merchandise to export to the colonies.

[According to Mathias, *First Industrial Nation*, p. 105, some direct connexion developed between commercial wealth in Glasgow and Liverpool, and industrial investment in the textile industries of their hinterland; merchants were in the partnerships of some mills; considerable mercantile credit flowed from the merchant to the manufacturer.]

[2] Ashton, *An Economic History*, p. 125.

[3] [L. Stone, 'The Nobility in Business, 1540–1640', in *The Entrepreneur. Papers presented at the Annual Conference of the Economic History Society at Cambridge, England, April 1957*, p. 14: it was between 1540 and 1640 'rather than later that the English nobility had its greatest influence on the growth of the economy'; moreover, most of their enterprise in mining and industry took place in the late sixteenth century.]

[4] Ashton, *An Economic History*, p. 41.

[5] Obviously, the improvement of transport was essential to industrial growth (mostly by sharply reducing the price of coal), so investment in roads and canals had an indirect influence on industrial investment.

[6] For the same reason, the landowners' role as 'passive' suppliers of fixed capital (leasing mills and blast furnaces to entrepreneurs, etc.) diminished.

that there was a psychological block, in that direct involvement in industry was felt to be beneath a gentleman. Eventually the net flow of capital may have been from industry into landowning, as the newly rich industrialists, such as Richard Arkwright, Samuel Whitbread I or T. Williams, hastened to buy large landed estates.[1]

Until the eighteenth century big landowners had supplied the iron industry with a large slice of its capital, but during the first half of the century they took an increasingly less active part in production,[2] while continuing to supply part of the fixed capital by leasing blast furnaces, forges and watermills to the ironmasters. But they subsequently retreated even further and, with one or two exceptions, they seem to have taken no part in the financing of the large ironworks which are typical of the Industrial Revolution.[3] As for the textile industries, investment by landowners seems to have been almost nil, although one or two instances are recorded in Scotland'[4]

Coleman, op. cit., p. 246, points out that in the nineteenth century, owing to technical progress, it was no longer possible to set up a competitive paper mill by renting a flour or fulling-mill and converting it; a special building had to be put up.

[1] Admittedly the nouveau-riche industrialists' investments in landed property sometimes provided a sort of reserve (e.g. for M. Boulton and S. Oldknow), and enabled them to obtain mortgage loans when they needed money (see also below, p. 185).

[2] e.g. R. L. Downes, 'The Stour Partnership, 1726–36. A Note on Landed Capital in the Iron Industry', *Economic History Review*, 2nd series, III (1950), pp. 90–6. This article studies the case of Sir Thomas Lyttleton who, in 1726, held three-sevenths of the capital of an ironworks in Worcestershire; he quarrelled with his partners, who were 'genuine industrialists', because he wanted to take out all his share of the profits each year, whereas the others wanted to let them accumulate and even to borrow in order to expand the business. Sir Thomas finally withdrew in 1736. The only exceptions are backward areas, like Wales, where, around 1750, landowners were still the most important ironmasters.

[3] Ashton, *Iron and Steel*, p. 209; John, *Industrial Development of S. Wales*, p. 8. See one exception around 1815, in A. H. Dodd, *The Industrial Revolution in North Wales* (Cardiff, 1933), pp. 144–5.

[Also Birch, *The Economic History*, pp. 86–90, and 'A Nobleman's Enterprise during the Industrial Revolution', *Bulletin of the John Rylands Library*, vol. 35, no. 2 (1953), pp. 316–33, on the Haigh Ironworks, in which the partners were the Earl of Balcarres, his brother and one Wigan founder; but this venture was unsuccessful.]

[4] Hamilton, *Industrial Revolution in Scotland*, pp. 126–7, 129. Revolution Mill is an exceptional case; it was built in 1788 in Nottinghamshire by the Rev. Edmund Cartwright, and financed, probably with landed capital, by his brother,

The situation was, however, different in the coal industry,[1] where, throughout the eighteenth century, a large part of the capital was supplied by landowners who themselves exploited the mines, and who included even members of the aristocracy, like the Duke of Bridgewater. Even when some of them preferred to lease the rights of working their deposits to capitalist entrepreneurs, the latter were often of the same social class; the Northumberland–Durham coalfields thus had their colliery gentry.[2] However, even in this industry, a withdrawal of landed capital is noticeable; in the St Helens area[3] it began before 1750; it happened after this date in South Wales, where the landowners who had hitherto dominated the coal industry began to give up working their collieries and leased them to English industrialists or merchants.[4]

It could be possible, however, that industrial entrepreneurs

Major John, and eighteen friends and relations, to exploit the power-loom. But the enterprise soon ran into difficulties; cf. W. H. Chaloner, 'The Cartwright Brothers. Their Contribution to the Wool Industry', *Wool Knowledge*, II (1953), p. 18.

[Chapman, *Early Factory Masters*, p. 95: 'The landed interest played a minor role in the textile enterprise of the Midlands in this period.']

[1] Landlords also invested in the copper mines of Cornwall and Anglesey; cf. Rowe, op. cit., pp. 20, 22; Barker and Harris, op. cit., p. 77.

[2] Ashton and Sykes, op. cit., pp. 1–3. But Hughes (op. cit., p. xviii) points out that this gentry of the North-East was of recent origin and had made their fortune in trade, eliminating the old catholic gentry. Moreover, they lacked liquid funds and had to borrow from solicitors, goldsmiths and merchants (ibid., pp. 158, 163).

[3] Barker and Harris, op. cit., pp. 24–5, 27, 45, especially on the decline and fall of the Cases of Redhasles, who had been the prominent coal-owners at the beginning of the eighteenth century. At the end of the century, however, some gentlemen were still exploiting their mines.

[4] John, *Industrial Development of S. Wales*, pp. 9–10, 36–7; also, his 'Iron and Coal on a Glamorgan Estate, 1700–1740', *Economic History Review*, XIII (1943), pp. 93–4, 103. As soon as 1749, the Mansell family disposed of its mines at Briton Ferry to a London merchant. The same sort of thing was happening in North Wales (Dodd, op. cit., pp. 195, 307). We do not know how far this withdrawal continued at the beginning of the nineteenth century, but D. Spring ('The English Landed Estate in the Age of Coal and Iron: 1830–1880', *Journal of Economic History*, XI (1951), pp. 3–24; especially pp. 4–6, 11, 14, 20–1) maintains that after 1830 landowners' interest and participation in industrial enterprises revived. He mentions some very large landowners who went in for mining on their own account and sometimes even entered the iron industry. These enterprises, however, seem to have been financed mainly by capital borrowed on mortgage, especially from insurance companies. Most squires preferred simply to let their mining rights.

drew from 'landed' sources part of their capital. Some writers have suggested this, pointing out that many eighteenth-century industrialists came from rural families.[1] However, many of them – like Abraham Darby I, R. Crawshay, D. Dale, J. McConnel – left the land early on and obtained no capital from it for their later enterprises. On the other hand, Samuel Whitbread I, son of a rich Bedfordshire yeoman, used the £2,600 inherited from his parents[2] for his initial outlay when he set up as a brewer in 1742; and some yeomen farmers, like the Peels or Joshua Fielden, combined farming with industry and developed the latter up to the 'factory' level.[3] But it is difficult to believe that income from the land made more than a marginal contribution to their success. My view is that, in the eighteenth century, the ownership or exploitation of a small rural property facilitated the entry of some entrepreneurs into industry and supplied them with some capital[4] (or perhaps gave them a means of obtaining more by mortgage); but this entry was only on a small scale – as an artisan or small merchant-manufacturer – so that if these yeomen-industrialists went on to found large enterprises, they did it with capital accumulated through industrial production.[5]

It was accepted for a long time that the English banking system, despite its precocious development, played no direct part in the financing of the Industrial Revolution; recent

[1] For example, Mantoux, op. cit., pp. 379–82.

[2] Mathias, *The Brewing Industry*, pp. 257, 261.

[3] Mantoux, op. cit., pp. 379–80; Redford, op. cit., pp. 50–1; Daniels, *Early English Cotton Industry*, pp. 141–2.

We know that J. Fielden was a small landowner, who owned a few weaving looms; about 1780 he bought some spinning-jennies and twenty years later was the head of a large cotton-spinning firm.

[Chapman, 'The Peels', p. 61; the yeoman-farming background of the Peel family is a legend; in the seventeenth century, they were woollen manufacturers, but also owned a farm, which much later Robert 'Parsley' Peel mortgaged to raise capital (possibly £2,000) for his calico-printing partnership.]

[4] This was probably the case with Joseph Rogerson who ran a scribbling mill at Bramley in Yorkshire (Crump, op. cit., pp. 6, 62), and with G. Beechcroft, one of the partners in Kirkstall Forge (Butler, *History of Kirkstall Forge*, p. 22); both of them were also farmers.

[5] Let it be said that marriages with landowning wives were also advantageous to both M. Boulton and J. Wilkinson, but their cases are rather exceptional! Cf. E. Roll, *An Early Experiment in Industrial Organization, being a History of the Firm of Boulton and Watt, 1775–1805* (London, 1930), pp. 10, 100; Chaloner, 'Isaac Wilkinson', p. 35.

research has modified this opinion by showing that the banks did often underwrite the expansion of existing concerns, as we shall see later. But as far as helping to found or start off new firms is concerned, L. S. Pressnell supports the traditional negative theory: 'The evidence,' he writes, 'is all against it.'[1] The story that Richard Arkwright, on his arrival in Nottingham, managed at first to interest Wright's Bank in his invention and that they some time later withdrew, remains typical.[2] M. Boulton did indeed obtain substantial credit from the London bank of Lowe, Vere, Williams and Jennings to develop Watt's steam engine and to set up the firm of Boulton and Watt, and a subsequent loan from Praed and Co. of Truro;[3] the Carron Company received some advances from several Scottish banks in its early years, supposedly on a short-term basis, but it used these partly for building purposes.[4] In the same way, John Marshall, in 1792–3, was allowed an overdraft (in April 1793, £3,783)[5] by Beckett & Co.'s bank. These seem to be isolated instances, however, to be explained perhaps by the

[1] L. S. Pressnell, *Country Banking in the Industrial Revolution* (Oxford, 1956), p. 337.

[2] Mantoux, op. cit., p. 228; Fitton and Wadsworth, op. cit., p. 63 (but both authors point out that the authenticity of the anecdote is unproven). See also Ashton, *Peter Stubbs*, p. 116, who notes, significantly, that it was not until P. Stubbs had secured a solid position and built his factory that the Warrington bank of Parr, Lyon & Co. began to advance him capital, and his account became a debit one instead of a credit one.

[3] Roll, op. cit., pp. 100–2; Pressnell, *Country Banking*, p. 331; J. Lord, *Capital and Steam Power, 1750–1800* (London, 1923), pp. 112–13. M. Boulton had great difficulty in obtaining advances from Lowe and Vere's bank during the 1778 crisis and had to find securities.

[When writing this passage, I had overlooked the article by J. E. Cule, 'Finance and Industry in the Eighteenth Century: the Firm of Boulton and Watt', *Economic History*, IV, no. 15 (February 1940), pp. 319–25; it proves convincingly that the steam engine enterprise of Boulton and Watt was not financed by the hardware manufactory of Boulton and Fothergill, and that no money was borrowed from banks for assisting it. Boulton's financial difficulties resulted from the disastrous course run by Boulton and Fothergill, and his borrowings were intended to rescue it; he was saved from disaster by the profits from the steam engine business and by its mortgaging in 1778.]

[4] Campbell, 'Financing of Carron Company', pp. 23–5, 29–30, 33. One of these banks even agreed to extend credit up to £17,000, provided that it became the owner of a quarter of the capital (but it went bankrupt shortly afterwards). However, we must not forget the peculiarities of the Scottish banking system. The part played by the London banker, John Dawes, in the founding of the famous Parys Mine Co. is also exceptional (Harris, op. cit., p. 141).

[5] Rimmer, op. cit., pp. 37, 55. Later on his partners, the Benyons, obtained a mortgage loan of £6,000 from a London bank.

personal credit of the beneficiaries who had already a strong local position. But, towards the end of our period, when the banking system had developed and consolidated, it was possibly more ready to back new enterprises; thus, in their early years, the Greenall–Pilkington glassworks on the one hand, and the firm of John Foster on the other, were allowed permanent and considerable overdrafts by their local banks.[1]

One last source of capital remains to be considered, which, for want of a better word, we shall call 'Miscellaneous'. I refer to capital provided by members of the professions, by tradesmen, by road hauliers, by fund-holders, not to mention the very rare instances of foreign capital (i.e. Dutch).[2] Such capital can be glimpsed especially in copper-and-coal mining, in the paper industry,[3] and it was perhaps also attracted by the boom in cotton-spinning after 1783.[4] It played no important part directly, but entrepreneurs found in it a useful source of supplementary capital and borrowed from relatives, friends and members of their own nonconformist sects. Such was the case with John Marshall in 1792–3, and W. G. Rimmer comments humorously that old ladies – rich widows or spinsters – were a very convenient source of capital for him. Probably this remark is widely applicable. . . .[5]

It is thus obvious that the founders of 'factory' industries obtained capital from diverse sources, but that these sources were of unequal importance; industry itself supplied most of

[1] Barker, op. cit., pp. 63, 77, 95; Sigsworth, op. cit., pp. 175–6, 178.

[2] T. S. Ashton, *An Economic History*, p. 127; also his *The Industrial Revolution*, p. 107; Roll, op. cit., p. 103; Lord, op. cit., p. 133.

[3] John, *Industrial Development of S. Wales*, p. 27; Barker and Harris, op. cit., pp. 34–5; Rowe, op. cit., p. 22; Coleman, op. cit., pp. 160–3.

[4] Wadsworth and Mann, op. cit., p. 495; Mantoux, op. cit., pp. 376–7.

[Chapman, *Early Factory Masters*, pp. 21–2, 77, 81, 92–6, 99, points out that Arkwright's spectacular success attracted to cotton-spinning a number of speculators without previous contact with the textile industries, but with money to invest; their background and resources were varied: retail traders, potters, brewers, builders, London commission agents of provincial hosiers, and also people from some declining industries of the Midlands area – lead, iron, silk.]

[5] Rimmer, op. cit., pp. 36–7. Admittedly such capital came, in fact, from land or from trade. In this way Samuel Whitbread I borrowed from his family and friends to set himself up in 1736 (Mathias, *The Brewing Industry*, p. 261).

[A. J. Robertson, 'Robert Owen and the Campbell Debt, 1810–1822', *Business History*, XI, no. 1 (January 1969), pp. 17–18; during his conflict with Archibald Campbell of Jura, Robert Owen was saved from bankruptcy by his four sistersin-law, David Dale's daughters, who were unmarried, but very rich.]

the capital for its own transformation; commerce provided an important supplementary reservoir, but the part played by landed capital, bank capital and 'miscellaneous' sources seems very small. Within industry the analysis made above confirms the thesis that capital moved from the 'secondary' to the 'primary' or 'basic' industries; commercial capital showed a similar backward motion. Thus we see a flow of capital into the primary iron industry coming from the light metal trades or from iron merchants; then from the primary iron industry into coal-mining. Cotton-spinning mills were similarly financed with funds amassed in the making or merchanting of textile goods.[1] The reasons for this are evident: the deficiencies of basic industries at the onset of the Industrial Revolution compared with consumer goods industries; bottlenecks in the production of semi-finished goods such as cotton yarn or bar-iron; high profitability from such productions once technical innovations had cut down costs; the desire of the users of these products to ensure a constant supply and to take a share in the high profits obtained in the primary industries.

Naturally, when examined in detail, capital flows are complex, and each industry, each industrial district has its own pattern of finance; the importance of 'merchant' capital in the South Wales iron industry is not found in other siderurgical areas; massive investment by merchant-manufacturers seems to belong only to cotton-spinning; coal-mining is an exception because of the preponderance of landed capital. These differences are due to the more or less capitalistic structure of each industry and to variations in profitability.

On the other hand, capital from diverse sources was used not only in each industry, but often in many individual enterprises. Of course we can find some which were founded solely on 'artisan' or 'commercial' capital, but generally speaking an entrepreneur had to rely on various sources to collect enough capital to found a sizeable new undertaking. We need only

---

[1] In the same way, industries making copper goods in London, Bristol and Birmingham financed to a great extent copper-smelting works (and even copper mines), mainly by founding curious co-operative societies, such as the Birmingham Copper Company (1780).Cf. John, *Industrial Development of S. Wales*, pp. 28–9; H. Hamilton, *The English Brass and Copper Industry to 1800* (London, 1926), pp. 219, 234, 236. In contrast, after 1820, cotton spinners tended to add power-weaving sheds to their mills (Ashton, *The Industrial Revolution*, p. 75).

G

mention M. Boulton, who financed Boulton and Watt with the help of 'industrial' and 'landed' capital, augmented by loans from friends and by bankers' advances; or John Marshall supplementing his original 'commercial' capital by borrowing from family and friends, by a bank overdraft and by the support of two successive groups of partners. The formation of a partnership was an entrepreneur's natural expedient when in need of capital; this pattern of business organization, which was predominant during the Industrial Revolution, provided, particularly for men of modest origin, an opportunity of supplementing the limited capital they had acquired as artisans or petty industrialists, through the support of richer individuals;[1] it was mainly in this way that much commercial capital came to be invested in industry. Thus in 1702 Abraham Darby I went into partnership with some Bristol merchants to establish his foundry; then with J. Peters and G. Prankard in 1709 to set up at Coalbrookdale; then with R. Champion in 1711 and T. Goldney in 1716 – the latter being both Bristol iron merchants.[2] In South Wales many ironworks were founded by partnerships which united ironmasters, like the Homfrays, and merchants from Bristol or London.[3]

Borrowing was another resort, loans being frequently obtained from relatives and friends; we need only cite once again the cases of John Marshall, Samuel Whitbread I and M. Boulton, all of whom are illustrations of Peter Mathias' excellent observations on the importance of kinship in the financial structure of eighteenth-century business.[4]

Loans obtained from outside the family were often secured by a mortgage; Abraham Darby mortgaged half of Coalbrookdale to T. Goldney to get a loan of £1,600, probably for

---

[1] The role played by partnerships in the take-off of business enterprises seems to have been peculiar to Britain, at least compared to France, where the one man or the strictly family firm was the rule.

[2] Raistrick, op. cit., p. 6. J. Wedgwood also had two successive partners at the beginning of his career, and in 1769, when he was founding Etruria, he joined with the Liverpool merchant, T. Bentley (Hower, op. cit., pp. 286, 288).

[3] John, *Industrial Development of S. Wales*, pp. 33–5.

[At an earlier period, A. Crowley III raised the capital for his Sunderland works in fairly small quantities from a number of diverse sources; M. W. Flinn, *Men of Iron. The Crowleys in the Early Iron Industry* (Edinburgh, 1962), p. 178.]

[4] Mathias, *The Brewing Industry*, pp. 261, 271; also Roll, op. cit., pp. 10–11, 100.

the construction of a blast furnace. M. Boulton mortgaged his own and his wife's lands, then the 'premiums' paid by some of the users of Watt's steam engines; Oldknow mortgaged his lands at Mellor to Richard Arkwright for a loan of £12,000 in order to build Mellor Mill.[1]

One can wonder, still, whether this system of finance was adequate to the needs of a fast-growing large-scale industry.[2] In a brilliant article published in 1935, Professor Postan maintained that the pioneers of the Industrial Revolution did suffer from a shortage of capital, which, for being 'local rather than general and social rather than material', was none the less acute. No 'general reservoir of national savings' existed in the eighteenth century, only 'a multiplicity of small disjointed pools'; there was no national capital market, only a number of local and specialized markets; in addition to this, psychological and institutional obstacles prevented most of the considerable capital which had accumulated in Britain (especially landed wealth) from being invested in industry; new enterprises, restricted to the personal savings of their founders, eked out by those of their family and friends, could hardly have profited from the fact that England was the richest country in Europe.[3]

It is debatable whether the main obstacles to the mobilization of savings were of a legal or psychological nature. A. H. John is inclined to favour the former theory, stating that many people would have been ready to invest in industry, had it not been for the risk of losing their entire fortune thereby, because unlimited liability was then the general rule.[4] On the other hand,

[1] Raistrick, op. cit., pp. 6, 50; Roll, op. cit., pp. 10, 100, 102–3; Unwin, op. cit., pp. 16–17, 85, 140, 147, 156; also Coleman, op. cit., pp. 162, 247–50, who draws attention to the frequency of mortgages as a source of capital in the paper industry. Mortgages were more commonly taken on land belonging to industrialists than on the factories themselves, and thus they are a contribution of landed capital to the formation of industrial capital (see also p. 178, n. 1).

[2] Of course, when talking about shortage or abundance of capital, we are using these terms relatively; they mean shortage or abundance in relation to other factors of production or to other countries.

[3] M. M. Postan, 'Recent Trends in the Accumulation of Capital', *Economic History Review*, VI (1935), pp. 2–5.

John has recently expressed similar views (*Industrial Development of S. Wales*, p. 57), in connexion with the industrialization of South Wales; also S. Pollard, 'Investment, Consumption and the Industrial Revolution', *Economic History Review*, 2nd series, XI (1958), pp. 218, 221–2.

[4] John, *Industrial Development of S. Wales*, p. 53. He points out, however, (pp. 54, 168) that joint stock companies launched in the Welsh iron industry in the

Ashton thinks that the Bubble Act did nothing to impede the rise of large-scale industry, because the latter did not need joint stock incorporation.[1] Pressnell adds that the limited-liability company would probably not have spread widely, even if there had been no legal difficulties, as is proved by the slowness with which English industrialists adopted it once the legal obstacles had been removed.[2]

Anyway, there is no doubt that in the eighteenth century

second quarter of the nineteenth century mostly failed, and that the personal element remained very strong, since most of the stockholders were inhabitants of the region.

[See also Birch, *The Economic History*, pp. 201–5; Cameron, op. cit., p. 35, thinks likewise that the mere existence of the Bubble Act hindered the flow of capital into industry.]

[1] Ashton, *An Economic History*, p. 119. Of course, it was possible to create a joint stock company by private Act of Parliament; and 'illegal' companies, created without authorization, were almost never prosecuted. In the mining industry they were fairly numerous (Dodd, op. cit., pp. 308–9). In manufacturing industry, one finds as many 'legal' as 'illegal' joint stock companies, but either way, they are exceptional. An example is the British Cast Plate Glass Company recently studied by Barker, op. cit., pp. 47–50, and Barker and Harris, op. cit., pp. 113 ff. It was founded in 1773 by Act of Parliament and built a very big plate-glass factory near St Helens, but it did not become prosperous until after 1782. It managed to attract capital from various sources, as it had, among the stockholders, members of the aristocracy, West and East India merchants (cf. p. 176), copper and coal magnates and, later, London bankers.

[The Equitable Trust was a form of company organization enabling promoters to avoid the terms of the Bubble Act; it has been discovered in activities such as insurance, road building, the brass industry, etc., where it was exploited for the purpose of raising capital and limiting liability; R. S. Neale, 'An Equitable Trust in the Building Industry in 1794', *Business History*, VII, no. 2 (July 1965), pp. 94–6.]

[2] Pressnell, *Country Banking*, p. 285; his opinion is supported by W. H. B. Court, *A Concise Economic History of Britain. From 1750 to Recent Times* (Cambridge, 1954), p. 36 [and by S. G. Checkland, *The Rise of Industrial Society in England, 1815–1885* (London, 1964), pp. 13–14, 203–4, who stresses that limited liability was not effective over much of industry before the last decades of the nineteenth century, and that the joint stock companies which proliferated after the repeal of the Bubble Act in 1825 were in public utilities and foreign mining companies. For the eighteenth century, P. G. M. Dickson, *The Financial Revolution in England. A Study in the Development of Public Credit, 1688–1756* (London, 1967), p. 489, stresses that the Bubble Act was a less serious obstacle to company flotation than was presumed and above all that the saving classes were mostly interested either in fixed interest securities or in the purely speculative chances offered by Government lotteries; and the rudimentary state of business organization precluded the offer to the investing public of many safe shares or debentures.] The question of the role and possibilities of joint stock companies remains open.

capital had a highly personal and specific character; it was far from being the abstract and mobile factor of production[1] it was to become in the nineteenth century; personal relationships were still at the bottom of most investments. On the other hand, one can wonder whether there was a real shortage of capital during the Industrial Revolution. To take some examples, Boulton and Watt had serious financial difficulties, but they managed to overcome them;[2] as for the Carron Company, its initial vicissitudes seem to be the result of special circumstances: over-ambitious plans at the outset, underestimation of building costs, and the founders being ruined in other ventures.[3] Reading records or histories of firms, one does not have the impression that the pioneers of the Industrial Revolution came up against insurmountable problems in raising the long-term capital they needed; what harassed them much more, it would seem, was the 'scarcity of money', of short-term credit, about which they complained incessantly.[4]

On the whole, the eighteenth-century capital market seems, to twentieth-century eyes, badly organized, but the creators of modern industry do not seem to have suffered too much from

[1] We must not, however, exaggerate the immobility of capital in the period under consideration, since, for instance, considerable sums were transferred from England to Wales.

[2] This argument is not, of course, decisive; what we need to know is the marginal cost to which Boulton and Watt would have obtained more capital. Or, inversely, by how much was the perfecting of the steam engine set back by lack of capital.

[3] Campbell, 'Financing of Carron Company', pp. 23–4, 27–8, 30–1.

[4] A point well taken by Wilson, 'The Entrepreneur', p. 115. This conclusion seems to agree with that of H. J. Habakkuk, *American and British Technology in the Nineteenth Century. The Search for Labour-Saving Inventions* (Cambridge, 1962), pp. 70–3, 174–6. He emphasizes that the fact that profits were the main source of fixed capital is not sufficient evidence for claiming *a priori* that they were adequate to finance all the investment that an industrialist wished to make; entrepreneurs who were frustrated by lack of capital leave no trace. There is no theoretical reason why financial institutions should adapt themselves immediately to the demands of industry, when the latter urgently needs capital. Finally, during the French wars it was difficult to borrow, and after 1815 the large savings of rentiers, and even some industrialists' savings, were attracted into Government stocks or into land. Habakkuk concludes from this that we cannot exclude the existence of a financial brake on the growth of British industry, but doubts if it was very powerful. In fact, in the eighteenth century, the rate of accumulation of capital was more rapid than the growth of other factors, in particular the labour force. Thus capital was relatively plentiful.

its imperfection.[1] We shall reach the same conclusion when we consider, after the problem of the initial outlay for the founding of enterprises, that of financing their expansion.

III

The simple answer to this question is the overwhelming predominance of self-finance. Enterprises increased their capital by ploughing back immediately, regularly and almost automatically the greater part, or even the whole of their profits. As we shall see, this increase was very rapid so that machinery and production were expanded at an accelerating rate. Thus most of the additional capital required for expansion was provided from industry's own resources, from the savings of the industrialists. This fact is so obvious as to be almost a cliché and the point is not worth labouring.

The widespread practice of systematically ploughing back profits is, of course, related to specific psychological attitudes and to a certain pattern of mentality: it is largely due to the 'frugality' of the pioneers of the Industrial Revolution. Their origins were often humble, and they were as hard on themselves as they were on others; business was their consuming interest and they continued to lead the simple lives to which they had been early accustomed, practising a stringent personal economy and a rigid austerity, which maximized their savings. They withdrew from their business each year only a small part of its profits for their personal needs, or else they paid themselves a small salary, hardly any higher than a skilled workman's wage. The case of the Walker brothers has become famous; at the beginning they paid themselves a wage of 10s. a week, and not until 1756, fifteen years after the founding of their firm, did they allow themselves a dividend of £140, about 2·5 per cent of their firm's capital value. This annual dividend was later increased, but at a slower rate than their capital

[1] In any case, English industry, compared with that of the Continent, seems to have overflowed with capital. I am grateful to J. R. Harris for pointing out to me that, from the beginning of the eighteenth century, there were large numbers of small 'capitalists' in South Lancashire who were willing to lend money to industry (on good security, of course) through intermediaries such as attorneys; this shows that local capital markets were relatively efficient and that small investors played a more important part than is usually realized.

grew: in 1768 it was £700, or 1·8 per cent of their capital.[1] There is an abundance of similar cases:[2] in the partnership deed signed by McConnel and Kennedy with the Sandfords in 1791, there was a proviso that the profits should be left to accumulate, and that if one of the partners wanted to withdraw his share, he would have to pay interest on it until he had replaced it in the firm; McConnel and Kennedy, as managers, received a salary of £40 a year.[3]

The fact that many, nay the majority of eighteenth-century industrialists belonged to noncornformist sects definitely reinforced their tendency to abstinence, hard work and thrift, and helped to keep them faithful to their simple and frugal way of life, even when they had made a fortune (as with the Darbys), and to discourage them from conspicuous expenditure or aping the upper classes; thus religion was a factor in the rapid accumulation of capital.[4]

We must not, however, over-emphasize the frugality of these early industrialists. Once they had built up their businesses and secured their fortunes, they nearly always relaxed some-what, withdrawing more money and adopting a more comfort-able way of life. Some of them bought landed estates and built themselves large mansions. Mathias describes how the great brewers withdrew considerable sums from their firms and did not at all restrict themselves to a spartan way of life.[5] At Marshalls, from the early years, between 1793 and 1804, the partners drew out a third of the gross profits each year, as an

---

[1] Ashton, *Iron and Steel*, pp. 48, 224; also his *The Industrial Revolution*, pp. 95–7; John (ed.), *The Walker Family*, pp. v, 2–9 ff.

[2] At Kirkstall Forge the partners only took a salary of £30 per annum; at Newton Chambers the 'wages' of the partners were 'absurdly low' – £80 per annum from 1799 to 1811 for G. Newton; and there were no dividends. At Marsh in Sheffield the partners received 29s. a week from 1816 to 1819, then £100 per annum and after 1825, £200; they were so accustomed to frugality that in the years around 1830 they could not manage to lessen their capital by increased withdrawals as they would have wanted. Cf. Butler, *History of Kirkstall Forge*, p. 28; Ashton, *Iron and Steel*, pp. 158, 160; S. Pollard, *Three Centuries of Sheffield Steel. The Story of a Family Business* (Sheffield, 1954), pp. 10, 12, 18.

[3] Daniels, 'The Early Records', pp. 177.

[4] Ashton, *Iron and Steel*, pp. 211, 218, 220, 223, 225.

[5] Mathias, *The Brewing Industry*, pp. 261, 264–5, 553. Benjamin Truman drew out on average only £2,000 a year from 1741 to 1750, while his profits were £6,780; in 1761–3, he drew out £3,744 a year and made two withdrawals of £34,000 altogether. Mathias adds that in the eighteenth century a rapid accumu-lation of capital was quite compatible with the life of a gentleman.

average, and let the other two-thirds accumulate; J. Marshall used to draw £1,800 a year, a large sum then, and, after 1804, £3,000 (between 1793 and 1804, however, his fortune had increased twenty times over!); between 1815 and 1828 his household expenses amounted to £6,000 a year. Rimmer estimates that from 1815 to his death in 1845 he devoted only a limited part of his resources to his flax-spinning mills and spent nearly £1 million in improving his social position.[1]

In spite of all this, there is no doubt that entrepreneurs, at the outset of the Industrial Revolution, reinvested immediately most of their profits (and even the interest on capital), in order to finance expansion; and even after these requirements were met, they left the greater part of their earnings with the firm, which then paid them interest, usually at the rate of 5 per cent. Most of the firms we have mentioned adopted this policy,[2] e.g. the Walker brothers, Newton Chambers, J. Marshall and Co., McConnel and Kennedy.[3] At Cyfarthfa also, in the 1790s, R. Crawshay systematically reinvested his profits each year, a custom kept up by his successors; in 1821 William Crawshay I wrote characteristically to his son that the profit was to be 'left on the spot . . . to support that which created it'.[4] At Pleasley Mill, profits made in the early years were never distributed, but either kept in reserve or reinvested. The first dividend was paid in 1796, after ten years of production, and then it was only £439 for a total annual profit of £1,439.[5]

This state of affairs enabled a number of enterprises – possibly most of them – to finance expansion entirely from their own resources. John points out that self-finance was the rule in the South Wales iron industry. Mathias makes the same observation about the brewing industry.[6] To which we can

---

[1] Rimmer, op. cit., pp. 47, 70, 91, 97–102. On the other hand, Sigsworth (op. cit., pp. 220–1) estimates that the Fosters never led a very austere life, but that was well into the nineteenth century and industrialists' habits had changed greatly since the beginnings of the Industrial Revolution.

[2] One finds many such examples from the first half of the eighteenth century onwards, the Stour partnership, for instance; Downes, op. cit., pp. 91–2.

[3] Ashton, *Iron and Steel*, pp. 48, 158; John (ed.), *The Walker Family*, p. v; Pollard, *Three Centuries*, p. 12; Daniels, 'The Early Records', pp. 177–8.

[4] Addis, op. cit., pp. 155–6. William Crawshay I and II disapproved of investing in landed property.

[5] Pigott, op. cit., pp. 37–40.

[6] John, *Industrial Development of S. Wales*, pp. 41–2; Mathias, *The Brewing Industry*, p. 252.

add that the Crawshays never borrowed, so that Cyfarthfa was completely self-financed.[1] John Marshall, who had borrowed a lot to start his flax-spinning mill, was able to finance his considerable expansion after 1794 from his profits;[2] the Marsh firm in Sheffield was able to do likewise on a lesser scale.[3]

Many firms, however, had to look outside for the capital they needed to expand. They could choose one of several methods. The first was to take new partners into the firm; it was the simplest way but it had serious disadvantages, especially for individualists whose dispositions were autocratic, like most entrepreneurs of the Industrial Revolution, as it could lead soon to disputes about the management of the firm and the distribution of profits. There are actually very few examples among the larger concerns, whose owners usually wanted as few partners as possible, so that one more often sees them manœuvring to oust irritating associates.[4] There is, however, one important exception: at the beginning of the nineteenth century, the great London breweries had embarked on a campaign destined to secure their outlets through control of the retail sales of beer (tying the trade). This necessitated an enormous capital outlay that could not be met by accumulated profits and they were forced to take in new partners, usually wealthy merchants and bankers.[5]

Firms more usually borrowed – on mortgage, bond or note of hand – from family and friends, solicitors and attorneys (or through their agency), or from other manufacturers or merchants with whom they had connexions. Such loans were normally made on a temporary basis, but they sometimes became quasi-permanent, or else a second loan was sought in order to pay the first. John considers that semi-permanent loan capital played a secondary but not unimportant role (compared

[1] Addis, op. cit., p. 159.

[2] Rimmer, op. cit., p. 47. Even when he had to buy out his partners, the Benyons, in 1804, J. Marshall drew almost entirely on his own resources.

[3] Pollard, *Three Centuries*, p. 18. This firm was allowed some short-term overdrafts by banks.

[4] For example, J. Marshall's quarrel with the Benyons ended in their separating in 1804; W. Crawshay I eliminated his partners, B. Hall and J. Bailey.

[However, D. S. Landes, *The Unbound Prometheus* (Cambridge, 1969), pp. 72-3, sees the partnership with friends or friends of friends as the preferred way of raising capital to expand.]

[5] Mathias, *The Brewing Industry*, pp. 300-4, 324.

with self-finance) in the expansion of the South Wales metal industry. In some firms, like the Llanelly Copper Company, the proportion of loan capital to paid-up capital was very high.[1]

The third method was for firms to obtain help from banks, whose contribution, as Pressnell's work and other recent studies (Mathias) have shown, was more important than had hitherto been realized. Firstly, many industrialists also became bankers, either by creating their own banks, or by going into partnership with bankers; John Wilkinson, Robert Peel, the Feredays, Walkers, Homfrays and Guests are all examples.[2] This extension of interests, clearly observable after 1793 and more so after 1797, was often necessitated by the scarcity of specie, which was indispensable for paying wages. In any case it allowed the 'industrial bankers' to receive deposits, issue bank-notes and tokens (these proliferated after John Wilkinson had set the example in 1787)[3] and start a circulation of bills of exchange. Such procedures provided them not only with means of payment, but also with capital, as repeated short-term loans eventually increased their long-term borrowing. Moreover, they frequently borrowed from the banks in which they were partners, for the needs of their own enterprises, and this practice of taking clients' deposits for their own use resulted in evading the laws on partnership and mobilizing capital from varied sources.[4]

On the other hand, country banks (and sometimes London

---

[1] John, *Industrial Development of S. Wales*, pp. 40, 42–6, 167. True, the Welsh ironmasters were in a strong position to borrow money, because their heavy equipment and their 'mineral leases' gave them security to offer creditors. Moreover, those who were former merchants had useful contacts in London and Bristol.

[Birch, *The Economic History*, pp. 208–9, stresses the vital role of loans on security in the iron industry, and pp. 61–2 mentions that, to finance the expansion of Coalbrookdale, from 1745 to 1770 some of the shares of the Darby family were mortgaged to other partners.]

Mathias also notes (*The Brewing Industry*, pp. 264, 267, 282–6, 291–2, 213) that all the large breweries depended heavily at times on borrowed money, but this was more to tide them over bad years than to finance expansion.

[2] Naturally many of them (such as S. Oldknow) did not take on all a banker's functions and confined themselves to issuing tokens and notes.

[3] [Much earlier, the Crowleys had issued leather tokens and 'current bills'; Flinn, op. cit., pp. 178–81.]

[4] Pressnell, *Country Banking*, pp. 13–29, 291–2, 322; Ashton, *An Economic History*, pp. 174, 182–3.

banks too) granted substantial credits to industrialists. True, they were theoretically on a short-term basis only; long-term loans were ruled out by liquidity requirements, by the inadequacy of the banks' own resources, by the problems resulting from unlimited liability and bankruptcy laws, and finally by the legal limitation of interest rates, which diverted banks' reserves into Government stocks. Banks considered factories a 'bad risk', and some made it a strict principle never to lend them money on mortgage. Consequently, financing of industry by the banks mainly took the form of discount of bills of exchange and temporary advances by means of overdrafts for fixed amounts. But the banks thereby supplied circulating capital which allowed industry to tie up in fixed capital a larger part of its own resources.[1]

Besides, what happened was that such short-term advances were converted to long-term loans after a time, either by being repeatedly renewed over the years, or by an overdraft being consolidated into a loan. As Mathias explains, this was the common fate of banking capital once it fell into the hands of manufacturers. Lastly, the banks did make direct loans on mortgage, personal bond or promissory note. Pressnell thinks that such loans may have been frequent, but it was unusual for banks to grant a first loan on a new mortgage, or new loans on an existing mortgage; generally, they were more ready to accept a mortgage as collateral or security for an earlier advance.[2] Examples of long-term loans by banks to industry, however, are few: there were some in South Wales, notably those made by the Brecon Bank to the Clydach and Plymouth (1813, £54,000, on mortgage) ironworks; from 1822 to 1876, the Llanelly Copper Company received bank credits equivalent to £25,000 in supplementary capital.[3] Pressnell thinks that the Cornish mines were also financed on a considerable scale by

---

[1] Pressnell, *Country Banking*, pp. 18, 285–6, 326; Ashton, *An Economic History*, pp. 183–4.

[2] Pressnell, *Country Banking*, pp. 294, 296–7, 299, 305, 308–9; Mathias, *The Brewing Industry*, p. 304. See also Campbell, 'Financing of Carron Company', p. 33, and R. Butler, *The History of Kirkstall Forge through Seven Centuries* (Kirkstall, 1945), pp. 69–71, which tells us that a Bradford bank granted this firm a loan against the deposit of five shares in a canal company, and a claim on them.

[3] John, *Industrial Development of S. Wales*, pp. 44, 48; Pressnell, *Country Banking*, pp. 308, 328–9.

[Birch, *The Economic History*, pp. 209–10.]

local banks such as Praed of Truro.[1] By contrast, the part played by banks in the textile industry seems to have been limited to short-term credit by discount.[2] As for the great London breweries, they were closely linked with banks, who sometimes financed their expansion, as for example, for the Anchor Brewery, but these were special cases, mainly because of the close family ties between brewers and Quaker bankers.[3]

In conclusion we can generalize John's observations on the Welsh iron industry; having noted that long-term bank loans to industry were exceptional, he goes on to say: 'But the total effect of tapping the banking system at so many points . . . is to reverse the accepted view of a rigid division between the growing industrialism and early banking system and to substitute one in which the latter, though not perhaps consciously, played a not unimportant part in the industrial development of this period.'[4]

Moreover, the development of credit as a whole and of the banking system, which was one of the concomitants of the Industrial Revolution, indirectly helped capital formation. The mere fact that industrialists could, firstly, buy their raw materials on credit and, secondly, obtain advances from the commissioners and merchants through or to whom they sold their goods, meant that they could procure thus part of their circulating capital and invest a larger part of their own resources in fixed capital.[5] This complex credit chain was, of course,

[1] Pressnell, *Country Banking*, pp. 322–5, 330–2.

[2] Ibid., pp. 334–6; also pp. 340–2 on the large loans made by Leyland, Bullins and Co.'s bank to Liverpool manufacturers. Coleman, op. cit., p. 254, considers the few overdrafts allowed to paper manufacturers by banks as exceptional.

[S. Shapiro, *Capital and the Cotton Industry in the Industrial Revolution* (Ithaca, 1967), pp. 60–1; in 1799 McConnel and Kennedy obtained a formal loan from their bank, but it was repaid quickly and was the only one from 1795 to 1825.]

[3] Mathias, *The Brewing Industry*, pp. 283–4, 294–5, 297, 300–5.

[4] John, *Industrial Development of S. Wales*, p. 49; also Ashton, *An Economic History*, p. 184. In the second quarter of the nineteenth century the banking system became stronger and more capable of supporting industry.

[5] See, for example, L. J. Williams, 'The Welsh Tinplate Trade in the Mid-Eighteenth Century', *Economic History Review*, 2nd series, XIII (1961), pp. 441, 447, which shows how an ironmaster, R. Morgan, obtained half his circulating capital from advances made by a Bristol merchant. Sigsworth (op. cit., pp. 221–2) points out that J. Foster, when starting in business, obtained circulating capital from credit granted by his wool suppliers. But in the case of S. Oldknow, Unwin (op. cit., pp. 7–8, 16) points out that the large commercial houses in London only granted temporary advances and refused to finance expansion.

held together by capital supplied to trade by banks, brokers and 'capitalists'. Also, the rise of the London discount market at the beginning of the nineteenth century enabled banks from industrial areas, which were short of capital, to have bills discounted in London, through the agency of bill-brokers, thanks to the surplus capital provided by banks from agricultural districts. This beginning of a centralized money market meant that more short-term, and indirectly more long-term, capital was available for industry.[1]

However useful these transfusions of 'external' capital may have been, the 'internal' resources of industry seem to have been even more predominant in financing expansion than for initial outlays to set up industrial concerns. Naturally, what permitted the Industrial Revolution to proceed at a relatively swift pace was that profits, the ploughing back of which made expansion possible, were at a high level. A study of profits during the Industrial Revolution is outside the scope of this paper. We may therefore only mention that all the firms we have discussed achieved extremely high net profits: in good years, they were often in excess of a 15 or even 20 per cent return on capital employed (at Cyfarthfa, in 1796–7, they reached 52 per cent!);[2] losses are correspondingly rare, except

[1] Pressnell, *Country Banking*, pp. 97–9, 102–8, 225, 401, 434–7; Ashton, *An Economic History*, p. 184; F. Crouzet, *L'Économie Britannique et le Blocus Continental, 1806–1813* (Paris, 1958: 2 vols), pp. 123–4.

[Dickson, op. cit., p. 485, points out to a circular process of long- and short-term lending, which had emerged embryonically by the 1750s: savings from the agricultural districts flowed into London to help finance the short-term needs of industry, but the contribution of the industrial districts to the London Fire and Life Insurance offices helped them to accumulate very large funds, a good part of which was returned to the agricultural districts under the form of mortgages to landowners.]

[2] John, *Industrial Development of S. Wales*, p. 41 n. 2; net profits for a *half-year* vary between 5 and 47 per cent of capital between 1792 and 1798, and are over 20 per cent for five of the eleven half-years for which John quotes figures. At Newton Chambers net profits in the good years between 1793 and 1815 are over 15 per cent – for example in 1793–5, 1799–1802, 1813–15 – in fact for eight of the sixteen years 1799–1815 (Ashton, *Iron and Steel*, op. cit., p. 160). Before this, from 1736 to 1746, one of the partners in the Stour Partnership received on average a return of 20·2 per cent per annum on his capital (Downes, op. cit., pp. 93–4). In the textile industry the net profits of Pleasley Mill reached 31 per cent of capital employed in 1801 and seem to have been over 10 per cent per annum for more than half the period 1797–1813 (Pigott, op. cit., pp. 37–8). With J. and T. Clark of Trowbridge, profits exceeded 20 per cent of capital for more than half the years 1804–20. See R. P. Beckingsale (ed.), *The Trowbridge Woollen*

in the lean years after 1815, and even in a poor year profits were respectable, especially when one remembers that the partners of a firm first assured themselves of a fixed interest (generally 5 per cent) on their capital, and only the earnings over and above this were considered as 'profits'; they were, in fact, *net* profits, and statistics dealing only with such figures tend to minimize the return on capital.[1] In the years 1792–1807 Benjamin Gott had an average return on the capital he had invested of 19 per cent,[2] and John Marshall seems to have fared no worse.[3]

It is true that these findings apply to 'progressive' firms in particularly profitable industries,[4] and no doubt many other firms had a less brilliant record. After 1815, moreover, profit margins became narrower as a result of the secular fall of the prices of manufactured goods. But although profits per unit of output dropped, there is no evidence that gross profits or return on capital were noticeably affected – except during

---

Industry as illustrated by the Stock Books of John and Thomas Clark, 1804–1824 (Devizes, 1951), p. xxxi.

The big London brewers also experienced very satisfactory profits: from 1741 to 1750 those of B. Truman averaged 29·75 per cent (his capital was admittedly small); Whitbread's *gross* profits exceeded 15 per cent for seventeen of the thirty-three years 1762–94 (Mathias, *The Brewing Industry*, pp. 264, 553). As for the big Ravenhead glassworks, it paid its shareholders dividends of between 20 and 25 per cent between 1807 and 1815 – but it enjoyed a quasi-monopoly (Barker, op. cit., p. 49).

These various rates should certainly not be taken as average profits – it seems impossible to calculate them – or even as representative; they are, however, fairly *common* rates. They have been calculated in relation to *real capital*, i.e. the total amount of money invested in the business (including reserves), and not to *nominal* capital.

[1] Furthermore, firms often worked out the depreciation of fixed capital in an erratic but rapid manner, so that many of them, especially in the metal industries (where fixed capital was important), earned even more than they appear to.

[2] Rimmer, op. cit., pp. 56 n. 1, 71 n. 1.

[3] Ibid., pp. 47, 56, 69–71, 160. From 1797 to 1804 Marshall's firm made total net profits of £70,899 and the partners received a return of 15 per cent on invested capital. From 1804 to 1815 John Marshall earned a total of £446,000, of which 71 per cent came from 'profits' and 18 per cent from interest on capital, while in 1804 his fortune had only been about £40,000. He was not satisfied, moreover, unless his capital was bringing in 15 to 20 per cent per annum.

[A. J. Robertson, op. cit., p. 30: under Robert Owen's management, from 1799 to 1827, New Lanark's net profits would have been £360,000.]

[4] Profits seem to have been lower in coal-mining but still satisfactory (cf. Ashton and Sykes, op. cit., pp. 245–6).

the severe post-war depression.[1] We must also remember how debatable E. J. Hamilton's theory is, that the Industrial Revolution was financed by 'profit inflation' caused by a lag of wages behind rising prices and resulting in forced saving. This thesis is based mainly on the comparison of food prices with the wages of workmen in the London building trade, which were not representative of fluctuations of prices and costs in manufacturing industry; and it does not take into account the secular fall in the prices of manufactured goods which started as early as the years 1799–1803.[2] In fact high returns on capital were the result of technological innovations which brought considerable economies in real production costs, while demand was buoyant for most of the period under consideration.[3]

Anyhow, the regular reinvestment of the largest part of these high profits ensured a rapid accumulation of capital within industrial concerns. We have tried to estimate it by using a number of statistical series drawn from firms' accounts, which show the evolution of their capital. They have been used in the preparation of Graph A and Table B on pages 198–9, in which we have calculated the average annual rate of growth of capital for these firms (and some others). Unavoidably these calculations are somewhat vitiated by arbitrary choices; fortunately in the majority of cases the amount of initial capital was known (in the case of Gott and Wormald we have started in 1792 when they went over to the factory system) and it

[1] A. D. Gayer, W. W. Rostow and A. J. Schwartz, *The Growth and Fluctuations of the British Economy, 1790–1850. An Historical, Statistical and Theoretical Study of Britain's Economic Development* (Oxford, 1953: 2 vols), pp. 653–4; also *Parliamentary Papers 1834*, XIX, p. 185; Rimmer, op. cit., p. 309, graph 8. [M. M. Edwards, *The Growth of the British Cotton Trade, 1780–1815* (Manchester, 1967), pp. 23, 190; in the cotton industry, profits reached a peak during the peace of Amiens, after which they fluctuated violently at a lower level; also Shapiro, op. cit., p. 252.]

At J. Marsh, gross profits were 20 per cent of capital in 1817–19, 23 per cent from 1822 to 1828, and 63 per cent in 1836 (Pollard, *Three Centuries*, pp. 10, 11, 21).

[2] E. J. Hamilton, 'Profit Inflation and the Industrial Revolution, 1751–1800', *Quarterly Journal of Economics*, LVI (1942), pp. 257, 259, 261–5; also his 'Prices and Progress', *Journal of Economic History*, XII (1952), pp. 339 ff.; and, in contrast, Ashton, *An Economic History*, pp. 198–200; Gayer *et al.*, op. cit., pp. 639–40.

[3] [S. Pollard, *The Genesis of Modern Management* (London, 1965), pp. 285–6, sees these high profits as an expression of the fact that possession both of capital and entrepreneurship was still so scarce as to have evident monopolistic elements.]

served as a *terminus a quo*; for the *terminus ad quem* we simply took, in some cases, the last available figure (e.g. for McConnel and Kennedy); in others, in order to eliminate the perturbations of the post-1815 crisis, we took the highest figure before

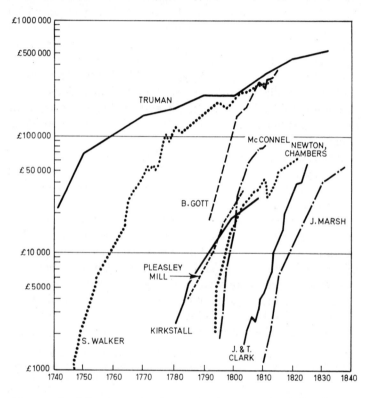

GRAPH A　The growth of capital of various industrial firms (semi-logarithmic scale with three modules)

that date. Such choices leave one open to criticism; moreover some series cover a very short period so that findings are sometimes influenced by business cycles and by the specific problems of each firm (such as the withdrawal of one partner which explains the irregularity in the Newton Chambers graph). Lastly, we cannot be sure that these series are really comparable, given the variations in accounting methods from

TABLE B *Rate of growth of capital of various industrial firms*

	Year	Capital £	Average rate of growth per year %
1 *Metal industries*			
Coalbrookdale Co.	1709	2,800 } 4·17	} 3·49
	1809	166,000	
	1851	366,000	
S. Walker and Co.	1746	600 } 16·92	} 9·86
(Rotherham)	1780	122,000	
	1812	299,000	
R. Crawshay and Co.	1790	14,000 } 11·17	} 6·50
(Cyfarthfa)	1813	160,000	
	1835	238,000	
Kirkstall Forge	1779	1,800	10·18
	1808	29,578	
Newton Chambers and Co.	1793	2,270	12·62
(Sheffield)	1821	63,306	
J. Marsh and Co. (Sheffield)	1813	1,013	17·63
	1838	58,000	
Cheadle Brass Co.	1734	3,600	4·95
	1804	106,000	
2 *Textile industries*			
McConnel and Kennedy			
(Manchester)	1795	1,770	29·80
	1810	88,375	
Pleasley Mill	1790	5,000	15·30
	1804	36,000	
Gott and Wormald (Leeds)	1792	20,000	13·73
	1815	397,000	
J. and T. Clark (Trowbridge)	1804	1,634	18·65
	1825	59,258	
J. Foster and Co. (Black			
Dyke Mills)	1834	11,185	16·10
	1867	1,463,155	
J. Marshall and Co. (Water			
Lane, near Leeds)	1794	14,000 } 15·70	} 9·15
	1803	52,000	
	1828	272,000	
3 *Breweries*			
Truman, Hanbury and			
Buxton (London)	1741	23,000	3·68
	1830	575,000	
Barclay Perkins (London)	1784	95,000	
	1830	759,000	4·68

N.B. I have abbreviated the names of firms, particularly because they often changed them.

Sources for Graph A and Table B

Coalbrookdale:[a] Raistrick, op. cit., pp. 6, 244, 297.

Walker:[b] John (ed.), *The Walker Family*, pp. 2–25.

Crawshay:[c] John, *Industrial Development of S. Wales*, p. 41; Addis, op. cit., pp. 83, 173.

Kirkstall: Butler, op. cit., pp. 27, 29, 110.

Newton Chambers: Ashton, *Iron and Steel*, p. 160.

Marsh: Pollard, *Three Centuries*, pp. 8, 10, 11, 18.

Cheadle Brass Co: Hamilton, *English Brass and Copper Industry*, pp. 246, 248.

McConnel and Kennedy: Daniels, 'The Early Records', p. 178.

Pleasley Mill:[d] Pigott, op. cit., pp. 37–8.

Gott: *Accounts of Co-partnership*, Gott MSS (Brotherton Library, Leeds). See also Crump, op. cit., p.255; Heaton, 'Financing the Industrial Revolution', pp. 9–10.

Clark: *The Trowbridge Woollen Industry*, p. xxxi.

Foster: Sigsworth, op. cit., p. 218.

Marshall:[e] Rimmer, op. cit., pp. 310–11.

Breweries: Mathias, *The Brewing Industry*, pp. 554–8.

Additional notes to Graph A

(a) [These figures must be completed and corrected by Birch, *The Economic History*, pp. 61–2, 65–6. Value of the concern: 1708: £2,804; 1740: £21,323; total capital value: 1798: £95,000; 1805: £111,000 (for Coalbrookdale only); net total value of the three concerns: 1809: £166,000; this means the value of the investments and undistributed profits which had been sunk into the firm, and not the capital strictly speaking.]

(b) After 1812, this firm declined and went into liquidation.

(c) Capital of the Cyfarthfa firm, the London house not included. [M Lévy-Leboyer, on p. 29 of the article quoted on p. 210 n. 3, gives £104,000 for this capital in 1798 and £193,000 in 1810.]

(d) In this case the figures are for paid-up capital.

(e) The rate of growth was slowed down when the Benyons withdrew in 1804, and other partners in 1824.

---

one firm to another;[1] the sample is in any case ridiculously small (it would, of course, be desirable that a scholar would gather, analyse and compare systematically, from the point of view of capital accumulation, surviving business accounts).

We must, therefore, treat these graphs and calculations with caution; interesting conclusions seem to emerge nevertheless. The clearest is the extremely high rate of growth of capital in the concerns considered; most of the graphs describe part

[1] A recent discussion has shown the pitfalls concealed by apparently simple account books and the possibility that they may have been falsified. Cf. A. Birch, 'Carron Company, 1784–1822: The Profits of Industry during the Industrial Revolution', *Explorations in Entrepreneurial History*, VII, no. 2 (1955), pp. 66–79; A. R. Hall, 'Note on Carron Company 1784–1822 . . . by A. Birch', ibid., IX, no. 1 (1956), pp. 44–6; A. Birch, 'Carron Company 1784–1822: A Reply', ibid., IX, no. 1 (1956), pp. 46–9; Campbell, *Carron Company*, pp. 137, 163–9.

Also, the authors from whom our data were borrowed had interpreted the original accounts in different ways.

of a parabola; and although the highest average annual rate of growth – that of McConnel and Kennedy at nearly 30 per cent – is obviously exceptional, rates ranging from 15 to 20 per cent are fairly common, especially among textile firms, over periods from 15 to 30 years. These almost vertical 'take-offs' are an essential feature in the process of the Industrial Revolution.

Secondly, growth rates are higher for the series which cover a short period than for those covering a long period (e.g. Coalbrookdale or the breweries); moreover the curves are almost vertical during the early years of a firm, but later on slope towards the right. In short, there is a more rapid growth in the early stages of a firm's history than in its later years. This is clearly marked in the cases of Walker, Newton Chambers, Marsh (in their first ten years the rate borders on 30 per cent per annum), Marshall, Gott, even McConnel and Kennedy. This slowing down of expansion is quite normal: it is more difficult to maintain rapid growth when a firm has reached a large size than during its 'take-off'; moreover, at the beginning, the owners of a business reinvest virtually all the gross profits, but after a while they want to live more comfortably, so draw out more. It also happens that the firm cannot absorb for its expansion all the capital it is accumulating, and then withdrawals must be increased to avoid heavy capital charges and new outlets must be found for the surplus resources. This seems to have happened quite often after 1815, when one finds big industrialists, like J. Marshall, William Crawshay II or the Fosters, investing their surplus capital in British or foreign Government stocks, later in railway shares or on the money market.[1] It also seems that after the early years of the nineteenth century the difficulties caused firstly by the Continental Blockade, then by the depression following the Napoleonic Wars, combined with the secular fall in profit margins, resulted in a slower accumulation of capital for some firms;[2] others, however, like Marsh or Foster, maintained a high rate of growth.

[1] Rimmer, op. cit., pp. 47, 94–6; Addis, op. cit., pp. 156–7; Sigsworth, op. cit., p. 224; also Heaton, 'Financing the Industrial Revolution', p. 9.

[2] See Rimmer, op. cit., p. 310, graph 11. In the iron industry there was sometimes a noticeable diminution of firms' capital after 1815; the same can be observed with B. Gott (Heaton, 'Financing the Industrial Revolution', p. 10).

We have little information about the pre-1780 period, but it seems possible that the accumulation of capital was slower before than after that date; Coalbrookdale and the breweries would seem to bear this out; on the other hand, the rate of growth of capital of S. Walker & Co. during their first decades is very rapid. Nor must we forget the enormous fortunes made in the eighteenth century by men like Josiah Wedgwood, R. Arkwright or Samuel Whitbread I who, starting with nothing, left £500,000 or so at their deaths.[1]

Thus only more detailed research would show if the growth rates of industrial concerns' capital were subject to significant variation during the Industrial Revolution (and notably if they reached a peak during the last twenty years of the eighteenth century) and also whether the rate was higher in the textile than in the metal industries, as our figures would seem to indicate. But it seems certain that in many cases this rate was bordering on 15 per cent per year over fairly long periods, which is really very high.[2] True, we have taken examples among particularly successful firms, whereas many others grew more slowly, stood still, or even disappeared. We must not forget that the death rate for firms was very high during the Industrial Revolution and that, as Mathias points out, referring to breweries, even the most lucrative business soon degenerated if it fell into incompetent hands, and a vast capital could be eaten away within a few years.[3] Moreover, although some innovators quickly made huge profits, for example, Richard Arkwright, there were others, like Boulton and Watt, whose capital increased only slowly.[4] It would therefore be unwise to generalize from these examples in order to estimate, even roughly, the long-term trend in capital formation in British industry

[1] McKendrick, op. cit., p. 408; Fitton and Wadsworth, pp. 94–5, 97, 178; Mathias, *The Brewing Industry*, p. 308. For the later period, Jedediah Strutt's three sons are supposed to have had a fortune of £1 million in 1813; R. Crawshay is said to have left £1·5 million on his death in 1811, and J. Marshall between £1·5 million and £2·5 million in 1845, of which almost £1 million came from his flax mills (Addis, op. cit., p. 19; Rimmer, op. cit., pp. 97, 321). [See also Edwards, op. cit., appendix E, p. 255.]

[2] [This guess-estimate is considered as valid by Cameron *et al.*, op. cit., p. 39.]

[3] Mathias, *The Brewing Industry*, pp. 265–8, 272.

[4] The same is true of Carron (see Hall, op. cit., p. 45) and, on the whole, of Coalbrookdale.

as a whole, or even in its different sectors.[1] Nor do we know the total amount of capital invested in the various industries or how it evolved. Contemporary accounts supply estimates: in 1803 R. Owen stated that the fixed capital of the cotton-spinning mills amounted to £9 million; in 1806 two iron-masters put the capital invested in the iron industry, one at £5 million, the other at £7 million;[2] and it would be useful to collect and compare these estimates, as M. Blaug successfully did for the cotton industry after 1830;[3] I fear, however, that contemporary estimates for earlier periods are flights of fancy (this possibly applies to those I have quoted) and therefore of little use.[4] Moreover, if the capital resources of firms accumulated steadily and swiftly, investment in fixed capital was realized much more irregularly, by successive stages, as is shown if one studies the fluctuations of investment.

IV

The study of investment in industry at the end of the eighteenth century and the beginning of the nineteenth century comes up

[1] Perhaps we could adopt 7 or 8 per cent per annum as the rate of growth of capital in the 'factory' industries, e.g. about half that of several large enterprises. But it is a wild guess.

[2] *Observations on the proposed tax on pig-iron, by an Iron-Master* (London, 1806); *Letter on the Iron Tax addressed to a Member of Parliament. By an Iron-Master* (Ibid.); G. D. H. Cole, *The Life of Robert Owen*, 2nd ed. (London, 1930), p. 123; *The Edinburgh Encyclopaedia* (Edinburgh, 1830), vol. VIII, p. 760. See also Deane, 'Capital Formation before Railway Age', p. 366, who points out that contemporary estimates put the rise in the cotton industry's capital at £8 million between 1783 and 1802, which meant that it rose from £1 million to £9 million, and in the capital of the iron industry at £6·5 million between 1791 and 1806.

[3] M. Blaug, 'The Productivity of Capital in the Lancashire Cotton Industry during the Nineteenth Century', *Economic History Review*, 2nd series, XIII (1961), pp. 359, 371.

The total capital of the cotton industry in 1834 is said to have been £22 million, of which £15 million was in fixed capital (over £10 million for the spinning mills alone). If one accepts that in 1782 £200,000 had already been invested in spinning mills, then one arrives at an average annual rate of capital growth of 7·6 per cent, which is not unlikely.

[4] Blaug (op. cit., p. 371) points out that it was estimated around 1834 that the capital–output ratio in the cotton industry was about 1. One could thus make rough calculations of the amount of capital by using estimates of the value of production. The ratio has, admittedly, changed, due to technical progress, but the trail is perhaps worth pursuing. One could also use the number of steam engines as an indicator of the formation of industrial capital, as Deane suggests in 'Capital Formation before Railway Age', p. 366.

against serious difficulties, because of the shortage of sources, and particularly of quantitative data. Admittedly Lord Beveridge and W. Hoffmann have built up indices, the one of activity in the 'construction industries' and the other of the output of producers' goods; but most of the statistics they used are, for our period, concerned with the import or transportation of raw materials and cannot be taken as representative of investment in industry or even in the economy as a whole.[1] As for the famous index of bricks output worked out by H. A. Shannon, it gives a true picture of building activity, but housing and public works obviously absorbed much more bricks than factory building, so these statistics are hardly relevant to our enquiry.[2] We are therefore restricted to qualitative data, in particular to information about the construction or enlargement of factories, the installation of new machinery, etc. It would be useful, also, to collect such data (especially the dates when industrial buildings were constructed) in a more systematic manner than has hitherto been attempted, with the help of provincial newspapers and of local, business and solicitors' records. In default of a precise chronology of investment, one can still sketch a graph of their short- and medium-term fluctuations.

Starting with an analysis of this sort, covering the years 1790–1850, Gayer, Rostow and Schwartz formulated a most interesting interpretation. According to them the process of investment is discontinuous by nature, and shows sharper fluctuations than current production; the large-scale increase in productive capacity is in fact concentrated on a small number of short periods, which occur in the late phases of expansion of a number of business cycles. Gayer and his team labelled the latter 'major cycles' to distinguish them from the 'minor cycles'

[1] Sir William Beveridge, 'The Trade Cycle in Britain before 1850', *Oxford Economic Papers*, no. 3 (1940), pp. 74–109, and no. 4 (1940), pp. 63–76; W. G. Hoffmann, *British Industry 1700–1950* (Oxford, 1955: trans. from the German by W. O. Henderson and W. H. Chaloner), chap. II, pp. 4–28 and table 54. See also the remarks in Gayer *et al.*, op. cit., pp. xi, 693, and W. W. Rostow, *British Economy in the Nineteenth Century* (Oxford, 1948), pp. 33–4 n. 1. In Beveridge's index, excessive weight is given to bricks production and shipbuilding; Hoffmann's index of producers' goods is heavily weighted in favour of coal and iron, and the figures he uses concern the transportation of these products.

[2] H. A. Shannon, 'Bricks – A Trade Index, 1785–1849', *Economica*, N.S., I, no. 3 (1934), pp. 300–18.

which usually separate them and during which investment is restricted; thus these bursts of intensive investment recur approximately every nine years.[1] This attractive thesis seems on the whole to be borne out by fact.

Discontinuity of investment first appears at the level of the firm; mainly, according to Gayer, because a concern lacks the necessary financial resources to undertake heavy construction (usually expansion and modernization of plant need to be made in large 'lumps') at short intervals, especially in the course of each business cycle. The only history of a firm to study this question in any detail, Rimmer's study of John Marshall's flax-spinning mills, shows that plant was increased or replaced during a small number of short periods – five between 1791 and 1840 – separated by fairly long intervals when the fixed capital hardly changed. J. Marshall built his first factory, *Mill A*, at Water Lane, in 1791–2; growth was rapid from 1793 to 1800; *Mill B* was built in 1794–5 at Leeds, and another at Shrewsbury in 1796–7. But from 1800 to 1814, capacity did not increase. In 1815, with his factories working at full capacity, and demand high, Marshall decided to build *Mill C* which increased his capacity by 55 per cent. In 1818 the fall in the prices of heavy yarn led him to change to the production of fine yarn, for which he installed new machinery, the gill frames, whence a reorganization of his mills, achieved in 1820–2. In 1825, in the middle of the boom, he decided to build a fourth mill, *D* (1826–7), but the 1826 crisis brought about the decision in September 1827 to change over to wet spinning, based on Philippe de Girard's invention, which involved a complete reorganization and re-equipment lasting from 1828 to 1835 and the construction of *Mill E*. Eventually, in 1838, Marshall decided to construct a huge new factory, Temple Mill.[2]

In the history of other firms that we know less well, the same discontinuity seems apparent; thus, from 1750 to 1755 or 1757,

[1] Gayer *et al*, op. cit., pp. 534–5, 540, 553–62; Rostow, op. cit., pp. 54–5. [This thesis has been criticized – but not convincingly – by R. C. O. Matthews, 'The Trade Cycle in Britain, 1790–1850', *Oxford Economic Papers*, N. S., VI, no. 1 (February 1954), pp. 4–10, 13; Matthews admits that the Gayer model is valid, on the whole, for manufacturing industry.]
[2] Rimmer, op. cit., pp. 33–4, 54–5, 85–6, 135–9, 142, 153–5, 165–80, 186–90, 196, 198, 200–3, 207–8, 212, 311, graph 12.

Coalbrookdale underwent considerable reorganization and expansion, marked by the construction of the Ketley and Horsehay blast furnaces; then investment seemingly came to a halt, to start again about 1783 with the installation of rolling mills and new steam engines; this was followed by a long pause.[1] At Kirkstall Forge there seems to have been three phases of investment, 1785–96, 1818, 1835–9, separated by long pauses.[2]

We must not, however, exaggerate the irregularity of investment by industrial concerns. Rostow has in fact noted that there were exceptions: for instance, after the invention of the hot-blast in 1828, the Scottish iron industry regularly increased its capacity, apparently unaffected by cyclical fluctuations.[3] On a different level, Samuel Walker's diary shows that his firm realized an amazing variety of small investments from 1741 to 1782, many of which were increasing its capacity.[4] At Pleasley Mill new machinery was bought almost every year of the two decades following 1790.[5] R. S. Fitton points out that the Strutts invested almost continuously during the Napoleonic Wars, repeatedly enlarging and rebuilding the Belper and Midford spinning mills.[6]

Moreover, according to Gayer the concentration towards the end of major cycles applies mostly to the 'decisions to invest'; the existing capacity is by then fully employed and a mood of optimism is prevalent; but the projects are often realized after the peak, during a depression, and tend sometimes to mitigate its effects. Many of the examples quoted support this thesis, particularly Marshall's decisions of 1791, 1796, 1818 and 1825; also S. Oldknow building Mellor Mill and

---

[1] Raistrick, op. cit., pp. 68–70, 96, 225–6.

[2] Butler, *History of Kirkstall Forge*, p. 139. [See also Shapiro, op. cit., p. 112.]

[3] Rostow, op. cit., p. 54. [R. H. Campbell, 'Investment in the Scottish Pig-Iron Trade, 1830–1843', *Scottish Journal of Political Economy*, I, no. 3 (October 1954), pp. 245–8; from 1837 to 1843, the expectation of profit engendered by the innovation of the hot blast and the previous boom greatly outweighed the expectation of loss, so that investment was heavy despite the depression.]

[4] John (ed.), *The Walker Family*, pp. 2–24, *et passim*.

[5] Pigott, op. cit., p. 39.

[6] Fitton and Wadsworth, op. cit., pp. 219, 221. See also Sigsworth (op. cit., pp. 191, 219–20), who points out that at Black Dyke Mills the number of power-looms was increased almost every year from 1841 to 1875, but with clearly marked peaks in 1847–55 and 1859. According to Pollard (*Three Centuries*, pp. 15–16, 20), Marsh put up new buildings almost every year from 1827 onwards, but his main investments were concentrated in 1827–9 and 1835–7.

B. Gott, Bean Ing in 1792; the Crawshays building three blast furnaces in 1824; Greenall and the Pilkingtons tripling the capacity of their glassworks in 1834–5.[1] Investment decisions do, however, occur also contra-cyclically, in periods of depression – as Gayer and his team have admitted.[2] This tends to happen when firms (like Marshall in 1827) adopt some technological innovation to enable them to combat depression more effectively by reducing costs.

The discontinuity of investment that can be observed on a micro-economic scale recurs at a macro-economic level,[3] and much of Britain's fixed industrial capital was installed during a few relatively short 'bursts' or 'waves' of investment. There is no point in looking for such movements in the first three-quarters of the eighteenth century, because industrial machinery was too primitive. The iron industry might be an exception, and some writers have noted bursts of growth, and especially the creation of new ironworks, during the War of the Austrian Succession, and still more the Seven Years War.[4] The first unmistakable wave of investment, however, occurs in the years 1783–92, though it had started before 1780 in the cotton and metal industries where it was to reach its height. Arkwright and his associates, the manufacturers whom he authorized to use his patents, and those who pirated his machinery, set up about twenty mechanized spinning mills, investing a capital estimated in 1782 at £200,000.[5] The American War of Independence may have checked such developments, but it encouraged investment in the iron industry, above

[1] p. 170 above and Addis, op. cit., p. 68; Barker, op. cit., p. 77. The decision to build the Carron ironworks had been taken in 1759 in a phase of prosperity (Campbell, 'Financing of Carron Company', p. 21). See also in W. H. B. Court, *The Rise of the Midland Industries, 1600–1838* (Oxford and London, reprinted, 1953), p. 257, a table of the steam engines that existed in 1835 in Birmingham; this shows that a large number of them had been set up in 1824, 1825 and 1826.

[2] Gayer *et al.*, op. cit., p. 649.

[3] Investment by firms is discontinuous but not erratic; it may be partly determined by circumstances specific to each enterprise, it may sometimes be contra-cyclical, but all things considered, the majority of investments are commanded by general factors and they happen simultaneously.

[4] John, *Industrial Development of S. Wales*, p. 332.

[5] Fitton and Wadsworth, op. cit., pp. 71, 77–8; Daniels, *Early English Cotton Industry*, p. 100.

[Chapman, *Early Factory Masters*, pp. 67–8, 72, 75: Arkwright built ten mills in the Midlands from 1769 to 1784; at least nine pirates and licensees worked on his model before 1781.]

all in South Wales, by hindering imports of Swedish and Russian iron and creating a demand for armaments. In any case the peace of 1783, and the suspension, followed by the cancellation, of Arkwright's patents were quickly followed by a boom in the cotton industry; numerous spinning mills, powered at first by water, and later by steam, were set up (in 1788 there were said to be 145), to say nothing of the many small carding or spinning workshops, the 'jenny factories'. In Scotland there was a strong burst of activity, starting with the building of the Deanston (1785) and the New Lanark (1786) mills; by 1787 Scotland had nineteen spinning mills. Imports of raw cotton in 1785–8 were three times what they had been in 1776–81. This boom was interrupted by the 1788 crisis, but after that it went on with renewed vigour until early 1793, and many mills were set up towards its end, in 1791–2.[1] The Welsh iron industry was also developing rapidly. Penydarren ironworks was set up in 1784, Blaenavon in 1789 and Ebbw Vale in 1791; elsewhere ironworks were being converted to the Cort puddling and rolling process – Coalbrookdale, for example, installed rolling mills – and in Scotland the Clyde and Muirkirk works were founded in 1786 and 1789 respectively.[2] It was thus a decisive decade, which saw the creation of large-scale industry, and the spread of mechanization. The cycle culminating in 1792 was definitely a 'major' one, although the total value of industrial investment cannot have been very high.[3]

By contrast, the 1793 crisis and the difficulties attendant on war with France slowed down new industrial investment, until about 1798 – though the iron industry was probably less

[1] Fitton and Wadsworth, op. cit., pp. 82–6, 198, 200–5; Unwin, op. cit., pp. 85, 103, 115, 119, 123; Mantoux, op. cit., pp. 251–2, 376–7; Hamilton, *Industrial Revolution in Scotland*, pp. 124, 126–7; M. L. Robertson, op. cit., p. 129.

[Chapman, *Early Factory Masters*, pp. 77, 143; eighteen mills were completed in the Midlands in 1783–4, then construction fell sharply, to rise again to eight mills in 1788 and thirteen in 1791–2; see also M. Lévy-Leboyer, *Les banques européennes et l'industrialisation internationale dans la première moitié du XIXᵉ siècle* (Paris, 1964), pp. 25–6, 28, 30–2.]

[2] John, *Industrial Development of S. Wales*, pp. 25–6; Raistrick, op. cit., pp. 95–6, 225–6; Hamilton, *Industrial Revolution in Scotland*, p. 163. From 1787 to 1793 R. Crawshay made £50,000 worth of investment at Cyfarthfa (Addis, op. cit., p. 11).

[3] Ashton, *Economic Fluctuations in England, 1700–1800* (Oxford, 1959), pp. 131–2, 165; Gayer *et al.*, op. cit., pp. 7, 16–17, 535.

badly affected.[1] However, the major cycle 1797–1803 stands out by a second wave of investment which reached its peak in the years 1799–1802. We know that in July 1799 eight new spinning mills were under construction in Manchester, the existing ones were being enlarged, machine-makers were working full-time; and at the beginning of 1802, twenty new mills were under construction.[2] Even more spectacular progress was to be seen in the iron industry, and in a sense this wave of investment belonged to iron, as the first one had to cotton. A sharp increase in the prices of pig- and bar-iron in 1796 (caused by the raising of protective customs duties, by the difficulties of importing from the Baltic, and by a growing demand, while technological progress was improving productivity) ensured huge profits for the ironmasters, stimulated and made possible considerable investment: new ironworks were set up, and the capacity of existing ones increased. Thus, nineteen blast furnaces were built in Shropshire from 1796 to 1806, and eighteen in Staffordshire between 1796 and 1800. In South Wales, five new ironworks were established between 1799 and 1802, and nine blast furnaces built between 1796 and 1800 in Glamorgan alone. Altogether at least sixty-seven blast furnaces were built between 1796 and 1802 in Britain, and in 1802, twenty-two others were under construction. Investment in copper mining and smelting and in pottery works was also active.[3]

On the other hand, when war with France broke out again with its attendant crisis in 1803, it was the start of a long period – the Napoleonic Wars – when new industrial investment seems to have been limited, even in good years like 1806 and 1809. Gayer's team in fact states that investment was almost nil and that no new 'factories' were built between 1808 and 1811; this is going too far, however, because in the cotton industry the first mills for power-weaving were being built at that time, while various firms were expanding or modernizing their equipment – but it was still nothing like the 1802 boom. Things were

[1] Gayer *et al.*, op. cit., pp. 8, 35.

[2] Crouzet, op. cit., p. 86. [Edwards, op. cit., pp. 13–14, 184: the peace of Amiens stimulated factory building and mechanization in spinning and finishing.]

[3] Crouzet, op. cit., p. 81; Gayer *et al.*, op. cit., pp. 41–3, 72; R. Meade, *The Coal and Iron Industries of the United Kingdom* (London, 1882), p. 609. The growth of the iron industry entailed a shortage of coal and the opening of new pits.

much the same in other industries: we know that several woollen mills were built in Bradford and Keighley, that steam power was introduced in many factories in the light metal trades at Birmingham, that two copper-smelting works were set up near Swansea; all this does not add up to much, and the capacity of the major industries does not seem to have increased significantly. During the last years of the Napoleonic Wars the situation remained unchanged, except for some expansion in the Staffordshire and South Wales iron industries.[1]

Napoleon's defeat was not followed by a significant wave of investment, even in 1818, a year of prosperity; quite the reverse: the post-war depression was characterized by a net disinvestment in the worst-hit sectors, such as the iron industry, and many ironworks either closed down or were pulled down.[2] Not until the major cycle culminating in 1825 do we see a 'tremendous expansion of plant', in the years 1824–5. Thanks to a strong demand for exports and to a burst of intense speculation, factories were working at full capacity and heavy investment was undertaken in several industries. Cotton is a case in point. The number of mills in Manchester increased from 49 in 1823 to 63 in 1826; tens of thousands of power-looms were installed. The iron industry benefited too, partly thanks to the demand from railways, and the coal industry was also stimulated; in 1824, 1825 and 1826, sixty blast furnaces were built.[3]

The 1825–6 crisis, however, put paid to the boom, and there followed, until 1832, a period of instability and chronic unemployment, for both men and machinery. Prices and profits dropped, bringing with them a marked falling-off of invest-

---

[1] Crouzet, op. cit., pp. 865–9; Gayer *et al.*, op. cit., pp. 58, 60, 69–72, 94. There was, in fact, in 1807 a *bubble* in floating joint stock companies, some of which were industrial. The majority of them, however, were stillborn.

[Edwards, op. cit., pp. 15, 185: it is unlikely that the total productive capacity of the cotton industry increased very much from 1803 until after 1815; Chapman, 'The Peels', p. 79, sees a contraction of fixed capital in this industry *circa* 1806.]

[2] Gayer *et al.*, op. cit., pp. 111–12, 127. Note, however, some important investment at Ebbw Vale. [Checkland, op. cit., p. 10: profitable outlets for investment almost ceased to exist.]

[3] Gayer *et al.*, op. cit., pp. 171–2, 185, 194 n. 6, 195–6, 198, 212, 230.

[M. Lévy-Leboyer, 'Quatre générations de maîtres de forges gallois: les Crawshay', *Revue du Nord*, XLVI, no. 180 (January–March 1964), pp. 30–4, on heavy investment at Cyfarthfa and Ynisfach from 1820 to 1825.]

ment. Though technological progress went on and industrialists were encouraged to improve productivity to offset the reduction of profit margins, Gayer thinks that in the cotton industry there was no substantial addition to plant, while in other industries fixed capital increased only sporadically.[1]

After 1832 came a new major cycle culminating in 1836, again characterized by considerable investment in the cotton and iron industries – sparked off for the latter by the first railway boom.[2] But this is outside our period, and anyhow we have said enough to show that a great deal of the investment which created large-scale industry in Britain was made, before 1840, during four relatively short periods. This conclusion agrees with that of Gayer, Rostow and Schwartz, except on one point: bursts of *industrial* investment are fewer and more spaced out than their 'major cycles', because some of the latter, for example 1808–11 and 1816–19, are mainly distinguished by investment in non-industrial sectors.[3]

It remains to identify the factors that caused these bursts of investment and their location over time. They seem to have been connected with technological innovations, and the attraction for capital of a possible reduction of costs. The two first bursts obviously coincided with the diffusion of Arkwright's, Crompton's, Cort's and Watt's inventions; it seems also that the bursts culminating in 1825 and 1836 were largely connected with the power-loom, the self-acting mule, the hot-blast process and railways. Innovation could play a direct part – as when an industry adopts a new technique on a massive scale – or an indirect one, when it creates either a new demand for industrial products (e.g. railways) or simply conditions favourable to industrial expansion (e.g. the building of canals in a region like South Wales).[4]

Secondly, investment waves come at a time when demand is high and industry's productive capacity is fully- or even overemployed. The investment, massive for its time, undertaken by the cotton industry in the decade 1783–92 is a direct result

[1] Gayer *et al.*, op. cit., pp. 171, 173, 212, 221–2, 224, 556 n. 1.

[2] Ibid., pp. 242–3, 259, 264. [Checkland, op. cit., pp. 17–19.]

[3] A more thorough analysis would perhaps confirm the existence of proper investment cycles in this period, connected with the 'long swings' which have recently been detected later in the nineteenth century.

[4] Gayer *et al.*, op. cit., p. 38.

of the bottleneck which prevailed in the production of yarn while people were crying out for cotton fabrics. As for explaining such high levels of demand, one must bear in mind, of course, the secular increase in internal consumption caused by the growth of population and by higher average incomes, but this does not account satisfactorily for the suddenness of these bursts of investment, which is rather linked to export demand. Throughout the Industrial Revolution 'the controlling element in the growth and fluctuations of the British economy . . . was its foreign trade' (Gayer), or, to be precise, exports of manufactured goods. Thus major business cycles begin with a gradual increase in exports, which is followed by an upsurge of investment; the two phenomena are moreover connected: increased exports cause a rise in both direct and derived demand and supply also entrepreneurs with the resources needed for investment; one sees very clearly a multiplier effect.

The buoyant state of British exports in the years following the 1783 peace, their recovery during the wars against the French Revolution after the 1793 crisis, and likewise the increased demand from abroad in 1822-5 and 1832-6, were thus decisive in unleashing waves of investment and supplying both the stimulus and the capital they needed.[1]

Monetary conditions seem to have played a much less important or direct part. On the whole, however, bursts of investment coincided with periods of easy credit, for example, after 1783 and after the suspension of cash payments in 1797.[2] Good harvests and low corn prices in 1797-8, 1820-3 and 1832-5 may have helped stimulate expansion during the subsequent major cycles by increasing consumers' real incomes.[3]

That these bursts of investment were often suddenly halted

---

[1] Gayer *et al.*, op. cit., pp. 16 n. 1, 532-4, 647. [Matthews, op. cit., pp. 17, 31-2, denies that exports were the most important source of fluctuations, of which they would be a symptom rather than a cause; he criticizes Gayer *et al.*, for neglecting imports movements, which have a direct effect on income levels through the foreign trade multiplier. But Checkland, op. cit., p. 15, maintains that the British economy was highly sensitive to conditions abroad. When foreign demand for British goods, especially textiles, was high, new investment in mills and machinery took place, with consequent incentives to other kinds of capital formation.]

[2] Ibid., pp. 559-60.

[3] Ibid., pp. 563-4; Ashton, *An Economic History*, pp. 60-1.

is obviously due to the crises of 1793, 1803, 1825 and 1836, which caused a sharp drop in demand, curtailed credit, and showed businessmen that their hopes of unbroken expansion were too optimistic. In addition, an investment boom brings with it unstable conditions, in which the least upset can provoke a crisis, since prices, wages and costs are rising and the money market becomes overstrained; a time comes when the prospect of new investment being profitable seems less likely and so investment tends to fall off, thus helping to create crisis conditions.[1]

One difficult question remains: that of the long period from 1803 to 1822 when investment, while far from negligible, never took on a boom-like character. It is surely no coincidence that this period was the time of the Napoleonic Wars and the depression that followed them. Gayer and his team did, in fact, claim that the French wars caused British economic growth to slow down, particularly where it concerned industrial plant, which was increased more slowly than in the years preceding the French wars, or in the period after 1820 – the time of greatest expansion in industrial capacity. Gayer maintains that if these wars had not happened, economic growth and technical progress would have been swifter – and differently orientated. The slowing down was not due solely to the disruption of foreign trade caused by military and political developments (notably the Continental Blockade) but also – and mainly – to the diversion of capital away from industry towards other sectors. On the one hand, the enormous sums absorbed in massive loans to the Government and forced exports of capital for military expenditures abroad, made productive investment at home relatively less important than before 1793 and after 1820; on the other hand, the influence of wartime conditions caused a shift of investment towards agriculture (owing to the high prices of corn which lasted

[1] Gayer *et al.*, op. cit., pp. 560–2.

[According to Matthews, op. cit., pp. 4–10, there is no proof that investment decisions stop because an excess capacity is forecast and because costs are rising; he emphasizes the mania element in boom years, like 1792, 1825, 1836, when industrial investment was stimulated by the mushroom growth of banks and the relaxation of standards by existings banks; likewise, Mathias, *First Industrial Nation*, pp. 236–7, thinks that investment booms tended to be killed off by mania in the Stock Exchange, followed by a crisis of confidence.]

throughout the wars), the building of merchant ships, harbours and docks and short-term financing of foreign trade. Typical of this period were short- and medium-term investment in foreign currency, and long-term investment in agriculture and Government stocks.[1] We should, no doubt, qualify this interpretation for the period of the war against the French Revolution, given the burst of investment from 1799 to 1802, but it is entirely borne out by my own research on the period of the Continental Blockade, the climax of the French wars, when the slowing down of growth is the most pronounced. I have already mentioned above that capital of industrial concerns seemed to accumulate more slowly during the Napoleonic Wars; moreover, it was then necessary to keep relatively more circulating capital because of the difficult conditions in foreign trade and this affected investment in fixed capital, just when inflation had made its costs rise.[2]

Some scholars, on the other hand, feel that the French wars speeded up Britain's economic growth; John supports this thesis, applying it especially to the War of the Austrian Succession and the Seven Years War. In his view, military demand encouraged the invention and the introduction of new metallurgical techniques, thus stimulating investment; consumer goods industries benefited also from the opening of new markets by British victories and the elimination of French competition. Furthermore, because of the primitive structure of the capital market, Government loans did not attract funds needed by industry and deficit finance actually encouraged investment.[3] It seems difficult, however, to accept these hypotheses, even for the mid eighteenth century, and Ashton holds the opposite view that wars, by damaging some indus-

[1] Gayer *et al.*, op. cit., pp. 648–9, 651–2. [Cameron *et al.*, op. cit., p. 27: during the Napoleonic Wars, the Scottish chartered banks invested heavily in Government securities, Bank of England and East India Company stock, thus reducing their capacity to lend to local industry and commerce.]

[2] Crouzet, op. cit., pp. 868–71. During the wars against revolutionary France, the elimination of French competition brought about a considerable increase in exports which in turn affected investment, making up for unfavourable wartime conditions. During the Napoleonic Wars, there was also an export boom in 1809, but the sudden crisis that was soon to follow in the summer of 1810 prevented it from encouraging investment.

[3] A. H. John, 'War and the English Economy, 1700–63', *Economic History Review*, 2nd series, VII (1955), pp. 329–44.

tries and diverting capital away from productive uses, had, all things considered, delayed the Industrial Revolution.[1] John, moreover, is the first to admit that his analysis does not apply to the American War of Independence, or to the revolutionary and Napoleonic wars.[2] The metal industries, however – although the influence of military demand should not be over-estimated – did benefit from the wars and this may explain their predominance during the 1799–1802 wave of invest-ment.[3]

The question of war and its influence on investment is con-nected with that of interest rates, on which there have been important recent discussions. Ashton maintained that the secular fall of interest rates throughout the eighteenth century gave a decisive impetus to the Industrial Revolution by lower-ing the threshold of profitability on innovations and invest-ment. He also stated that medium-term fluctuations in interest rates (determined by variations in the volume of Government borrowing) influenced the decisions to invest, not only in the building trade or in public works, where the cost of capital is an important element of costs, but also in most industries; obviously such fluctuations do not affect much the profitability of industrial investment, but in wartime industry suffers from a shortage of capital because the legal maximum rate of interest, imposed by the Usury Laws, diverts all the available savings

[1] Ashton, *Economic Fluctuations*, pp. 69–71, 73–9, 83. [Same opinion in C. Wilson, *England's Apprenticeship, 1603–1763* (London, 1965), p. 277: the higher cost of borrowing in wartime did not rule out business investment altogether, but it made some types of investment less attractive; Mathias, *First Industrial Nation*, p. 47: war produced lags in construction investment.]

[2] John, 'War', p. 344.

[3] Crouzet, op. cit., pp. 82–3. Also L. S. Williams, 'A Carmarthenshire Iron-master and the Seven Years War', *Business History*, II (1953), pp. 32, 43, and 'The Welsh Tinplate Trade', pp. 440–1, shows that orders for armaments were not as profitable to ironmasters as is often said, notably because of delays by the Government in discharging its debts; Campbell is also of this opinion in *Carron Company*, pp. 141–2. See also R. O. Roberts, 'Copper and Economic Growth in Britain, 1729–84', *National Library of Wales Journal*, X (1957), pp. 1–10, which shows that the growth of the copper industry was not faster during the War of the Austrian Succession, the Seven Years War and the American War than in peacetime.

[Flinn, op. cit., pp. 46, 74, stresses that 'war was . . . the foundation on which the Crowley fortune was built' and that the rise of Ambrose Crowley III to the rank of largest iron manufacturer in Europe resulted mainly from the profitable naval supply trade; but this is a special case.]

H

into Government stocks.[1] This theory has been sharply criticized but it remains broadly valid.[2]

We have already noticed that during the revolutionary and Napoleonic wars – when the interest rate hovered around 5 per cent – loans to the Government diverted much of the available capital away from productive investment, and Pressnell further points out that there were then long periods when it was impossible to borrow on mortgage.[3] Conversely there is a correlation between the lowering of interest rates from 1783 to 1792 and the burst of investment that characterizes this period; similarly, after 1815, interest rates dropped rapidly to reach a lowest point in 1824, which coincides with a new burst of investment.[4]

Unfortunately many other important problems remain – and will no doubt remain – unsolved for lack of statistical data. It is, for example, impossible to determine the ratio between net and gross capital formation; we have no information about the longevity of fixed capital in our period, and we can only assume that machinery was quickly replaced, given the swift-

[1] Ashton, *The Industrial Revolution*, pp. 9–11, 58; *An Economic History*, pp. 27–9; *Economic Fluctuations*, pp. 84–6, 104–5.

[2] i.e., the diversion of capital into Government stocks in wartime. And this happened despite the fragmentation of the capital market which sheltered the provinces from the tension which prevailed on the London market during the wars (John, 'War', pp. 341–3); but this argument is more valid for the middle than for the end of the eighteenth century. Despite also the fact that much investment was financed 'internally' from firms' own resources, and was thus hardly sensitive to variations in the market interest rate; it seems, however, that provincial businessmen did watch the level of the interest rate in London. Cf. L. S. Pressnell, 'The Rate of Interest in the Eighteenth Century', in Pressnell (ed.), *Studies in the Industrial Revolution*, pp. 195, 198–9.

[K. G. Davies, 'Joint-Stock Investment in the Later Seventeenth Century', *Economic History Review*, 2nd series, IV, no. 3 (1952), p. 292: in the eighteenth century, the third year of a war was marked by a contraction of the capital market, as the Government stepped in and compelled capital away from private investment into the public funds; see also Landes, *The Unbound Prometheus*, p. 64 n. 2, and above, pp. 213–14.]

[3] Pressnell, ibid., pp. 183–4; H. J. Habakkuk, 'The Eighteenth Century', *Economic History Review*, 2nd series, VIII (1956), pp. 434–6, accepts the validity of Ashton's thesis about the most severe periods of war, but thinks that for the rest of the time, interest rates had little influence upon investment. [Also A. J. Robertson, op. cit., p. 30; but A. H. John, 'Insurance Investment and the London Money Market of the Eighteenth Century', *Economica*, N.S., XX, no. 78 (May 1953), p. 157, thinks that inflationary profits permitted the continuance of borrowing for agricultural improvements, despite the high rate of interest.]

[4] Gayer *et al.*, op. cit., p. 652.

ness of technological progress, and this naturally restricted *net* capital formation.[1] As for the structure of capital formation, producer goods industries absorbed an increasing proportion of investment during the Industrial Revolution; they therefore expanded more quickly than consumer goods industries, and capital, as we have seen, moved from 'secondary' to 'primary' industries. It does not seem possible, however, to go further than this.

Another problem – important because of its connexions with technological progress and economic growth – is that of capital intensity in industry. The Industrial Revolution certainly made British industry more capital intensive, when compared with other factors, especially labour; it was labour-saving. We do not know, however, the exact extent of this change, and some innovations, moreover, were also capital-saving; this needs to be precisely estimated, bearing in mind variations according to periods and industries. We also need to know the effect of the capital and labour factors on entrepreneurs' decisions to invest. In a path-making study of the cotton industry in the mid nineteenth century, Blaug states that technological innovation increased the real capital invested per workers' *capita*, but not per net unit of output. This, he thinks, was caused by progress in the machine-making industry, which reduced the cost of machinery; he thus challenges the idea that the Industrial Revolution was dominated by capital-using innovations.[2] Investigations of this nature could usefully be made for the period prior to 1830 and for other industries.

Meanwhile, the problem has been tackled on a more general level in a recent thought-provoking study by H. J. Habakkuk. He suggests that until about 1800 the rate of capital accumulation was faster than the growth of the available labour force. The result was a relative shortage and an increasing cost of labour, in other words a bottleneck which led manufacturers to develop and adopt innovations that were labour-saving and more capital intensive. By this means they hoped to avoid slowing down the accumulation of capital owing to narrowing

[1] J. Marshall, in 1798, had only 13 out of 126 frames dating from before 1793; in 1811 all those that were pre-1801 were replaced (Rimmer, op. cit., pp. 46, 84 n. 1).

[2] Blaug, op. cit., pp. 358–60, 365–7, 369–70.

profit margins. Thus, an increased demand for British manufactured goods was met, not by an extension of the domestic system, but by the creation of the factory system. The abundance of capital in relation to labour would explain, combined as it was with the improvement of internal transport and the fast rise of foreign trade, the growth 'over a broad front' that took place in the last twenty years of the eighteenth century.[1]

After 1800, however, and even more after 1815, the supply of labour was more elastic, the shortage of labour vanished and there was even a great deal of underemployment. Capital could be accumulated without any pressure from wages, and capacity went up noticeably; this was favourable to technological progress, by offering many opportunities for trying out and applying new techniques. But the trend was more towards diffusing and improving existing techniques than discovering and adopting more advanced methods, especially those which were labour-saving, because the incentive for the latter had lost strength. This resulted in a slowing down of technological progress during the years after 1815. In order to offset the effects of a superabundant labour force, more substantial investments should have been made than was the case, but various obstacles prevented this, in particular an insufficient demand for manufactured goods because of the low purchasing power of British and foreign consumers after 1815.[2]

Habakkuk maintains that, as a general rule, abundance of capital compared with other factors – particularly labour – creates the most favourable conditions for technological progress, because the bottlenecks which occur force the development and adoption of innovations that increase capital intensity and save on manpower. Such innovations, moreover, offer the best prospects of sustained progress and conform more closely to long-term economic trends – while this is not the case with inventions which save capital or natural resources.[3] This hypothesis could be the starting point for some extremely

---

[1] Habakkuk, *American and British Technology*, pp. 132–3, 185–6.

[2] Ibid., pp. 135–6, 138–42, 177–8, 180, 188.

[3] Ibid., pp. 135, 162–3, 165, 168, 185–6. Technological progress, therefore, will be more rapid when resources are fully stretched and bottlenecks threaten to slow down the accumulation of capital.

interesting research, and it is to be hoped that scholars will soon take it up.[1]

One last, more or less insoluble problem is the percentage of the national income invested in industry. All we know is that at the end of the eighteenth century it was extremely small (remembering moreover the very low cost of machinery); P. Deane thinks that the annual flow of new capital into the major industries did not exceed £2 million or about 1 per cent of national income.[2] The percentage increased, however, especially after 1820. This is proved by the secular change in the nature of business cycles caused by the growing weight of investment that Gayer, Rostow and Schwartz noticed at about that time.[3] The contribution of expanding manufacturing industries to national income had also increased: according to Deane the net value of industrial production accounted for slightly more than a quarter of British national income in 1812, and something over a third around 1830–40.[4]

V

In this paper I have tried only to draw a picture of the present state of research about capital formation in Britain during the Industrial Revolution. It has perhaps also thrown light on some aspects of the latter. Thus, industry would seem to have financed from its own resources most of its mutation, and this

---

[1] We could apply it to France, for example, which, compared with England, lacked capital and natural resources, but where labour was relatively plentiful; we should have to see whether this situation held up technological progress and favoured innovations that economized on capital and raw materials, thus making it difficult to go over to labour-saving innovations later on, when they became necessary.

[2] Deane, 'Capital Formation before Railway Age', p. 366; this figure includes investment in shipbuilding as well. This author reckons (pp. 367–8) that the percentage of total net capital formation (including agriculture, transport and building) to national income remained stable – around 3 per cent – in the first half of the eighteenth century; after that it increased gradually to reach 5 per cent by the end of the century, and was approaching 10 per cent around 1830–40. The Industrial Revolution was accomplished without this ratio ever reaching the 12 per cent of national income that some writers consider essential for the take-off of an underdeveloped country.

[3] Gayer *et al.*, op. cit., pp. 568–71.

[4] P. Deane, 'Contemporary Estimates of National Income in the First Half of the Nineteenth Century', *Economic History Review*, 2nd series, VIII (1956), pp. 342, 348, 350.

emphasizes the spontaneity of the Industrial Revolution, its characteristically organic growth within the already dynamic and complex economic structure existing in England around 1760. Its autonomy was not, however, complete, and the influence of foreign trade – as much in supplying supplementary 'merchant' capital as in giving exports-led impetus to bursts of investment – seems to have been of great importance. The Industrial Revolution also seems to have been a swift and continuous process as far as the speeding up of capital accumulation is concerned, but discontinuous and relatively slow when it comes to investment operations. The picture is rather one of energetic 'take-offs', but by stages, with some slipping back, than of a smooth ascent. The most pronounced irregularities, however, were caused by outside circumstances – in particular the French wars.

It is the task of comparative economic history to test whether the same characteristics are to be found in other countries at the outset of their industrialization. They should discover if landed capital and banks played such a small part as they did in England, if the return on capital was as high and accumulation as rapid. As far as France is concerned, its Industrial Revolution was financed from industry's own resources to the same, or to an even greater, extent as in Britain, because capital was less mobile and people's outlook was not so favourable to investment.[1] And investment was still more irregular, with outbursts – 1802–10, post 1820 and around 1840 – separated by clear-cut phases of inactivity caused by political 'catastrophes'.

Discussion

Dr Chaloner of the University of Manchester emphasized the importance of the comparatively neglected period before the Industrial Revolution, from 1690, say, to 1760. He noted the low cost of entry in this period and the high rate of accumulation achieved by such entrepreneurs as the Crowleys and the Walkers. Such figures as we have seem to indicate that the proportion of fixed capital to circulating capital was very low

---

[1] However, in the *département du Nord*, the part played by landed capital seems to have been more important than in Britain; capital from Belgium was also significant.

in this period; moreover that credit was more important in providing the working capital than has hitherto been realized.

Dr Chaloner also drew attention to a point made by Professor Habakkuk in his *American and British Technology in the Nineteenth Century* (Cambridge, 1962), that is, the contrast between the sturdy British capital equipment of the mid nineteenth century and the flimsier, shorter-lived American equipment. British enterprise could afford such outlays by that time, noted Dr Chaloner, thanks to previous earnings; but during the Industrial Revolution, plant was often built for short duration (corresponding to short leases) and allowed to run down to the point of dilapidation. Dr Chaloner wondered whether excessive investment in the elaborate plant of French *manufactures* in the eighteenth century was not a factor in French industrial retardation.

Mr Eversley (University of Birmingham) cautioned against the danger of underestimating the burden of capital requirements in the early period of industrialization. £600 might seem little to us now; it was a large sum in the eighteenth century. He noted on the other hand the contribution of an often neglected source of industrial enterprise and capital: yeomen using the cash received from liquidation of their land after enclosure to set up in manufacture or trade.

Dr Harris (University of Liverpool) also stressed the contribution of agriculture to industrial development, particularly the investment of revenues from the land in fixed capital – manufacturing plant, mining installations and the like.

He also emphasized the role of credit for the provision of both working and fixed capital. In this regard he suggested research into the role of money scriveners, in Lancashire for example, who collected large and small amounts from people of all walks of life and consolidated these into substantial industrial loans. He agreed with Dr Chaloner that mortgage loans on buildings or equipment were rare; that mortgages were based almost exclusively on land.

Professor Crouzet agreed that the contribution of agriculture to industrial development was a subject of great importance, but one that still had to be explored. He noted that the balance of investment flows between the two sectors fluctuated; that at times – during the Napoleonic Wars, for example – the current ran towards agriculture; that before the 1790s and after 1815 it probably ran the other way. The question, of course, is how strong the current.

Postscriptum

After the completion of this paper, Phyllis Deane and W. A. Cole published their *British Economic Growth 1688–1959. Trends and Structure* (Cambridge, 1962), which contains many interesting views and clarifies those set out in Deane's article, quoted above. The authors think that the relative level of capital formation in Britain increased slowly and gradually from the end of the seventeenth century until about 1783, rising from 3 to 5 per cent of national income. From 1783 to 1802 it increased more rapidly than before, but not as rapidly as W. W. Rostow claims, at the most by 1·5 per cent of national income, of which, at the beginning of the nineteenth century, it represented possibly 7 per cent. During the Napoleonic Wars and the subsequent depression there was no progress. A radical change in the level and structure of capital formation took place with the beginning of the Railway Age after 1830 only. It may seem surprising that the growth of the British economy should have clearly accelerated at the end of the eighteenth century, even though the level of capital formation had only made a small advance. But Deane and Cole think that savings were then used in a more productive fashion, and machinery more continuously and intensively. These authors also point out that, according to contemporary estimates, the capital invested in machinery could have represented 2 to 2·5 per cent of the national capital at the very beginning of the nineteenth century, 3·5 per cent around 1812 and 4 per cent around 1832 (see pp. 260–4, 268, 271–2, 276–7, 304, 308–9).

I should add that information has kindly been supplied to me by Rondo Cameron and S. B. Saul which would tend to show that in Scotland 'landed' and 'colonial' capital played a bigger part in financing 'modern' industry than this paper would suggest.

7 The Attorney and the Early Capital Market in Lancashire

B. L. ANDERSON

[First published as chapter 3 of J. R. Harris (ed.), *Liverpool and Merseyside: Essays in the Economic and Social History of the Port and its Hinterland*, Frank Cass & Co. Ltd, London, 1969.]

I

IT IS some twenty years since the question of the supply of capital in the English economy of the eighteenth century was first seen as crucial for explaining the origins of the Industrial Revolution.[1] Earlier writers were most concerned with the formation of capital and emphasized the fact that the threshold of entry into industrial activity was normally quite low for the entrepreneurs of that period.[2] But little attention was given, outside of banking, to the distribution of capital, and the self-financing habits of individual businessmen tended to be interpreted as a sufficient explanation of sustained, industrial capital formation taking place in an environment of capital scarcity.[3] Subsequent research, while reiterating the importance of non-industrial capital in the growth process, has so far failed to throw much light on the nature and effectiveness of the capital market in the eighteenth century.[4] As one writer has remarked, 'Very little has been written in any organized way on the development of the capital-market in the early stages of industrialization. . . . Financial intermediaries other than

[1] T. S. Ashton, *The Industrial Revolution 1760–1830* (1948), p. 11.

[2] H. Heaton, 'Financing the Industrial Revolution', *Bulletin of the Business Historical Society*, XI (1937).

[3] M. M. Postan, 'Recent Trends in the Accumulation of Capital', *Economic History Review*, VI (1935).

[4] S. Pollard, 'Fixed Capital in the Industrial Revolution in Britain', *Journal of Economic History*, XXIV (1964).

the banks are largely ignored . . . and about the local markets in which long-term capital was provided through solicitors and other intermediaries in the early days of industrialization we are also very much in ignorance.'[1] The same writer also makes the important point that if, as is often assumed, the landed classes were not directly concerned with investment themselves then it is even more important to know in what ways savings might be transferred to entrepreneurs in industry and trade.

Through the seventeenth and eighteenth centuries a growing number of instances show that the legal profession was concerning itself with financial intermediacy and, when taken together, these suggest that a capital market was coming into being in England, outside of London and apart from the growth of the national debt. The financial activities of the lawyers developed over a long period but even as early as the fifteenth century they were showing a peculiar capacity for acting as a bridge between the merchants and the nobility, and the most outstanding among them were on a par with the greatest London merchants.[2] By the early seventeenth century the country attorney was also able to channel landed profits into trade by way of legal fees, as was the case with Thomas Stampe of Lincoln's Inn, sometime recorder of Wallingford, who invested in the Guinea trade.[3] At the same time the diary of Walter Powell of Monmouth shows that he was managing his clients' estates as well as making short- and long-term loans. Money-lending formed a considerable part of the practice of James Casen, a seventeenth-century Norfolk attorney, while at the turn of the eighteenth century Joseph Hunt of Stratford-upon-Avon combined scrivening with estate management. In fact, wherever the activities of such men have been investigated this financial intermediacy seems to be an almost invariable part of their work, and some of them must have operated on a considerable scale. In the early years of the eighteenth century Peniston Lamb of Nottingham amassed a fortune of £100,000 and at the middle of the century

---

[1] A. K. Cairncross, 'Capital Formation in the Take-off', in W. W. Rostow (ed.), *The Economics of Take-Off into Sustained Growth* (1963).

[2] S. Thrupp, *The Merchant Class of Medieval London 1300–1500* (1948), p. 263.

[3] A. Harding, *A Social History of English Law* (1966), p. 208.

John Cooper of Salisbury became very prosperous as a money-scrivening attorney. Even later in the century the financial expertise of the attorney was in demand and the notebook of Robert Lowe records some thirty borrowing transactions in Nottinghamshire between 1781 and 1800.[1] By this time, however, the attorney was exploiting new investment opportunities. For example, in the 1790s Robert Alcock of Halifax was dealing in the shares of the Rochdale Canal Company and Robert Hobbes of Stratford-upon-Avon was involved in arranging transfers of shares in the Birmingham and Warwick Canal Company in the first years of the nineteenth century.[2]

II

The century after the Restoration saw significant developments taking place in the organization and practice of the legal profession in England. Whereas previously the attorney, as an officer of the court, had performed a function similar to that of the modern common law clerk, almost wholly concerned with procedure, by the late seventeenth century he was beginning to encroach on the numerous activities which traditionally belonged to 'counsel'. The aspirations of the country attorney to interpose himself between the pedestrian practice of procedure and the high flights of advocacy had met with considerable success by the eighteenth century and he had come to play an important part in the affairs of the local community. The influence of law was finding its way into so much of economic life at this time, the demand for legal experience and techniques had increased to such an extent after the Civil War, that the attorney came to occupy a pivotal position in local affairs and his social status was moving perceptibly nearer the ranks of the rural gentry and the urban élite. In town and borough attorneys were to be found performing the duties upon which municipal government depended. They filled the offices of clerks of the peace, town and corporation clerks, and came to monopolize the stewardships of the manorial courts,

[1] M. Birks, *Gentlemen of the Law* (1960), pp. 181–205.
[2] Ibid., and my 'Aspects of Capital and Credit in Lancashire during the Eighteenth Century' (Liverpool M.A. thesis, 1966), p. 176.

which introduced them to the circles of landed society.[1] Their involvement in local government administration meant that they could be extremely influential in local politics, particularly as election agents.[2]

The progress of these developments tended to be, if anything, more rapid in those areas farthest removed from London which were beginning to show signs of facing the Home Counties on new and improved economic terms. Throughout this period provincial society was demanding men of versatile talent to grapple with its emergent problems of administration and business and the country attorney seems to have been best equipped to deal with them.[3] In Lancashire, for example, where the number of barristers was relatively small and professional monopoly less effective, the attorney found it easier to take on more of the work of advising clients, handling straightforward conveyancing and arranging mortgages. It is the financial activities of the attorney with which this essay is chiefly concerned, for in Lancashire, at least, there is evidence that he was making a singular contribution to the economic life of the eighteenth century.

The concern of attorneys with financial matters no doubt emanates from their involvement with the large amount of real estate dealings made necessary by the long and complex processes of land sale and recovery following the Civil War.[4] Such business brought them the acquaintance of merchant and county families, which not only enhanced the social prestige of attorneys, but also led to many of them accumulating fortunes comparable with those of their clients. The key factor in the great volume of real estate business which passed through the hands of the Restoration lawyers was the practice of 'entailing' estates. This legal technique had been in existence as early as the thirteenth century, but it was not until the seventeenth century that entails were perfected with the help of a trust protected by the court of Chancery, when it was widely used

[1] S. and B. Webb, *English Local Government: The Parish and the County* (1960), passim.

[2] M. Cox, 'Sir Roger Bradshaigh and the Electoral Management of Wigan, 1695–1747', *Bulletin of the John Rylands Library*, 37 (1954).

[3] R. Robson, *The Attorney in Eighteenth Century England* (1959), p. vi.

[4] H. J. Habakkuk, 'Landowners and the Civil War', *Economic History Review*, XVIII (1965).

by landowners during the Civil War to safeguard their estates.[1] The principal advantage gained from this 'strict settlement' was the possibility of mortgage without the loss of rights of redemption and the implications of this legal breakthrough for the owners and holders of land were decisive for the development of the mortgage in its modern form. By the middle decades of the seventeenth century the process by which large amounts of land in institutional and private hands were sold on an open market had almost run its course.[2] In the late seventeenth and eighteenth centuries the characteristic feature of the land market was the relatively low level of sales, partly as a result of decreasing social mobility and increasing tendencies towards consolidation of ownership among the landed classes, and partly because of the reassertion of legal restrictions on alienation which, incidentally but most importantly, offered the alternative of the mortgage as a method of raising long-term loans on the security of land.[3]

After the Restoration the mortgage market grew rapidly and became part of the process by which eighteenth-century landowners made indebtedness the normal condition of real estate management. At the same time this growing volume of mortgage business gave attorneys numerous opportunities to employ their various techniques in order to make land into a security for debt, opportunities which were quickly seized upon and frequently exploited to the limit as the corresponding increase in litigation during this period shows. Arranging mortgages and drawing up the necessary documents, whether the funds so raised were to be used for commercial or industrial investment, for agricultural improvement, or for personal consumption, had to be carried out by the legal profession, for although it was not until 1804 that outsiders were prevented from practising conveyancing this function had been monopolized by the profession during the course of the eighteenth century. Conveyancing embraced not only the

[1] G. A. Grove and J. F. Garner (eds), *Hargreaves on Land Law* (1963), pp. 64–6.

[2] L. Stone, 'Social Mobility in England, 1500–1700', *Past and Present*, 33 (1966).

[3] H. J. Habakkuk, 'The English Land Market in the Eighteenth Century', in J. S. Bromley and E. H. Kossmann (eds), *Britain and the Netherlands* (1959), vol. II.

business of transferring or mortgaging property but all the work of the Conveyancing Room which included the business of trusts and consequently the need to become acquainted with clients' financial affairs and advise on loans and investments.[1] In addition, many lawyers undertook the provision of personal loans at interest, either on their own account or as intermediaries; nevertheless, the mortgage remained the most typical form of their security dealings in the eighteenth century. It was not the academicians or the lawyers of Parliament and the bureaucracies who were important in this context, but rather the provincial 'men of business', most of them trained in provincial practice, who had knowledge of the whole range of local problems. These attorneys came to dominate the county mortgage market in the eighteenth century through their intimate knowledge of local society and their ability to tap reservoirs of savings in order to accommodate an increasing demand for loanable funds. It was these attorneys of whom Johnson spoke when he asked: 'What is their reputation but an instrument of getting money?'[2]

In this way the provincial capital market of the eighteenth century was based on the mortgage market at the centre of which stood the money-scrivening attorney, characterized as much by his familiarity with business practice and local affairs as by his knowledge of the law. It would be incorrect to suppose that the careers of all or even most country lawyers indicate a class of successful financial entrepreneurs at this period and the modest achievements of a majority would barely justify the conclusion that they were the most significant organ of local finance. Yet in Lancashire, as presumably elsewhere, the names of a large number of attorneys and scriveners occur so frequently and in such contexts that it is certain their financial activity was ubiquitous.[3] Future research might well show that the number of attorneys and others who rose to first rank in this field bears comparison with the number of successful industrial entrepreneurs in the eighteenth century. In any event, the following evidence on the nature of the attorney's activities lends some support to the proposition that he

---

[1] E. B. V. Christian, *Solicitors: An Outline of their History* (1925), p. 129.

[2] Quoted in Robson, op. cit., p. 53.

[3] See my M.A. thesis, appendix 1.

functioned as an intermediary for inter-personal lending and that his practice was, in all important respects, a capital market.

III

Isaac Greene of Childwall Hall (1678–1749) is one of the most outstanding examples of a successful lawyer in Lancashire. Descended from an old yeoman family, his father Edward Greene entered business as a mercer in Liverpool in the late seventeenth century and prospered sufficiently to apprentice his only son Isaac to Daniel Lawton, a Prescot attorney, in whose large practice he gained his early experience. Isaac Greene's association with Edward Blundell, a Prescot barrister, was the first step towards personal success, for it enabled him to take over the work of the Molyneux family's legal affairs from Blundell, around which he built up a substantial practice of his own.[1] Greene's clientele varied considerably in terms of social status but most of his business appears to have been done with people requiring a mortgage in order to make or repay loans. For example, when one of the local gentry, Thomas Worthington of Coppull, needed to settle his debts he mortgaged certain lands in his possession to Thomas Lydiate of Lydiate for £700. Later the mortgage was transferred to Richard Bristow, a London goldsmith, and Isaac Greene, both of whom were acting for clients, the former for one Thomas Kemp of London and the latter for two local gentlemen, William Haydock and Thomas Banks.[2] This association of a Lancashire lawyer with a London goldsmith is an interesting illustration of the opportunities for collusion in the organization of loans which existed at the time. Greene's expertise made him invaluable as a trustee and the small but ambitious yeoman anxious to safeguard the gains of a lifetime was among those who sought the attorney's services. Such a man was Thomas Moss who, by the time of his death, had acquired the 'Ship' inn and other property in Prescot together

[1] R. Stewart Brown, *Isaac Greene: A Lancashire Lawyer of the Eighteenth Century* (1921).
[2] Indenture of Assignment, 1 April 1710, Misc. Deeds, 37, Blainscough, Captain Case Deeds (Wigan Public Library).

with Hayes House in Whiston, and who held the office of Bailiff-Serjeant of Widnes by purchase. As one of the trustees administering the Moss estate Greene was charged with placing the residue out at interest.[1]

It is to be expected that Greene drew most of his clients from local landed society but his interests did not end there for it appears that he was also involved in financing local industry. The site of one of the earliest glasshouses in Lancashire, the Sutton Glasshouse estate, had been mortgaged by the founder-owner John Leafe I to a London physician named Dr Palmer, presumably for the purpose of financing its early growth. Under John Leafe II the estate was reconveyed on payment of £100 to Joshua Palmer of the Middle Temple, son of the original mortgagee, and Greene was called in to manage the affair. The fact that Greene's own land adjoined the Leafe property and that he possessed the coal rights of the manor of Eltonhead in which it stood gave him a vested interest in the transaction and makes it possible that he was personally involved in the financial affairs of this glassmaking family.[2]

Business of this sort is a sufficient explanation of Isaac Greene's success, a measure of which can be gained from his acquisition of land over the years. At the age of 40 he had made himself the owner by purchase of the manors of Childwall, Much and Little Woolton, West Derby, Wavertree, Everton and Eltonhead, as well as considerable lands in Rainhill, Whiston, Sutton, Windle, Hardshaw, Thornton, Sefton and Lunt, where it is known he was an energetic improver, figuring prominently in local enclosure agreements. Greene's marriage into the ancient family of Ireland of Hale brought him that manor, and when in 1751 his estate was estimated at £60,000, this probably only referred to the personalty. At his death Greene's estate was inherited jointly by his two daughters, Ireland and Mary, who divided the properties between them in 1751. Ireland Greene took Hale, her mother's portion, and

---

[1] Will of Thomas Moss of Prescot, yeoman, 1730, *Lancashire and Cheshire Record Society*, 22 (1890).

[2] 'An Abstract of the Title to the Glasshouse Estate in Sutton . . .' 920MD155; also Glasshouse Sutton (1675–99), 1762, 1920SAL681; both in Liverpool Record Office.

later married into the Blackburne family who dominated the salt trade of the Mersey in the eighteenth century. Mary Greene received the remainder of her father's estate and in 1757 married Bamber Gascoyne whose eldest son of the same name was to be a Member of Parliament for Liverpool in the period 1780–96. The latter's only daughter, Frances Mary Gascoyne, eventually married Lord Salisbury.[1] It is an interesting reflection of the openness of English society in the eighteenth century that the provincial attorney Isaac Greene, son of a mercer, was in his lifetime able to establish strong professional links with merchant and county gentry and to bring together what were later to become the Lancashire estates of the Marquess of Salisbury.

In many respects the contemporary career of John Plumbe of Wavertree Hall (1670–1763) shows marked similarities to that of Isaac Greene. Plumbe also came originally from a yeoman family; his grandfather Thomas Plumbe was a small freeholder in Cuerdley and had purchased more land in Whiston in 1646. After the Restoration Plumbe's father enlarged his patrimony further, and was able to bequeath to his eldest surviving son a messuage, tenement and land in Whiston, and another tenanted holding in Prescot.[2] From these modest beginnings John Plumbe went on to accumulate substantial landed property through inheritance and by purchase; at the same time he built himself an extremely successful legal practice and even adventured in trade. As with Isaac Greene, Plumbe gained some of his early experience in the stewardship of a manorial court, namely that of Nicholas Blundell of Crosby: Blundell's journal and disbursement books reveal the steady growth of Plumbe's influence in the affairs of that family in the early decades of the eighteenth century.[3] He also used his family connexions to further his professional interest and one incident shows something of the character of the attorney at this period. His uncle, Oliver Lyme of Prescot, described as being 'afflicted with many indispositions of the

---

[1] Salisbury MSS, 920SAL18/1 (Liverpool Record Office).
[2] For the early history of the family see 'Genealogical Memoranda Relating to the Families of Plumbe and Tempest' (1898), 920PLU (Liverpool Record Office).
[3] 920MD74–5 (Liverpool Record Office).

body and singularly with great infirmities in his eyes', engaged Plumbe, 'an attorney at law and man of business', to manage his concerns and negotiate his transactions. John Plumbe's relations with his uncle, a noticeably litigious character, were far from being satisfactory, however, and disputes continued to arise between them until finally, in May 1710, Lyme took his grievances to arbitration. He was awarded £100 per annum for four years, £48 per annum for life, and an immediate payment of £300, but Plumbe soon began to find legal loopholes in the bonds he had been required to give and, by June 1712, he had ceased making payments.[1] This example is significant not so much because of its hint at sharp practice on the part of an attorney, a professional defect which linked his name with a string of malodorous adjectives, but because it is typical of the sort of situation in which he developed his aptitudes for management and trusteeship.

Fortunately, the nature and scope of Plumbe's financial activities as an attorney-landowner can be described more fully from a series of account books which, though incomplete, range from 1697 to 1757 and show the part played by a financial intermediary in accommodating many people, drawn from all social levels, with loans and investments both large and small.[2] For more than half a century Plumbe was involved in short- and long-term lending, both on his own account and for others, usually at the official and generally accepted rate of 5 per cent interest. Sometimes, however, he appears to have charged no interest at all on very short loans made to people of small means. On 22 December 1699 he lent £20 to one Richard Mercer which was repaid to him on 25 January the following year. It seems likely that the money was borrowed for seasonal expenditure and the fact that no interest was charged may be attributed to seasonal goodwill.

Plumbe appears to have been chiefly engaged in taking in and putting out at interest much larger sums of money, frequently on mortgages of long duration. Deposits with him did not usually lie idle for long before being taken up, and the evidence suggests that the local market for funds was in a buoyant condition. Typical of the way in which Plumbe organized his

---

[1] Lancaster Chancery Petition (1712), P.L.6.52/7 (Public Record Office).
[2] Plumbe–Tempest Deeds and Papers, 920PLU9 (Liverpool Record Office).

activities is the example of Mrs Elizabeth Prescott, a widow of Liverpool, who deposited £50 with him on 12 July 1701. The whole of this deposit could not be put at interest for some months and, in the interval, Plumbe financed his carrying of it by fragmenting it into a number of small short-term loans: his practice was to maintain throughout the interpersonal character of a transaction, so that each individual deposit found a particular taker, and perhaps because of this joint-investment through him was quite common. One such fragment of Mrs Prescott's deposit, a mere £3, was borrowed by John Seacome, a Liverpool gentleman, who repaid it on 29 November 1701; this loan was obviously 'called in' because on the same day Plumbe mentioned that he had been able to find a mortgage for the money. The sum needed was £60, however, and Mrs Prescott made up the difference of £10 before the whole was placed out on mortgage with a certain William Hardy of Fazakerley. On 12 December 1701 Plumbe wrote: '. . . Paid Mr Lawton's man for Wm. Hardy, the money I rec'd of Mrs Prescott for which I took a mortgage to her from him – £60.' This mention of Mr Lawton refers to Daniel Lawton, a Prescot attorney with an adjoining practice, and indicates that Plumbe had in fact found a contact among the clients of the Prescot attorney, which implies that he was not simply an intermediary in his own area but was also in communication with attorneys operating elsewhere. Another instance occurs on 21 June 1703 when he records the receipt of £100 from Alderman Houghton of Liverpool who was delivering the sum for the Reverend Richard Richmond, incumbent of Walton parish: Plumbe sent Richmond's deposit to Joseph Lancaster, a Warrington attorney, to be put out in that area. Lawyers Radcliffe and Horwich from elsewhere in the county are also mentioned in similar contexts, while Isaac Greene, as well as Daniel Lawton, had dealings with him on a number of occasions: indeed Plumbe was receiving funds from as far away as Rochdale, while in Ireland he had a business rendezvous at the Exchange tavern in Dublin where he made payments for Liverpool merchants trading to that port.

The personal details of most of Plumbe's clients have proved difficult to trace and remain largely unknown, nor is any indication given in his accounts and memoranda of how loans were used by recipients. Among the most noteworthy of his clients were Madame Sarah Clayton and Thomas Cobham, two important mine owners on the coalfield, and the Reverend Richard Richmond who, in July 1716, made £500 over to Plumbe as an annuity fund for his family. The prospect of an annuity was a powerful incentive to long-term lending in the eighteenth century, and provided a substantial proportion of the capital needed to finance mortgages. Two other important names appear in the memoranda for 1750, John Chadwick of Birkacre, the charcoal ironmaster, and John Okill of Liverpool, the timber merchant and shipbuilder, but again no details of their affairs are given. Plumbe's dealings with such prominent individuals did not prevent him from finding a use for almost anybody's savings, however small; on 17 March 1739, for instance, he put £5 out at interest to a certain William Payne of Prescot for one of his servants. Great or small, there is no evidence that any of his clients were dissatisfied with the service he provided, in fact the same Mrs Prescott mentioned above subsequently became a consistent depositor with Plumbe, to the extent of almost £500 between 1702 and 1712, when her son Ralph Prescott, a linen-draper, became a client and began to make deposits.

The money-scrivening activities of John Plumbe not only provide information about debt-management but also offer a useful insight into the private structure of debt in the eighteenth century. The surviving accounts are set out below and show, at irregular intervals, the details of Plumbe's security holdings at year's end. It cannot be assumed that these represent a complete picture of his security holdings in the years for which they are available, or that all the securities listed are his alone and not held by him for others, while the breaks in continuity mean that very short-term business does not appear. What does emerge clearly is that, in general, mortgages were numerically fewer than bonds, promissory notes, etc., but of greater proportional value and duration, and that the 5 per cent interest charged remained constant over the whole period with the exception of the particularly reliable or long-standing client who was charged 4·5 per cent. The occasional cash breakdown which occurs, particularly that for 1737, shows an interesting resemblance between Plumbe's 'budore' and the vault of any small, provincial banker at this period. The final table shows the result of an attempt to gather a number of scattered figures together and to present them as an incomplete series of annual accounts, showing receipts, disbursements and cash balances. Another category, showing cash held besides the annual balance, has been construed as representing a fluctuating reserve which gives some slight indication that Plumbe's liquidity ratio was 'normally' high and increasing up to 1740, and low and declining thereafter: possibly no such ratio existed in fact, and if it did it was by no means sacred, but it may be significant that when Plumbe purchased some land in 1733 he paid for it by realizing two bond debts rather than by reducing his cash reserves. This may possibly reflect changing investment opportunities over the period, but equally it could be explained in terms of the necessity to guard against a bad security or to realize investments made through him at short notice.

The occupations and domiciles of only a few of Plumbe's debtors have been discovered, nevertheless it is clear that much of his business was done with the local landed classes; for the rest, a number of his clients are identifiable as merchants and master craftsmen, usually engaged in watchmaking and the pottery manufacture. The largest and longest mortgage loan mentioned was made to James Brettargh of Prescot – one of those country gentry whose family had seen better days – in August 1748 when, on his own account, Plumbe lent an initial sum of £1,658 7s. od. on a mortgage of the Brettargh family property called the Holt estate in Little Woolton: by January 1756 the principal to carry interest had risen to £2,190. The reason for the mortgage is to be found in the fact that Brettargh's widow was in receipt of a £40 annuity from the Holt estate when she made her will in 1758.[1] The soundness of the investment can be gauged from the fact that as late as 1789 Plumbe's daughter Elizabeth Smarley was able to bequeath all the interest money on the Brettargh mortgage to her grandchildren.[2]

[1] Will of Ann Brettargh of Prescot, widow, 1788, *Lancashire and Cheshire Record Society*, 44 (1902).
[2] Will of Elizabeth Smarley of Liverpool, widow, 1789, ibid.

THE SECURITIES OF JOHN PLUMBE

Outstanding at the end of 1732

				£	s.	d.
	30 May	1712	Case & Huddleston's bond	10	0	0
	15 March	1720	remainder of John Winstanley's bond	9	5	7
Pd.	4 April	1724	Humphrey Topping's bond	5	0	0
	2 December	1724	remainder of J. Pemberton's note	4	0	0
	27 June	1726	Mr Haskayne's bond	40	0	0
	1 May	1728	David Hall's contract	17	0	0
	5 March	1728	Barton's bond	100	0	0
Pd.	13 March	1730	Mr Radcliffe's bond	200	0	0
	16 March	1730	Mr A. Radcliffe's note	50	16	7
Pd.	7 March	1731	Mr Lawton's bond	90	0	0
	20 August	1731	remainder of Mr Plumbton's bond	13	10	0
Pd.	18 March	1731	John Leadbetter's bond	70	0	0
Pd.	24 August	1731	Robert Taylor's bond in my son's hands	10	0	0
Pd.	10 November	1732	Mr Caryl Hawarden's bond	30	0	0
	28 December	1732	Mr Payn's note & warr't acc't	20	0	0
			BONDS AND NOTES, etc.	739	12	2
	30 November	1726	Robert Barnes's mortgage	45	0	0
	18 June	1730	Richard Lonsdale's security	12	0	0
	1 July	1731	John Hales's mortgage	46	0	0
	1 July	1731	Daniel Jenkinson's mortgage [1]	215	0	0
			MORTGAGES, etc.	318	0	0
			CASH IN HAND	230	11	8
			TOTAL	1,288	3	10

'Memo. May 1733 – I took in Mr Radcliffe's and Mr Lawton's [attorneys] to pay towards my purchase of Halsall's in Aughton – £280.'

[1] Daniel Jenkinson of Liverpool, innkeeper.

	£	s.	d.
Outstanding at the end of 1737			
Samuel Bolton's assignment in sec's	30	0	0
Richard Kingsley's bond	20	0	0
Mr Paine's warr't acc't for sec. of	20	0	0
Henry Watkinson's bond[1]	35	0	0
John Grayston's bond[2]	10	0	0
Mrs Kelsall's note for £10 and John Balmer's £3	13	0	0
William Fairclough's note	2	0	0
Randle Brownsword's note	1	7	0
John Morecroft's note	3	0	0
John Part's note		10	0
Other old securities not to be depended on	21	0	0
	154	17	0
CASH NOW BY ME	369	0	0
TOTAL	523	17	0
In guineas in my Budore 260	273	0	0
more in my pocket 6	6	6	0
more 5 moidurs at 27s. each	6	15	0
Silver in the Budore	70	0	0
more in my pocket		12	0
more in a bag	8	0	0
more in silver for market money abt.	4	7	0
	369	0	0
	£	s.	d.
Outstanding at the end of 1739			
Worthington's bond	50	0	0
Watkinson	35	0	0
Payne's bond	15	0	0
Grayston	18	0	0
Kelsall	10	0	0
Balmer	8	0	0
Glover's bond	10	0	0
Robert Plumbe	5	0	0
	151	0	0
CASH BY ME	645	14	0
In guineas by me 571½	600	1	6
Portugal Gold	20	2	0
In Silver about	25	10	6
	645	14	0
TOTAL	796	14	0

[1] Henry Watkinson of Halsall, husbandman.
[2] John Grays[t]on of Liverpool, mariner and later shipbuilder.

Outstanding at the end of 1740	£	s.	d.
Henry Watkinson	35	0	0
Mr Ince	60	0	0
Mr Glover	10	0	0
Robert Gore	10	0	0
Robert Plumbe's note	5	0	0
Lonsdale's note	2	5	0
	122	5	0

Debts desperate since last year			
Worthington	50	0	0
Payne	15	0	0
Grayston	10	0	0
	75	0	0
TOTAL	197	0	0

Outstanding at the end of 1747	£	s.	d.
June 1737 Henry Watkinson's security	35	0	0
6 December 1742 Ralph Balshaw's bond	10	0	0
10 August 1743 Mr Pritchard's bond	300	0	0
Roger Horrock's warr't acc't remains with int.	10	0	0
1 August 1748 Mr Brettargh's mortgage and bond	1,658	7	0
16 December 1746 William Penketh's bond	200	0	0
MORTGAGES AND BONDS	2,213	7	0

Robert Marshe's remains due besides int.	5	13	6
John Fazakerley's ,, ,, ,, ,,	54	0	0
Charles Tong's ,, ,, ,, ,,	29	2	0
John Goor's note desperate	6	4	0
Richard Page	1	0	0
PROMISSORY NOTES	95	19	6

Nicholas Fearns on balance besides int.	21	7	6
James Bolton – poor	13	0	0
Mr Paine's security – dead at London	20	0	0
Josiah & John Worthington's bond	50	0	0
OTHER SEC.'S LOST OR DESPERATE	104	7	6
CASH IN HAND	209	2	3
TOTAL	2,622	16	3

Outstanding at the end of 1748	£	s.	d.
6 December 1742 Ralph Balshaw's bond	10	0	0
10 August 1743 Mr Pritchard	300	0	0
Roger Horrock's bond	3	3	0
16 December 1746 Mr Penketh's bond	200	0	0
1 August 1748 Mr Brettargh's mortgage	1,658	7	0
Arrears of Rent from tenants clear	252	18	7
Others subject to Taxes	597	18	10
and several securities desperate	–		
	3,022	7	5

Outstanding at the end of 1750	£	s.	d.
Balshaw	10	0	0
Pritchard	300	0	0
Penketh	200	0	0
17 April 1749 more by note from Forbes	260	0	0
20 June 1749 Mr Clare's bond assigned	30	0	0
Robert Okill's bill	19	11	0
1 August 1748 Mr Brettargh's mortgage	1,658	7	0
	2,477	18	0
CASH IN HAND	264	6	0
TOTAL	2,742	4	0

	Principal	Interest		
Outstanding at the end of 1756	£	£	s.	d.
William Penketh	200	10	0	0
Mr Brettargh's mortgage	2,020	101	0	0
20 September 1751 Robert & Thomas Barton	30	1	10	0
Joseph Finney's mortgage	100	5	0	0
Thomas Aspinwall's bond	20	1	0	0
Mr Crosby's bond @ £4 10s. p.c.	600	27	0	0
Thomas Brownbill's bond	100	5	0	0
Thomas Topping	100	5	0	0
Thomas Appleton	200	10	0	0
John Fogg	100	5	0	0
John Webster	100	5	0	0
Robert Fogg with suretys	100	5	0	0
some with other suretys	150	7	10	0
William Simpson's mortgage & bond	600	30	0	0
Thomas Tipping's mortgage	100	5	0	0
James Farrer's bond	50	2	10	0
Daniel Mackneal	500	25	0	0
December 1755 Peter Gerrard	100	5	0	0
	5,170	255	10	0
2 February 1756 John Livesley's bond	300	15	0	0

31 January 1756 Brettargh settled account to carry
   int. from this day is to be £2,190

               Cash   £448 18 8

Outstanding at the end of *1757*	£	s.	d.
James Brettargh's mortgage			
(the Holt estate in Little Woolton)	2,190	0	0
9 June 1752 Joseph Finney's mortgage[1]			
(messuage and other buildings in Thomas St)	100	0	0
27 March 1754 William Simpson's mortgage			
(several houses on Liverpool Common)	600	0	0
27 December 1754 Thomas Tipping's mortgage			
(ground in Liverpool and gave bond for)	100	0	0
MORTGAGES	2,990	0	0

			£	s.	d.
16 December	1746	William Penketh	200	0	0
20 September	1751	Robert Barton	30	0	0
17 July	1752	Thomas Aspinwall	20	0	0
3 May	1753	Mr Crosby	600	0	0
3 August	1753	Thomas Topping	100	0	0
26 November	1753	Thomas Appleton	200	0	0
18 July	1754	John Fogg	100	0	0
3 August	1754	John Webster	100	0	0
6 October	1754	Robert Fogg	100	0	0
3 March	1755	James Farrer	50	0	0
20 October	1755	Daniel Mackneal	500	0	0
9 December	1755	Peter Gerrard	100	0	0
2 February	1756	J. Livesley (and another for £200 not			
		included)[2]	300	0	0
30 October	1756	D. Kenyon	300	0	0
		BONDS	2,700	0	0
		CASH	460	0	0
		TOTAL	6,150	0	0

The money-scrivening activities of John Plumbe represent his most important, but not his only, excursion into business affairs. He was also involved in an oyster fishery concern with his brother-in-law, Thomas Townley of Royle, and William Hesketh of Means, near Poulton-le-Fylde. In the early years of the eighteenth century a patent had been applied for by Robert Davys of Chester and Thomas Townley, who maintained that they had been at some expense in searching several areas of the sea between the mouth of the Ribble and the Piel of Fouldrey

---

[1] Joseph Finney of Liverpool, watchmaker.
[2] John Livesley of Liverpool, pottery manufacturer.

for an oyster bed below the low-water mark. By 1729 Plumbe was actively involved and accountable for a quarter part of the concern, another quarter part being taken by Townley and a half share by Hesketh, but the venture does not appear to

RECONSTRUCTED ANNUAL ACCOUNTS OF JOHN PLUMBE
1729–57[1]

Year	Receipts			Disbursements			Annual balance			Cash besides annual balance		
	£	s.	d.	£	s.	d.	£	s.	d.	£	s.	d.
1729	581	5	11	630	1	5½	− 48	15	6			
1730												
1731												
1732	437	13	4	399	6	2	+ 38	7	2	192	4	6
1733												
1734												
1735												
1736	405	7	8	378	9	10	+ 26	17	10			
1737	409	13	7	336	16	9	+ 72	16	10	369	0	0
1738												
1739	455	3	6	293	12	5	+ 160	11	1	645	14	0
1740	542	3	1	1,061	7	9	− 519	4	8	144	10	0*
1748	3,942	15	3	752	1	4	+3,190	13	11	66	16	0
1749												
1750	4,780	7	4	528	12	1½	+4,251	15	2½	264	6	0
1751												
1752												
1753												
1754												
1755												
1756											448	18	8
1757											460	0	0

* N.B. Receipts increase more than seven-fold over 1740–8.

[1] The trend of the accounts is indicative of the prevailing situation in agriculture – see G. E. Mingay, 'The Agricultural Depression 1730–50', *Economic History Review*, VIII (1956). Most of the data relating to the 1740s is missing but it would seem that 1739–40 was a major turning-point in Plumbe's career: during the thirties a growing concern with 'desperate debts' is evident and, at the same time, a strengthening of his liquidity position. It is clear that Plumbe began deficit spending in 1740 but whether on investments, on subsidies or on both is not known. The most remarkable feature of the 1740s, however, was the complete change in the order of magnitude between 1740 and 1748, particularly with regard to receipts; in the absence of further evidence it is impossible to be certain but such a change indicates something more than merely recovery to a pre-depression level of income.

have been particularly successful.[1] Plumbe was also eminent in the more orthodox practice of the law and as an attorney he frequently represented the Liverpool Common Council and many prominent private individuals in lawsuits. Yet he was also a considerable landowner and his professional achievements must, in some measure, be attributed to the social repute gained from the possession of land: all his business activities were ultimately founded upon landed wealth and cannot be considered in isolation from his position as a rentier.[2]

In the eighteenth century a shrewd attorney and man of affairs was peculiarly well placed for accumulating substantial landed property from the nucleus of a modest patrimony, and the fortunes of John Plumbe cannot have been untypical. By 1720, with the deaths of his elder brothers William (d. 1719) and Thomas (d. 1712), he had inherited the family property in Whiston, Prescot and Cuerdley. At that date he was already resident at Wavertree Hall, whose manor he had purchased together with those of Aughton and Uplitherland. In 1694 he had married Sarah, the daughter of Peter Marsh, niece and co-heir of James Vernon of Vernon Hall, West Derby, which increased his landed wealth still further. From these areas Plumbe expanded his landownership at the expense of older declining families, his Liverpool property being acquired chiefly from the Moore family and his lands in Aughton and Scarisbrick from the Heskeths. It is significant that Plumbe's final purchase of such estates was usually preceded by a period of heavy mortgage lending on his part to secure the financial dependence of the family concerned. In the case of the Heskeths, for instance, Plumbe lent Alexander Hesketh of Aughton no less than £2,400 from 1715 until he finally purchased the manorial rights of Aughton and Uplitherland in 1718. Over the same period Hesketh's Ormskirk property and his lands in Scarisbrick, Aspinwall, Tarleton and Snape were mortgaged to Plumbe.[3] Prior to 1715 the Hesketh estate had been mortgaged to and recovered from Richard Legh of Lyme, a

---

[1] 'Papers of an Oyster and General Fishery off the Fylde . . . 1727–50', 920PLU14 (Liverpool Record Office).

[2] Similarly with Isaac Greene, see G. E. Mingay, *English Landed Society in the Eighteenth Century* (1963), pp. 92–3 and 104.

[3] Plumbe-Tempest Deeds and Papers, 920PLU A2/3–15 and A1/35–42 (Liverpool Record Office).

Cheshire squire, and when the Heskeths went down to Plumbe it was not without a struggle.[1]

Rents were undoubtedly Plumbe's major source of income; certainly some of the bond and note debts recorded among his securities were for interest-bearing rent arrears, and there is evidence that he possessed a number of characteristics associated with the progressive 'gentleman' farmer of the period. Just occasionally he was willing to accept payment of rent in kind, but more usually he allowed credit for work done in marling, etc.; similarly, if a tenant improved the property, Plumbe would not pay him for the improvements or reduce his rent, but instead would give credit on rents due. In this way he appears to have subsidized his tenants and sometimes rent arrears were very heavy, as with James Marsh who farmed the Aughton Hall estate and parts of the demesne in Aughton and Scarisbrick at a rent of £105 per annum. Marsh owed Plumbe £306 18s. 4d. for rent on 1 January 1747/8, and he himself was sub-letting to at least five other tenants.[2]

What little is known of the attorneys Greene and Plumbe as landowners would appear to lend support to the view that in the century following the Restoration many landed estates were units of ownership rather than production, and that the professional classes were among the most important of what new entrants there were into the upper levels of landed society.[3] Neither belonged to established landed families of high repute in the county and both may well be typical of those who acquired land at the expense of the declining sections of the squirearchy, and who, as gentlemen farmers, were not by any means exclusively involved in agriculture. In the case of a landowning attorney his rent income was likely to be supplemented from money-scrivening rather than, as happened in other cases elsewhere, from lucrative army posts and government pensions. Scrivening, like banking, was a technique rather than a full-time occupation in the eighteenth century and, even within the legal profession itself, quite different sorts of men might practise it. Greene and Plumbe both pursued

---

[1] 'Papers of legal actions between J. P. Plumbe and the Hesketh family in defence of his title . . . 1724–44', 920PLU10 (Liverpool Record Office).

[2] John Plumbe's Account Book (1748), 920PLU9 (Liverpool Record Office).

[3] H. J. Habakkuk, 'English Landownership 1680–1740', *Economic History Review*, X (1939–40).

their careers in the environment of landed society and eventually joined its ranks themselves, but there were others whose landed links were much less apparent and who exhibit rather different traits.

IV

Daniel Lawton and Edward Deane were two attorneys who operated large practices in south-west Lancashire during the first half of the eighteenth century. They merit attention, in particular, because both carried on their activities from Prescot, a town that was well endowed with attorneys at this period, a fact that may, to some extent, account for its importance as a financial centre. Before the navigation of the Sankey Brook, Prescot stood on the main line of supply of coal to Liverpool, and the accounts, memoranda, etc., of Lawton and Deane give some notion of the wide scope of activities that were open to financial intermediaries on the edge of a developing coalfield, ranging as they do from the handling of bankruptcy cases and business partnerships to attending to apprenticeship indentures and local Poor Law matters.[1] A number of the small coalmining partnerships which abounded on the Lancashire coalfield before the monopoly movement of the 1750s appear among the clientele of Lawton and Deane. In September 1751 articles were drawn up between Robert Gwyllym and Robert Roper, the executors of Cobham and Makin, one of the most important partnerships, for carrying on their coalmining business in Sutton.[2] Similarly, in the summer of 1753 a partnership agreement was drawn up between a certain Mr Barton of Poulton-le-Fylde and three local men, John Halliwell, William Lomax and John Shepherd, for working Barton's coal-pits in Blackrod.[3] Although clear instances of direct financing are difficult to isolate in such cases, it is certain that Edward Deane and the Lawton brothers, Daniel and William, were deeply involved in the legal and financial affairs of many of them. In 1749 one or other of them advised

[1] The Account Book of a Prescot Attorney (1745–52), in possession of Dr J. R. Harris.
[2] Ibid., p. 140.
[3] Ibid., p. 141.

Nicholas Cross, a Mr Fisher, Samuel Smith, a Mr Rowe and others, all part-owners of a ship and its insurance policy, about the mortgages which encumbered the vessel and drew up a Chancery petition for them.[1] Again, in 1752 they assigned the share of John Chorley of Prescot in a sailcloth-making concern called Messrs Matthews, Leather and Chorley, to a certain William Webster.[2]

This kind of work enabled the attorney to delve deep into the private business affairs of a large number of people, with the result that he gained a rare and intimate knowledge of the financial position of individuals while at the same time cultivating those personal contacts so essential, for instance, when raising a mortgage loan. In November 1750 Thomas Golden of Hardshaw, being indebted to the daughters of Isaac Greene on a mortgage, engaged Deane to raise a sum of money with which to pay it off. After consulting Alexander Leigh, the Wigan attorney, best known for his financing of the Douglas Navigation, and the Greene sisters' own attorney, Mr Taylor, Deane eventually managed to obtain a loan from Nicholas Fazakerley, the famous Preston lawyer. In the course of negotiating this loan a dispute arose over the time taken to get the money and the rate of interest to be charged, but after an inspection of the securities was made Deane managed to raise £900 from Fazakerley with Golden's Hardshaw estates as collateral.[3] One of the Prescot attorneys' most important clients was John Wyke, the celebrated watchmaker and toolmaker of that town, who was to become one of Liverpool's earliest bankers, building up a flourishing business there after 1758. In June 1745 Deane obtained a £200 mortgage for Wyke on property the latter had only recently acquired in Prescot: a certain Mr Garnett of Farnworth supplied the loan and before its arrival Deane personally met Wyke's occasions for money.[4] The same Mr Garnett was not always so fortunate in his lending for he is mentioned as being one of sixteen creditors involved in bankruptcy proceedings against Henry Marsh, a local businessman, in 1749–51; Marsh owed Garnett £100 on mortgage.[5] It is interesting to note that another of Marsh's creditors was a

[1] Ibid., p. 35.   [2] Ibid., p. 57.   [3] Ibid., pp. 105–6.
[4] Ibid., loose leaf insert. For Wyke see also F. A. Bailey and T. C. Barker, 'The Seventeenth-century Origins of Watchmaking in South-West Lancashire', in J. R. Harris (ed.), op. cit., chap. 1, p. 12.   [5] Ibid., p. 26.

Mr Plumbe of Bolton-le-Moors who was being represented by his relative the Reverend Thomas Plumbe of Aughton, the second son of William Plumbe, attorney, and grandson of John Plumbe discussed above.[1]

The Prescot lawyers also had connexions with Henry Wiswall of Ormskirk, a scrivening attorney who practised throughout the first half of the eighteenth century and who appears to have often had an excess of deposits over loans. As early as 1709 Wiswall is described as 'one that is much concerned in the letting out of moneys upon securitys' and in that year a Liverpool slater, Gabriel Westhead, son of a glovemaker of Lathom, borrowed £14 from him on the security of a leasehold tenement in Lathom worth £8 per annum. The money which Westhead received had been put out at interest with Wiswall by a Prescot tobacconist named Thomas Taylor. In 1749 James Tyrer, a Liverpool merchant, borrowed £142 from Wiswall on land security and Daniel Lawton acted as intermediary for the loan. When Tyrer needed more money to pay off his creditors Lawton transferred the mortgage from Wiswall to Thomas Barron, another more substantial Prescot lawyer. Barron paid Tyrer £142 and interest for Wiswall and accepted an assignment of the mortgage for securing a further £180.[2]

Because almost anyone with the necessary personal credit and connexions was able to arrange mortgages and make loans in the eighteenth century, the attorney was wont to associate with all manner of people in his search for clients. For example, Thomas Taylor of Manchester, the Greene sisters' attorney, was assisted by his uncle, Thomas Hulme, the parish clerk of Salford, who appears to have concerned himself with attracting local savings, while Taylor found securities on which loans could be made. An entry in Hulme's memorandum book for 4 February 1783 reads: 'I now am Dr to Mrs Smith twenty pounds which I will endeavour to put out to Interest for Her with my Hundred pounds as soon as Mr Taylor can find proper security.'[3] The association of Hulme and Taylor brought them a varied business: at the same time as he is lending £300 on

---

[1] The Account Book of a Prescot Attorney (1745–52), p. 36.
[2] Ibid., pp. 39, 45–6, 221–2.
[3] Memorandum Book with will of Thomas Hulme, 1786.

mortgage to a John Makinson of Blackburn, Hulme is also making shorter loans: for instance, on 20 April 1782 he lends £100 to a Thomas Gates of Norbury which is to be repaid on 2 February 1783 with £3 18s. od. interest. On at least one occasion Thomas Taylor is found going to London to collect a debt and this may account for his representing the Greene sisters in the affair concerning Thomas Golden's mortgage, mentioned above, since at that time they resided there. The collecting of debts, often for trivial amounts, was an important part of the everyday business of a country attorney in the eighteenth century, an age when the problem of small debts was very acute. One of the legacies of Elizabeth Arnold, a Liverpool widow, was a debt for £2 9s. od. owed by 'a man in London and which Mr Statham (attorney) is imployed to recover'.[1] Debt recovery could adversely affect relations with clients as is shown by one experience of the Prescot attorneys in the case of a sum of money placed out with them by the executors of one Mary Tarleton in the name of her grandson, William Simkin of Great Sankey. When Simkin wanted the money at his coming of age in 1750 the lawyers had some difficulty in calling the loan in; the penalty for delay was a smaller percentage, to judge from the complaint of one of them when settling the accounts: 'But now I think myself ill used in having no allowance for managing the money for 10 yrs. together, tho' I was to have had it @ 4 p.c., for there was risk which they refused to consider.'[2]

The extent to which the legal profession in the eighteenth century concerned itself with financial matters naturally varied a good deal: with some their activities resemble those of a financial entrepreneur rather than an attorney, while in many cases local government and administration occupied a large part of their professional careers. Henry Brown of Liverpool (1745/6–1822), for example, was almost entirely concerned with municipal affairs.[3] Nicholas Fazakerley of Prescot, whose career covered a period rather earlier in the century was, on the other hand, able to combine civic and financial business:

[1] Will of Elizabeth Arnold of Liverpool, widow, 1786, *Lancashire and Cheshire Record Society*, 44 (1902).

[2] The Prescot Attorney's Account Book, p. 66.

[3] G. T. Shaw, 'Henry Brown: A Liverpool Attorney of the Eighteenth Century', *Transactions of the Lancashire and Cheshire Historic Society*, 16 (1900).

a recorder of Preston, he was also deeply implicated in managing the affairs of the Lancashire recusants; he was a celebrated money-lender and is traditionally supposed to have left a large fortune. The money-scrivener and financial intermediary was most commonly found among this latter type of attorney who flourished particularly in the first half of the century and who, by virtue of the very range of his activities, was always something of an interloper. Consequently, such men had no monopoly of activities which lay on the margins of law and finance; indeed many of them were probably no different from a seventeenth-century conveyancer like Sir Orlando Bridgeman, who attained power and wealth while remaining outside the legal profession.[1] These 'merchants of capital' could thus appear in many guises by the eighteenth century, though that of the scrivening attorney was the most characteristic.

It is the quite distinct function which such men performed and the special ability they showed in the management of loanable funds that is significant, representing an important element in financial communications that was often instrumental in releasing funds from tightly-knit personal groups and channelling them to investment opportunities within the county and beyond. In this way, for example, a Liverpool widow, Elizabeth Sharples, was placing large sums of money out at interest through an intermediary named Edward Veal of Wingheays, near Poulton-le-Fylde. Some of those who borrowed the money are mentioned as being in arrears over interest payments; they were John Wesby of the Burn, who owed £150 on bond, Robert Hoole of Kirkham, who owed £20 on bond, and Thomas Roe, a Poulton attorney, who owed £100 on bond.[2] This sort of investment from centres of wealth to outlying areas where funds were less plentiful went on side by side with the investment of capital seeking more intensive utilization in areas of rapid growth, though the latter type probably became increasingly important as the century proceeded. An early instance of this was the £260 belonging to a Preston spinster, Susanna Doughty, who heard that Thomas Ball of Ormskirk, later of Liverpool, attorney, 'was a person very much made use of by several persons for the placing out

[1] A. W. B. Simpson, *An Introduction to the History of the Land Law* (1961), p. 217.
[2] Will of Elizabeth Sharples of Liverpool, widow, 1731.

their moneys at interest, and that he would be a very proper person to be employed in putting out the money, having the character and reputation of a very careful, substantial honest man'.[1] Some of her money was lent to Richard Norris of Speke, a mayor of Liverpool, and may well have helped finance the famous slave-trade voyage of the *Blessing* in 1699.

V

The functions associated here with the attorney appear, at first sight, to be very close to those of his contemporary the country banker. Both professions may be said to have consisted of specialists in techniques already practised in combination with other activities by a variety of people: just as it is difficult to estimate the numerical importance of financial intermediaries who came from many walks of life, and whose activities are often difficult to disentangle from the normal business of merchants, tradesmen, country gentry or professional men, so it would be unwise to attach too much significance to the number of bankers, properly so called, at the end of the century.[2] The attorney and the banker, however, while both provided valuable financial services in the emergent capital market of the eighteenth century, came from essentially different moulds.

There appears to be no evidence to suggest that anyone in England before the seventeenth century regularly performed that dual function, which is fundamental to modern banking, of borrowing from some people in order to lend to others at a profit. There were thus no English counterparts of the Venetian 'campsores', for in England the Jews, and the Lombards after them, were merely lending their own capital. Banking as opposed to money-lending was first carried on in this country by the scriveners and goldsmiths: the scriveners were clerks who took care of the legal minutiae of conveyances, bonds and other transactions, and who were thus able to arrange borrowing and lending.[3] Although the scriveners were probably

[1] Lancaster Chancery Petition (1701), P.L.6.48/6 (Public Record Office).

[2] L. S. Pressnell, *Country Banking in the Industrial Revolution* (1956), p. 12.

[3] H. C. Gutteridge, 'The Origin and Historical Development of the Profession of Notaries Public in England', *Cambridge Legal Essays* (1926), pp. 123–33. Also M. Beloff, 'Humphrey Shalcrosse and the Great Civil War', *English Historical Review*, LIV (1939).

among the very first bankers, the chief instrument of modern banking was introduced by the goldsmiths when, just prior to the Civil War, the London merchants began to deposit money with them; a new departure, this may be attributed, on the one hand, to a decline of the trade in plate, and, on the other, to an increasing need for financial security on the part of the merchants.

After the Civil War the goldsmiths began to act not merely as depositaries paying interest but also as agents for making payments to third parties, and soon a cheque system was effectively in being, arising out of a special use of the bill of exchange which was already in existence. It is, of course, difficult to distinguish between banking and broking aspects of the financial structure at this period, and in the activities of the goldsmith it is possible to find much that is characteristic of both banking practice and financial intermediacy. Similarly with the scriveners, who were probably the first to perform the basic banking functions, yet who later became more important as agents for loanable funds and advisers on investment portfolios. Thus at first both practised two functions together which gradually grew apart, and which would now be considered as separate. Nevertheless, it is possible to distinguish different emphases in the work of each of them and, at the risk of oversimplification, the deposit and remittance activities of the seventeenth-century goldsmith stand in a direct line of precedence with the banking of the eighteenth century, while the financial agency and brokerage business of his contemporary, the scrivener, were wholly, or in part, taken over and extended by the money-scrivening attorney of the eighteenth century.

In practice, of course, these two functions took some considerable time to disentangle themselves from the corpus of financial work, indeed the process of clarification had not been completed by the time the joint stock banks and an institutionalized capital market came to serve the very different economy of nineteenth-century Britain. Thus the kinds of services which the banking specialists were providing towards the end of the eighteenth century were not in themselves new, but rather an integration of existing techniques in response to an urgent need arising in the first phase of industrialization. The provision of a local means of payment and facilities for the transfer of payments were among the most pressing problems confronting the early entrepreneurs; it is not surprising, therefore, that the country bankers were typically engaged in note-issuing, discounting and remittance activities, and were rarely to be found consistently channelling savings to the points of investment demand, even in the short run. As a result, deposit banking cannot have amounted to very much in eighteenth-century England, and this situation appears to have prevailed until the advent of joint stock banks after 1826. The precocity of the Scottish banks at this period is shown by their more favourable attitude towards granting loans, particularly their 'cash-credit' facility;[1] yet Scottish industry does not appear to have benefited from a greater degree of financial freedom than existed elsewhere. By contrast, London's private bankers, particularly the old-established ones in the West End who came to serve the landed interest, were greatly involved in the market for government securities: the same was true of the City bankers, whose mercantile links were much stronger, and who carried out most of the London agency business when country banking expanded after 1750.[2] It is significant that the younger firms created in the banking boom of 1769–73 and afterwards were the ones who took most of the agency business, yet for much of the century it seems that the private bankers of the capital were the willing tools of public finance.

The Lancashire banks, when they appeared, were part of the response to a general acceleration of industrial and commercial activity which involved, in particular, an increased demand for discounting facilities. Note-issue was never very important in Lancashire and even Bank of England notes came into use much later than elsewhere; in part this can be attributed to the widespread mistrust of note-issues, but probably more important was the fact that there was no great need for them. Bills of exchange, coin and, later, banker's drafts were much the most popular means of payment, and it was in these that the

---

[1] For comparisons, see R. Cameron, 'Banking in the Early Stages of Industrialization', *Scandinavian Economic History Review*, XI (1963).

[2] D. M. Joslin, 'London Private Bankers 1720–1785', *Economic History Review*, VII (1954).

Lancashire bankers specialized. The draft was the only new instrument which they brought to bear on the monetary situation in the county and this never became popular, reissue being almost always in the form of bills, so that in the early years of the nineteenth century its importance was small.[1] Coin and bills of exchange had, of course, long been provided before the arrival of the banks, together with discounting facilities in Lancashire and London, so that there is no reason to suppose that they radically altered, rather than merely supplemented, existing facilities.[2] What is more, it seems unlikely that the banks fitted easily into the credit and currency system of Lancashire, for even during the crisis of 1793 it was the Corporation of Liverpool, not its bankers, who finally resorted to a note-issue.[3] It is also worth noticing that the mercantile communities of Lancashire, and not its bankers as such, rallied to defend the bill of exchange system when it was threatened.[4]

The timing of the appearance of banking in Lancashire and the origins of the early bankers illustrate the type of individual who stood nearest to the specialist, and the functions he was most concerned with during the century. In Liverpool, for example, banking grew out of the needs of local commerce, and most of the city's early bankers were merchants such as William Clarke, engaged in the linen trade, the first banker to appear in a Liverpool Directory.[5] John Wyke, acknowledged to have been the first banker in Liverpool, was a merchant-middleman, and a watch and machine toolmaker. Similarly, a number of Manchester's earliest bankers were traders, in particular tea dealers such as John Jones, the son of a non-conformist minister. The first Manchester bank, founded in December 1771, was launched by Edward Byrom, son of a physician, William Allen, son of a tradesman, Roger Sedgwick, another physician's son, and Edward Place, son of a

---

[1] T. S. Ashton, 'The Bill of Exchange and Private Banks in Lancashire, 1790–1830', *Economic History Review*, XV (1945).

[2] Pressnell, op. cit., p. 177.

[3] F. E. Hyde and S. Marriner, 'The Port of Liverpool and the Crisis of 1793', *Economica*, XVIII (1951).

[4] S. G. Checkland, 'The Lancashire Bill System and Its Liverpool Protagonists, 1810–27', *Economica*, XXI (1954).

[5] J. Hughes, *Liverpool Banks and Bankers, 1760–1837* (1906), pp. 56–9.

clergyman.[1] The professional middle-class element was marked from the beginning in banking as shown, for example, by the number of attorneys who moved into it during the course of the century. The fact that bankers usually only made specific practices which had previously been grafted on to the main body of a business, should not be taken to apply only to merchants and traders who, no doubt, were in the forefront of the eighteenth-century credit expansion and, therefore, among those most likely to specialize in banking. Although very little is known about the progress of credit in the internal economy of the period, it was almost certainly as crucial, in its way, as the growth of credit in foreign trade. Hence, attorney-bankers such as George Tyndale, a partner in the Exchange Bank of Bristol, and Charles Henry Hunt, the Town Clerk of Stratford-upon-Avon who founded a bank there in 1790, are significant not so much for themselves as for the tradition of which they were the last exponents, and which finally petered out in 1890 when the last solicitor-banker, Joseph Dickinson of Alston, sold out to the Carlisle City and District Banking Company.[2]

It has been suggested that one reason why banks were not founded in greater numbers outside London was because attorneys were offering some banking services to provincial society throughout the greater part of the eighteenth century.[3] The evidence examined here suggests that this was in fact the case, and that country banking was essentially a response to the phenomenal increase in the demand for payments facilities, consequent upon population growth and industrialization, with which existing arrangements were inadequate to cope.

The real importance of the scrivening attorney, however, lies not in his ability to apply rudimentary banking principles before the spread of country banking, but in his role of broker for negotiating secured loans. The English banking system was largely a response to industrialization rather than a causal factor, the banks were capital-servicing rather than capital-forming institutions, and if the problem of how long-term capital requirements were met in the eighteenth century is to

[1] L. H. Grindon, *Manchester Banks and Bankers* (1878), pp. 23–31.
[2] Pressnell, op. cit., p. 44.
[3] Birks, op. cit., p. 186.

be solved, more attention needs to be focused on the working of the mortgage market with which the scrivening attorney was intimately connected. An important link in continuity between the scrivener and the attorney in the seventeenth century seems to have been the former's uncertain hold on conveyancing business, which was more and more taken over by the ascendant attorneys.[1] The evolution of easy mortgaging by the end of the seventeenth century gave the attorney an immense opportunity to build on the art of the scrivener and subsequently 'by most of the scriveners becoming attorneys, and most of the attorneys practising as scriveners, the business of the two professions became united in the same persons'.[2] There was never any conflict of interest between banking and financial intermediacy during the eighteenth century, for their respective spheres, if they sometimes overlapped, were basically distinct. On the contrary, they must frequently have complemented one another; indeed, Thomas Hulme of Salford, mentioned above in connexion with scrivening, was at the same time investing in the Manchester bank of Scholes and Cundall, and mentions receiving a dividend of £418 3s. 6d. on his own account, plus £354 12s. 5d. on account of Edward Kenyon, an Altrincham attorney. In this way the early country banks may have provided yet another investment outlet for local savings managed by financial intermediaries.

The part played by rural-based savings in financing the early stages of the Industrial Revolution, in particular capital raised on real security, has been given scant consideration to date, yet it is now clear that money-scrivening attorneys, among others, were able to effectively mobilize such resources fully a century or more before the industrial and technological changes of the later eighteenth century. The business interests of the London firm of scriveners, Sir Robert Clayton and John Morris, between 1650 and 1700, for example, extended over the south-east and Midland counties.[3] The Lancashire attorneys practised mainly between 1700 and 1760, their interests appear to have been confined to the county and, significantly, they did much

---

[1] Harding, op. cit., p. 179.

[2] Christian, op. cit., p. 122.

[3] D. C. Coleman, 'London Scriveners and the Estate Market in the Late Seventeenth Century', *Economic History Review*, IV (1951).

more mortgage business than the London concern, and their clientele was more varied. Much remains to be done before all the implications of the money-scrivening attorney's important position in the financial life of the eighteenth century can be known. Many more detailed studies of his activities need to be undertaken before his significance as compared with other contemporary channels of finance can be appreciated. Finally, it would be useful to know how widespread were the business connexions of the attorney, outside of his purely scrivening activities, and what, if any, were his contributions to entre-preneurship.

Select Bibliography

Most works dealing with the Industrial Revolution contain some data on capital formation or some discussion of the relevant problems. Only the more useful and important in this respect are listed in the following bibliography, which moreover does not include the articles reprinted in this volume. References to many more books and articles will be found in the footnotes to the Editor's Introduction and to the other articles, especially chapter 6. No attempt has been made to cover the extensive theoretical literature on capital formation.

I *General Works on the Industrial Revolution*

ASHTON, T. S. *The Industrial Revolution 1760–1830* (1948).

ASHTON, T. S. *An Economic History of England: The Eighteenth Century* (1955).

DEANE, P. *The First Industrial Revolution* (1965).

DEANE, P. and COLE, W. A. *British Economic Growth 1688–1959: Trends and Structure* (1962; 2nd ed., 1967).

FLINN, M.W. *Origins of the Industrial Revolution* (1966).

HARTWELL, R. M. *The Causes of the Industrial Revolution in England* (1967).

HARTWELL, R. M. *The Industrial Revolution and Economic Growth* (1971).

HICKS, J. *A Theory of Economic History* (1969).

HOBSBAWN, E. J. *Industry and Empire. An Economic History of Britain since 1750* (1968).

LANDES, D. S. *The Unbound Prometheus* (1969).

MATHIAS, P. *The First Industrial Nation. An Economic History of Britain 1700–1914* (1969).

POLLARD, S. and CROSSLEY, D. W. *The Wealth of Britain 1085–1966* (1968).

PRESSNELL, L. S. (ed.) *Studies in the Industrial Revolution. Essays presented to T. S. Ashton* (1960).

II *Works on Capital Formation (some of these only partly deal with the problem)*

ANDERSON, B. L. *Aspects of Capital and Credit in Lancashire during the Eighteenth Century* (Liverpool M.A. thesis, 1969).

BLAUG, M. 'The Productivity of Capital in the Lancashire Cotton Industry in the Nineteenth Century', *Economic History Review* (1961).

BROADBRIDGE, S. *Studies in Railway Expansion and the Capital Market in England 1825–1873* (1970).

CAIRNCROSS, A. K. 'Capital Formation in the Take-off', in W. W. Rostow (ed.) *The Economics of Take-Off into Sustained Growth* (1963); also in *Factors in Economic Development* (1962).

CAMPBELL, R. H. 'The Financing of Carron Company', *Business History* (1958).
Capital Formation and Economic Growth. A Conference of the Universities – National Bureau Committee for Economic Research (1955).

CHAPMAN, S. D. 'Fixed Capital Formation in the British Cotton Industry 1770–1815', *Economic History Review* (1970); reprinted in Higgins and Pollard, see below.

Conference on Research in Income and Wealth. *Problems of Capital Formation. Concepts, Measurements and Controlling Factors* (1957).

CULE, J. E. 'Finance and Industry in the Eighteenth Century: the Firm of Boulton and Watt', *Economic History* (1940).

DAVIES, K. G. 'Joint-Stock Investment in the Later Seventeenth Century', *Economic History Review* (1952).

DEANE, P. 'New Estimates of Gross National Product for the United Kingdom 1830–1914', *The Review of Income and Wealth* (1968).

DEANE, P. and HABAKKUK, H. J. 'The Take-Off in Britain', in Rostow (ed.) *The Economics of Take-Off*, see above.

DUPRIEZ, L. H. (with the assistance of D. C. Hague) *Economic Progress* (1955).

FELIX, D. 'Profit Inflation and Industrial Growth: The Historic Record and Contemporary Analogies', *Quarterly Journal of Economics* (1956).

HAMILTON, E. J. 'Profit Inflation and the Industrial Revolution 1751–1800', *Quarterly Journal of Economics* (1942).

HAWKE, G. R. and REED, M. C. 'Railway Capital in the United Kingdom in the Nineteenth Century', *Economic History Review* (1969).

HIGGINS, J. P. P. and POLLARD, S. (ed) *Aspects of Capital Investment in Great Britain 1750–1850. A Preliminary Survey* (1971).

HOSELITZ, B. F. 'Entrepreneurship and Capital Formation in France and Britain since 1700', in *Capital Formation and Economic Growth*, see above.

JOHN, A. H. 'Insurance Investment and the London Money Market of the Eighteenth Century', *Economica* (1953).

JONES, E. L. 'Industrial Capital and Landed Investment. The Arkwrights in Herefordshire 1809–1843', in Jones, E. L. and Mingay, G. E. (eds) *Land, Labour and Population in the Industrial Revolution* (1967).

KUZNETS, S. 'Notes on the Take-Off', in Rostow (ed.) *The Economics of Take-Off*, see above; reprinted in *Economic Growth and Structure. Selected Essays* (1966).

KUZNETS, S. *Modern Economic Growth. Rate, Structure and Spread* (1966).

KUZNETS, S. 'Capital Formation in Modern Economic Growth (and Some Implications for the Past)', in *Third International Conference of Economic History. Munich, 1965*, vol. I (1968).

LEWIS, W. A. *The Theory of Economic Growth* (1955).

LORD, J. *Capital and Steam Power 1750–1800* (1923; 2nd ed., 1966).

LUTZ, F. A. and HAGUE, D. C. *The Theory of Capital* (1961).

MARX, K. *Capital. A Critical Analysis of Capitalist Production* (English translation; 5th ed., 1896).

MITCHELL, B. R. 'The Coming of the Railway and United Kingdom Economic Growth', *Journal of Economic History* (1964).

POLLARD, S. 'The Growth and Distribution of Capital in Great Britain, *c.* 1770–1870', in *Third International Conference*, see above.

POLLARD, S. 'Investment, Consumption and the Industrial Revolution', *The Economic History Review* (1958).

ROBINSON, J. *The Accumulation of Capital* (1956; 2nd ed., 1965).

ROSTOW, W. W. *The Stages of Economic Growth* (1960).

SAVILLE, J. 'Primitive Accumulation and Early Industrialization in Britain', *The Socialist Register* (1969).

SHAPIRO, S. *Capital and the Cotton Industry in the Industrial Revolution* (1967).

STERN, W. M. 'The First London Dock Boom and the Growth of the West India Docks', *Economica* (1952).

STERN, W. M. 'The Isle of Dogs Canal: A Study in Early Public Investment', *Economic History Review* (1952).

SWANN, D. 'The Pace and Progress of Port Investment in England 1660–1830', *Yorkshire Bulletin of Economic and Social Research* (1960).

WILLIAMS, E. *Capitalism and Slavery* (1944).

III *Monographs*

ASHTON, T. S. *Iron and Steel in the Industrial Revolution* (1924; 3rd ed., 1963).

BARKER, T. C. and HARRIS, J. R. *A Merseyside Town in the Industrial Revolution: St Helens 1750–1900* (1954).

CAMERON, R. C. *et al. Banking in the Early Stages of Industrialization* (1967).

CHAPMAN, S. D. *The Early Factory Masters. The Transition to the Factory System in the Midlands Textile Industry* (1967).

COLEMAN, D. C. *The British Paper Industry 1495–1860* (1958).

DICKSON, P. G. M. *The Financial Revolution in England. A Study in the Development of Public Credit 1688–1756* (1967).

EDWARDS, M. M. *The Growth of the British Cotton Trade 1780–1815* (1967).

FITTON, R. S. and WADSWORTH, A. P. *The Strutts and the Arkwrights 1778–1830. A Study of the Early Factory System* (1958).

FLINN, M. W. *Men of Iron. The Crowleys in the Early Industrial Revolution* (1962).

GAYER, A. D., ROSTOW, W. W. and SCHWARTZ, A. S. *The Growth and Fluctuations of the British Economy 1790–1850* (1953).

HABAKKUK, H. J. *American and British Technology in the Nineteenth Century. The Search for Labour-saving Innovations* (1962).

JOHN, A. H. *The Industrial Development of South Wales 1750–1850. An Essay* (1950).

MATHIAS, P. *The Brewing Industry in England 1700–1830* (1959).

PRESSNELL, L. S. *Country Banking in the Industrial Revolution* (1956).

RIMMER, W. G. *Marshalls of Leeds, Flax-spinners, 1788–1886* (1960).

SIGSWORTH, E. M. *Black Dyke Mills. A History of John Foster and Son* (1958).

UNWIN, G. *Samuel Oldknow and the Arkwrights. The Industrial Revolution at Stockport and Marple* (1924).

DATE